Water, Leisure and Culture

Leisure, Consumption and Culture

General Editor: Rudy Koshar, *University of Wisconsin at Madison*

Leisure regimes in Europe (and North America) in the last two centuries have brought far-reaching changes in consumption patterns and consumer cultures. The past twenty years have seen the evolution of scholarship on consumption from a wide range of disciplines but historical research on the subject is unevenly developed for late modern Europe, just as the historiography of leisure practices is limited to certain periods and places. This series encourages scholarship on how leisure and consumer culture evolved with respect to an array of identities. It relates leisure and consumption to the symbolic systems with which tourists, shoppers, fans, spectators, and hobbyists have created meaning, and to the structures of power that have shaped such consumer behaviour. It treats consumption in general and leisure practices in particular as complex processes involving knowledge, negotiation, and the active formation of individual and collective selves.

Water, Leisure and Culture

European Historical Perspectives

Edited by
Susan C. Anderson
and
Bruce H. Tabb

Oxford • New York

First published in 2002 by
Berg
Editorial offices:
150 Cowley Road, Oxford, OX4 1JJ, UK
838 Broadway, Third Floor, New York, NY 10003-4812, USA

© Susan C. Anderson and Bruce H. Tabb 2002

Berg is the imprint of Oxford International Publishers Ltd.

Library of Congress Cataloging-in-Publication Data
Water, leisure and culture : European historical perspectives / edited by Susan C. Anderson
and Bruce H. Tabb.
    p. cm. – (Leisure, consumption, and culture ISSN 1468-571X)
Includes bibliographical references (p.   ).
    ISBN 1-85973-535-5 (cloth) – ISBN 1-85973-540-1 (pbk.) ✓
    1. Water use–Europe–History. 2. Water–Social aspects–Europe–History. I. Anderson,
Susan C. II. Tabb, Bruce H., 1959- III. Series.
    GB720 .W38 2002
    333.91'0094–dc21

                                                                                    2002007245

British Library Cataloguing-in-Publication Data
A catalogue record for this book is available from the British Library.

ISBN 1 85973 535 5 (Cloth)
        1 85973 540 1 (Paper)

Typeset by JS Typesetting Ltd, Wellingborough, Northamptonshire
Printed in the United Kingdom by Biddles Ltd, Guildford and King's Lynn

Contents

Contents

List of Illustrations

Acknowledgements

The editors gratefully acknowledge the financial support of the University of Oregon's Office of Research and Faculty Development, in particular, Thomas Dyke and Paula Burkhart, and of the College of Arts and Sciences through the Hertline Fund. In addition, we are grateful for Carmen Mayer-Robin's proof-reading of our translation, for Anthony Michaels's reproduction of the maps and illustrations and for the thoughtful comments on various chapters from George Sheridan, Fabienne Moore, Susan Crane, John Walton, Virpi Zuck, Alexander Mathäs, Ron Unger and Paal Bjørby. We also thank Marcia Alexander for her assistance in the office and Kathy Saranpa for her fine indexing. This book would not have come about without the encouragement of Maike Bohn, Kathryn Earle and Rudy Koshar.

Map of Europe

Introduction: The Pleasure of Taking the Waters

Susan C. Anderson

Reisen [heißt] . . . fremdes Wasser zu trinken. Andere Orte, anderes Wasser. (Tawada 66)

Dancing on the beach after a swim in the Mediterranean, taking the waters in fashionable Baden-Baden, boating on the Black Sea, sauna bathing in Helsinki, diving into a pool in Berlin – the myriad ways of delighting in water imply a variety of cultural meanings. Water figures in notions of hygiene, health, the sacred, the sublime, all of which play a role in the practice of leisure as a social activity, as the following essays will show. Especially over the last two hundred years – as broader segments of European society have gained access to free time – the seaside, lakes and mineral springs have attracted groups, or even crowds, of visitors on holiday. In addition to the spiritual gratification shared leisure experiences afford, congregating by water has helped forge bonds between people whose paths would not otherwise have crossed.[1] The varieties of commingling, in turn, have shaped the ways that water is 'packaged' and marketed for leisure.

This volume presents case studies about the structuring of leisure around water in its various manifestations – from ice to liquid to steam – which offer fresh insights into divergent ideas of cultural, social and political identities in Europe. Important is the transdisciplinary dialogue at work here. Recreational water in Europe takes shape from a number of focal points. British historians in the first section address hierarchies of class evident at beaches and spas, while Dutch and Finnish scholars explore water's communal qualities. In the second section, British and American art historians and German landscape architects focus more on bodies of water as aesthetic problems but within specific national contexts. The last essays, by historians from Greece, Italy and France, highlight the spa or beach as product. And geographers and tourism experts from Bulgaria present accounts of the Black Sea Coast or Moldovan resorts as embroiled in a highly charged atmosphere of contesting market and societal forces.

The range of approaches and disciplinary perspectives exemplifies heterogeneous views about what comprises a cultural history of water in modern Europe.[2]

While each case is European in that it illustrates conditions in certain parts of Europe, the contributors evince disparate concepts of history. Diverse institutional and political contexts may account for such a variety of approaches. For instance, the manner by which a Greek economic historian addresses the shift from mineral-spring to beach tourism in twentieth-century Greece differs markedly from the way a British historian evaluates a seashore in late nineteenth-century Spain or from the mixture of lyrical and empirical-historical styles a French historian employs to assess the Côte d'Azur. While many authors emphasize local differences and contingencies in describing changes in perceptions and practices, others employ a narrative of collective progress or regress. Most chapters address changes occurring in specific regions or towns. They often reveal divergent perceptions and practices within one nation, such as the differing paths of beach tourism in Rimini and the Costa Smeralda from the nineteenth century until the present. Conversely, one can see transnational similarities in the ways some Europeans have gathered around water, such as along Spanish or English beaches in the nineteenth century. This anthology thus presents both a multitude of meanings ascribed to water and leisure in Europe as well as a variety of 'European' and 'American' approaches to European cultural history.

Such a history of water has a prominent social dimension. As the first part, 'Collective Identities', demonstrates, Europeans have gone to beaches and spas as much to socialize and be seen as to enjoy the water. The ways they relax and their choice of destination intersect with beliefs about what is appropriate for their social role. Water helps them maintain boundaries around themselves and those with whom they wish to identify. For centuries Europeans bathed in mineral waters in the belief that they could cure disease or improve fertility. Springs often assumed an aura of sacredness, drawing medieval pilgrims to visit for both spiritual and physical regeneration. The spas built around them were more often than not reserved for the wealthy. However, modest lodgings by some European springs in the nineteenth and twentieth centuries allowed the poor to partake of their curative powers as well (see Steward, 'Culture of Water Cure'; Dritsas, 'Water, Culture and Leisure'). Despite centuries of spa use, however, modern spas were not merely a continuation of an unbroken tradition. They were a new phenomenon related more closely to Enlightenment ideas and changes in the marketplace (Blackbourn, 'Fashionable Spa Towns'). Fashionable spas in the nineteenth century can be connected to the emergence of an international elite of aristocrats, politicians and wealthy bourgeois, who travelled from spa to spa in varying configurations (Blackbourn, 'Fashionable Spa Towns'). However, this very fashionableness repelled other spa guests, who disapproved of aristocratic dissoluteness and immoderation. In nineteenth-century Habsburg Austria, middle-class visitors chose spas for their therapeutics rather than their modishness, for example the resorts at Carlsbad or Gräfenberg that based their regimen on discipline and simplicity (Steward, 'Culture of Water Cure'). Spas thus existed within a web of interconnected, though at times conflicting, medical, philosophical, aesthetic, social and religious discourses.

Similar to spas, early beach resorts often strove to maintain class distinctions but not always with success. Visitors to the beach went to watch others as much as they did to bathe in the sea. Swimming for sport did not come into vogue until the eighteenth and nineteenth centuries, because the sea had been regarded as dangerous and the beach desolate.[3] Such views began to change in the wake of scientific discoveries about water's medicinal and hygienic benefits. Romantic notions of nature helped alter aesthetic perceptions as well. The seaside took on an aura of alluring mystery, and this helped draw people to the beaches. In nineteenth-century San Sebastián the desire for unobstructed seascapes and pure water intersected symbolically with a wish for clean breaks between social classes, but complete separation was not feasible. The cosmopolitan tourists and Basque entrepreneurs were mutually dependent (Walton, 'Waters of San Sebastián'). Likewise, municipal efforts to prevent contaminated water from flowing into San Sebastián's tourist areas can also be viewed metaphorically as attempts to police the morally or socially unruly (Walton, 'Water of San Sebastián').

Water can also unite. While the seaside and mineral springs often became connected with distinct social groups, other ways of interacting with water have been linked to ideals of regional or national solidarity transcending social class. Ice in the Netherlands has had a democratizing function, especially with regard to skating. Indeed, in nineteenth-century The Hague, elitist attempts to create exclusive skating rinks based on class or gender differences failed, because longstanding beliefs about skating's value as marker of a common Dutch identity proved stronger (Furneé, 'Thrill of Frozen Water'). National identity and universal access are also linked in the Finnish sauna tradition, which continues to be a major force in how Finns and non-Finns imagine Finnishness (Leimu, 'Finnish Sauna').

Another facet of water's cultural history is the aesthetic. Water is a longstanding metaphor in art and literature, evoking, among many others, ideas of limitless expansion or the unknowable. [4] Closer study can reveal political tensions at play behind these. The section 'Aesthetics and Ideology' shows that images of the seaside or designs of ornate fountains possess an ideological dimension affecting notions of political affiliation. For instance, nineteenth-century British art and literature both reflected and helped propagate ideas about the English seaside as symbol of British freedom. Illustrations of sea bathing could make the sea appear available to all British, even though beaches were segregated and leisure time was a scarce commodity (Payne, 'Seaside Visitors'). Yet, 'British' as sea bathing was supposed to be, Europeans living in other countries with coastal beaches imagined themselves as being similarly connected to their own land and seascapes. Nineteenth-century Swedes often conceived of their national connectedness through textbooks and artworks. Notable are the mid-century changes of opinion about the value of Sweden's rugged coasts and new ideas about sea bathing as a proving ground for both masculinity and Swedishness (Facos, 'Sound Mind'). Differing geographic configurations, nationalist ideals, moral-religious beliefs and local conditions help account for dissimilar modes of representing coastal waters.

Landscape design and architecture are also bound to social and political trans-formations. In twentieth-century Germany artificial waterfalls, 'organic' lakes and eco-ponds have been used to help educate or influence the public (Wolschke-Bulmahn, 'Water in German Garden Design'). One noteworthy case is the proposed 'thermal palace' in 1920s Berlin, which promised Berliners of all walks of life the chance to improve their health through bathing and balneological treatments without having to leave the city (Gröning and Wolschke-Bulmahn, '*Thermen-palast*'). This rich and intriguing find exemplifies competing German notions about swimming's social function, that is as being liberating or destabilizing. It provides fodder for comparison to other forms of mass leisure in Weimar Germany. Buildings for pools and spas can also bear traces of the daily life of past gener-ations. Changes in Budapest's spa architecture reveal connections between the region's Ottoman, Habsburg and Marxist pasts and concepts of hygiene (Switzer, 'Hungarian Spas'). At present the spas' very marketability as curative establish-ments is depleting the water table, which relates to the environmental concerns stressed more prominently in the last section.

The myriad functions of recreational water have given rise to a plethora of accoutrements for easing the enjoyment of it – hotels, restaurants, rental equip-ment, swimwear – and an industry for developing and managing all this. Water has become a recreational commodity to be marketed, advertised and sold. Vacations appear disconnected from the realm of work only under the careful supervision and planning of the tourist industry, and the success of tourism threatens, through pollution and overcrowding, the natural assets that attract tourists in the first place. Furthermore, pleasure itself is an amorphous term. For instance, it implies rest to people seeking curative spa treatments, but activity defines it along trendy stretches of seaside. As leisure has changed from a privilege to an extension of everyday life, recreational bodies of water have altered their meanings as well.

The third part, 'Ecology and Economics', demonstrates how notions of owner-ship and community affect the ways planners imagine the coastal and lakeside resorts they develop, such as along Bulgaria's Black Sea Coast (Marinov and Koulov, 'Water Recreation Resources') or Moldova's rivers (Vodenska, 'Water and Leisure in Moldova'). Tourism helps create perceptions of specific sites that can transform the image of a whole geographic area and of the leisure practices appropriate for it. The essays in this section refer to bodies of water that have long attracted visitors from throughout Europe and beyond. They dismantle stereotypes by documenting the competing interests at work in spinning the allure of the Black Sea or the Mediterranean. In the case of Moldova, poverty prevents the majority of citizens today from enjoying their country's leisure resorts. They are at an even greater disadvantage than when they were subject to Soviet vacation policies. The two contributions from Eastern Europe outline present hierarchies determining who has access to pristine waters and call for policy changes along with critical reflection.

Along the Mediterranean today the mass appeal of the beach has come to replace the luxury and/or healthfulness of the spa as attitudes, material conditions and consumer trends have changed. However, some Greek resorts are now working to revive interest in mineral springs (Dritsas, 'Water, Culture and Leisure'). Questions of pollution and overdevelopment play a significant role as do types of investors and visitors. The disparate paths of two Italian coastal resorts, one for tourists of all social and income levels, the other exclusively for the wealthy, show how their outcomes were closely bound to local geography and financial investment patterns from the nineteenth century until the present (Battilani, 'Rimini'). In contrast, current changes in beach tourism along the French Riviera reflect mutating consumer tastes within the context of concepts of leisure that have developed since the 1950s. The Club Med has come to embody an international idea of the French Mediterranean experience, and its emphasis on activity has also helped to transform tourist ideals. Yet, the fact that hardly any Club Med villages exist on the French Côte d'Azur implies that its image of secluded, untouched nature is more fantasy than reality.

The economics of recreational water in France, Italy, Greece, Moldova and Bulgaria reveal how regional, and to a certain extent national, infrastructures, community values and institutions have interacted to help create distinct settings for leisure according to age, income, nationality, political affiliation etc. Vacationers who can distance themselves the farthest from polluted shores are the most privileged.

At times, partaking of water for pleasure parallels how groups cohere, such as wading in pools in people's parks or braving the elements on the nineteenth-century Swedish coast. In other cases, the opposite is true, such as the differences between pre-World War I day visitors and long-term spa guests. Like the notions scrutinized in these pages, there is no single European concept of recreational water. Intimately linked to culture, region, ideology, etc., its multifarious significations disclose ways of thinking and living in specific places and times. The meanings of using water for pleasure thus present examples of much broader changes in European society, changes that have allowed the different classes and ethnic groups both 'to become more familiar with each other's ways of living' (Gundle 273) and to maintain distance from each other. These explorations of using water for pleasure display facets of the fluctuating, interactive confluences of people, cultural discourses and marketing practices that comprise modern Europe.

These analyses also figure as partial responses to what the editors of this volume see as broader socio-historical and cultural questions. What can the ways people relax around bodies of water tell us about these people and their tastes? How do the ways they give value to their free time affect water use? How can changes in perceptions of nature over time, according to social status or by region help us understand various cultures? What can the manners in which humans have 'taken the waters' in a recreational or therapeutic setting reveal about their attitudes toward medicine, cleanliness, aesthetics, social hierarchies, consumerism? We have chosen to initiate a discussion of such questions by concentrating on modern Europe and hope this volume will stimulate further study on water and leisure in other cultural contexts.

Notes

1. See MacCannell 13.
2. Recent academic studies show links between mythical narrative and ideas about water's physical properties, between notions of how fluids circulate in the body and concepts of how rivers and oceans flow around the earth (Schama 243–382). In the field of leisure, scholars have addressed the history and significance of certain types of water-based recreation (e.g., Lenček/Bosker or Urbain, *plage* [beaches]; Leeuwan [swimming pools]; Walton, 'Consuming'; 'Resorts' [seaside resorts]; Wolschke-Bulmahn/Gröning, 'Ideology' [nature gardens]; Leimu [saunas]; Croutier or Steward [spas]; Aaland [sweat bathing]) and the alternative worlds they call to mind (Löfgren 112).
3. Lenček/Bosker discuss this in detail; up until this time swimming had been practised chiefly for military purposes (Leeuwan).
4. See, for example, Böhme's discussions of water as cultural force in Germany and Theweleit's references to floods in western literature, philosophy, psychology and art; see also Anderson/Tabb.

Part I

Collective Identities

2

Fashionable Spa Towns in Nineteenth-century Europe

David Blackbourn

The crowned heads and social elites of nineteenth-century Europe flocked to fashionable spas in the summer. They were joined by cultural luminaries, professional gamblers and figures from the *demi-monde*. That coming together of different worlds perhaps explains why spas attracted the literary imagination, for among those who wrote about them were Lermontov, Turgenev, Dostoevsky, Chekhov, Zola, Maupassant, Fontane and Thomas Mann. These watering places have recently enjoyed new attention, from the authors of coffee-table books and writers for the magazines of quality newspapers, a revival of interest reminiscent of the earlier English obsession with the country house as an object of longing and symbol of an imagined better past (Croutier; *Fr. Rundschau*; *Süddeutsche*).

But fashionable spas also deserve attention from historians. They are places where several different lines of historical enquiry intersect: perennial arguments about the relations of bourgeoisie and aristocracy in nineteenth-century Europe; the recently revitalized history of high politics and court society; the growing cultural-historical literature on travel, attitudes towards nature, taste and consumption. This essay discusses why people went to spas. It also looks at the development of spas as businesses, what people found when they got there and how they behaved. The golden age of spa culture was notably transnational in character, which raises two other questions. First, can we see at these fashionable places anything like the development of an 'international culture'? Secondly, spa towns were where European political elites could be found in the summer months when wars were generally begun. What connection was there, if any, between the world of luxury that reached its high-point in the *belle époque* and growing international tension that found its release in the summer of 1914?

Spas were not nineteenth-century creations. It is a commonplace that people have taken the waters since the times of the Babylonians, and many later fashionable watering places had classical antecedents. They include Bath, Wiesbaden and Vichy. Read the spa publicity of the nineteenth century, or nostalgic modern accounts, and you are presented with a misleading picture of continuity: the spa

9

town X was first developed by the Romans; Montaigne visited in the sixteenth century and praised the effect of its waters on the liver; Casanova or Goethe had a love affair there (in neither case a terribly exclusive claim to fame); then in the nineteenth century it became the favourite summer destination of the Ruritanian ruling house. As we know, the nineteenth century had a talent for inventing line-ages and traditions (Hobsbawm/Ranger). It is therefore worth underlining the discontinuous history of spas. The fashionable seaside watering place, for example, was wholly a product of the eighteenth century. It was invented in England, then spread to France and Germany (Walton, *English Seaside Resort*; Corbin; Prignitz). But there are other instances of discontinuity. Spas were founded in the sixteenth century that did not flourish until the end of the seventeenth, such as Bad Pyrmont; and Pyrmont is one good example – others include Schlangenbad, Teplitz and Spa itself – of places that subsequently lost the celebrity they had once enjoyed (on Pyrmont, see Kuhnert). Conversely, many great spas of the nineteenth century were essentially newcomers. Marienbad did not take off until the 1820s. A celebrated early visitor noted that 'it was as if I had found myself in the North American forests, where a town is built in three years' (Goethe, quoted in Hahn/Schönfels 100). The German trio of Bad Ems, Bad Homburg and Bad Kissingen arose even later. Two general points deserve emphasis. First, individual spas were subject to quite sudden fluctuations of fortune. Second, the modern spa culture with which I am concerned arose in the eighteenth century as a product of the age of absolutism, Enlightenment and commercial revolution, reaching its apogee in the nineteenth century.

Why did people go? They went, naturally, on account of the waters themselves: to bathe in them (especially warm springs and seawater), or to drink them, a practice that became more widespread from the eighteenth century. Taking the waters was not necessarily the primary motive, but it was what made a spa town distinct from other destinations, even if the line is sometimes hard to draw. The health imperative itself changed over time. We can plot the shifting diagnoses that might prompt a cure, from the 'melancholia' and 'hypochondria' of the eighteenth century to the 'nervous diseases' and 'neurasthenia' of the nineteenth (Lepenies; Shorter, esp. 201–32; Mirbeau). We can also see a broader shift from the idea of taking the waters for health in the eighteenth century to taking the waters for sickness in the nineteenth, as the active cure-seeker became the passive patient, a process reflected in the growing professional authority of spa doctors and the expansion of hospitals, clinics and sanatoriums at spa towns. Finally, we can chart the mutations of balneology, from the extraordinary range of water-cure regimes that marked the Enlightenment period, through the Romantic insistence on the 'spirit of the springs' (exemplified in the 'whole-body regime' of the German doctor Christoph Wilhelm Hufeland), to the development of scientific-positivistic spa medicine in the nineteenth century, with its detailed chemical analysis of mineral water content and its specialized water-cure procedures (spray-bath, drip-bath, trickle-bath and so on). As nineteenth-century balneology became more technologically complex and specialized, it provoked a series of reactions in the name of a return to simplicity. One example was the Spartan regime at the Austrian spa of Gräfenberg, founded by Vinzenz Priessnitz in 1820. The impulse towards a more natural, holistic medicine also drove the 'water doctor' and Benedictine monk Sebastian Kneipp, author of *Meine Wasserkur* (*My Water Cure*, 1886). By the 1890s his Bavarian spa at Bad Wörishofen was drawing 30,000 visitors a year, who took cold showers, applied cold-water poultices and waded through wet grass before feasting on sauerkraut, black bread and mint tea (Reis; Schomburg).

Medical debates over taking the waters had an important international dimension from the beginnings of modern balneology in the early eighteenth century. Consider the case of the Hahn family, a medical dynasty from Silesia that played a major role in popularizing water cures. The patriarch, Siegmund Hahn, had studied in the Netherlands and knew the work of the English 'water doctor' Sir John Floyer, a passionate early advocate of cold-water bathing. Hahn's writings on the subject drew on Floyer; and, like those of his younger brother Johann Siegmund, they were to be periodically rediscovered by later German-speaking balneologists, from Priessnitz to Kneipp. The work of yet another member of the family, Siegmund's son Johann Gottfried, proved influential in the English-speaking world. It helped to bring about the 'Wright regime' developed by the Jamaican military doctor William Wright, which was further refined by the Englishman James Currie, then carried to Austria by the Viennese doctor Joseph Frank (Graetzer; Langer). This family history sketches in just a few features on a complex intellectual map of mutual borrowings and refinements. The map would be further complicated if we plotted the lines that connected these figures with balneologists at work in Switzerland (Schleuchzer, Tissot, Herpin) or France (Scoutetten, Fleury).

Not all water-cure advocates or spa doctors were confident cosmopolitans. Spas could be small-minded, inward-looking places, especially out of season, riven by petty medical feuds like the one that divided the Vogler and Döring families of Bad Ems over several generations (Sarholz 266–7). The limited horizons of some spa doctors were mocked by Heinrich Hoffmann (of *Struwwelpeter* fame) in an 1860 satire on the fictitious spa town of Salzloch, an account purportedly written by 'Dr Polykarpus Gastfenger, Medical Counsellor and Spa Doctor to the Principality of Schnackenberg, Member of the Aquatic Society, the German Shower-Association, the Men's Club and the Skittle Club of Schnackenberg, as well as Corresponding Member and Honorary Member of many other learned societies' (Hoffman). But many things worked against this kind of provincialism. Growing university research on water and its properties, international scholarly congresses, more frequent translations of foreign works and growing numbers of journals – all made it more likely that doctors, at least in the more important spas, would feel themselves to be part of a larger world. Thus Dr Armand Mora of Dax in France travelled to examine for himself the spa facilities of England, Belgium, Germany and Italy (Mora 49). That was the underlying logic of competition between the spas to offer the latest technique or installation. Holistic, low-tech spas such as Bad Wörishofen were also, whether they liked it or not, part of this international marketplace. They were selling simplicity, already a desirable commodity for parts of fashionable society in the late nineteenth century.

Despite the changes over time, and despite variation from place to place in the degree of emphasis placed on the cure itself, there was a common denominator in the medical advice offered to spa-goers. Water, they were told, was the antidote to the diseases of 'civilization' – boredom and 'nerves', stress and anxiety, gluttony and overindulgence in stimulants like alcohol, tobacco and coffee. And yet, people also went to spas to enjoy the pleasurable fruits of 'civilization': food, drink, shopping, dancing, sociability. The spa culture that emerged in the eighteenth century was defined partly by the concerns of Enlightenment medicine, but it owed at least as much to two other influences: the absolutist court and the new consumer society that was developing in urban Europe. The contribution of the court can be seen in the presence of crowned heads, in the Baroque architecture and geometrical parks of the earliest fashionable Continental watering places and in the endless 'diversions' (fireworks, *fêtes*) designed for the jaded palates of aristocratic courtiers. These elements persisted in some form even after spas outgrew their close links to the court, as they had already begun to do during the eighteenth century. What the new consumer culture contributed was equally important. The spa reproduced an urban way of life in a rural setting: theatre, reading room, luxury shops, coffee house. Here, in concentrated form, was 'the world of goods' and a place where civilized ideas could be exchanged. A more exclusive and controlled environment than city 'pleasure gardens' like London's Vauxhall, it offered the satisfactions of urbanity to a growing public that wanted to consume and converse as well as take the cure (Brewer/Porter; McKendrick/Brewer/Plumb; Kuhnert).

From the beginning, then, the spa-going public had mixed motives. And we should not underestimate the fact that they went to fashionable watering places simply because they were fashionable. The pursuit of novelty, that distinctive eighteenth-century trait, was the motor of the spas' popularity. Spa doctors and treatments were one important ingredient in what made a place fashionable; but so were social reputation and diverse material or cultural attractions. The spa season was defined by the larger rhythm of the social season, which took its cue ultimately from European court calendars (Davidoff; Werner). The spa was also one among a growing number of possible destinations for better-off travellers. Travel, no longer confined just to the aristocratic grand tour, was already being widely referred to as a 'mania' during the Enlightenment. In the nineteenth century the mania became routine. Russians travelled west and English south, Europeans travelled to North America and North Americans to Europe. Baedeker in hand, travellers were guided through Europe's historic cities and landscapes. The Holy Land and 'Arabia', once accessible only to the most intrepid, drew larger numbers; within Europe marginal places gained a new cachet. It is particularly hard to separate cleanly the attraction of the spas from the draw of two other increasingly fashionable European destinations: the Mediterranean rivieras and Alpine resorts (Löschburg; Krasnobaev/Robel/Zeman; Pemble; Bausinger/Beyrer/Korff; Stowe).

That is a summary version of why people went to spas, what might be called the demand side. But what about the supply side? For the spas, as for other fashionable venues, new means of communication were a key enabling element. Many spas were hard to reach before the railway age because of their mountainous location or otherwise difficult terrain. That was true of Gastein in the Austrian Alps, Wildbach in the Black Forest, Plombières in the Vosges and Cauterets in the Pyrenees. It took four days to reach Bad Ischl from Vienna before a railway link was established in 1877 (Wechsberg 100). As early as 1843, Heinrich Heine – an enthusiastic visitor to Norderney in its early years – observed: 'It seems to me as if the mountains and forests of every land are moving closer to Paris. I can already smell the fragrance of German linden trees; the North Sea breaks in front of my door' (cited in Küster 32). A generation later railway and steamship had transformed the nature of travel, redefining the numbers of visitors a spa might expect. At the end of the eighteenth century even the most sought-after spas accommodated very few: 400–600 a year at Ems and Carlsbad, 600 at Pyrmont, 600–1,200 at Spa, 1,000 at Baden-Baden. The numbers crept up steadily in the first decades of the nineteenth century; then they took off. In the period from roughly 1840 to 1870, visitors increased from 20,000 to 56,000 at Baden-Baden, from 2,500 to 23,000 at Vichy, from 5,000 to 12,000 at Ems, and from 5,000 to 11,000 at Aix en Savoie (Gerbod 140–1; Sarholz 187, 140–1).

A decisive shift therefore took place in the middle years of the nineteenth century, the first railway age. Another upward spike in the numbers began around the turn of the twentieth century. By 1905, the modest spa town of Bad Soden in the Taunus mountains received four times as many visitors as Baden-Baden had received a century earlier, while Baden-Baden itself was drawing almost 70,000 long-stay visitors. These heady increases were fuelled by the long economic boom that began in the 1890s, but the consolidation of the rail network also played an important part. Wiesbaden's official spa guide for 1910 referred to the 'hundreds' of express and passenger trains that ran every day, and continued: 'Wiesbaden is now directly connected to the lines that carry the heaviest world traffic, indeed in a certain sense it has become one of their nodal points' (Fuhs 361). It is tempting to dismiss such hyperbole, but grandiose claims of this kind – and Wiesbaden was not the only town to make them – might also be taken at face value, as the expression of a genuine sense that transformed communications had pulled the world together. That, after all, had been Heine's point in the 1840s, and it was a perception that underlay much of the 'poetry of steam' rhetoric we encounter in nineteenth-century Europe (Blackbourn/Eley 186–7; Schivelbusch). It is not necessarily a sign of hypocrisy that the emphasis on 'one world' was also good for business.

By 1900 spas were advertising not just their accessibility but the fact that they could be reached in comfort. The trajectory of their nineteenth-century expansion was inseparable from the growing paraphernalia of international rail travel: timetables and guides, Cook's offices and *wagons-lits* – aspects of what one writer has called 'travel capitalism' (Böröcz 708–41). Ease and security were equally important when spa guests reached their destinations. Post-Romantic visitors wanted Nature – but Nature tamed.[1] Landscaped areas of greenery were laid out and efforts made to prevent interruptions from floods or rockslides (although these efforts were never completely successful, and nothing could be done about the minor earthquakes to which many spa regions were prone). Paths were marked out in the surrounding countryside, directing visitors to suitable 'views' and 'panoramas' (Merrylees 109–25; Fuhs 440–59; Sarholz 371–2; Sternberger; König). Funicular railways allowed easy access to features such as Wiesbaden's Neroberg and the Malberg at Bad Ems. The spa was a business that required major investment in infrastructure – medical facilities, pump rooms, hotels, parks, promenades. There was no single pattern of who invested, developed and profited. It might be noble landowners, the local municipality or individual bourgeois entrepreneurs, such as the combination of Norwich and London money that transformed Cromer in East Anglia from a small resort dominated by a few prominent Quaker families into a fashionable watering place that attracted, among others, the Empress Elizabeth of Austria, Lord Curzon and Oscar Wilde (Girouard 79–90). (There is no record that the last two ever met, which is probably just as well.) In German-speaking Europe we find every variant. Aachen was developed by the local municipality, Driburg by private entrepreneurs.[2] Mostly, however, the German princes retained control of the spas, reaching agreement with the municipality over day-to-day concerns like policing. Capital was raised to invest directly in new installations, or the rights were leased to concessionaries for a fixed sum. The income from mineral springs or assembly rooms might be arranged in this way. The classic example was the casino, often run by Frenchmen who crossed the Rhine after gambling was banned in France in the 1830s, such as Jacques Bénazet and his son in Baden-Baden, or François Blanc in Bad Homburg. Until they were also made unlawful in the new German Empire, casinos brought in revenue to cash-strapped rulers and reduced their dependence on representative institutions, just as state lotteries had done in an earlier period. After gambling was banned, German spas diverted investment towards medical facilities and expanded the lucrative sales of bottled water. By the late nineteenth century Bad Ems, Schlangenbad and Schwalbach were selling millions of litres a year worldwide, a revenue stream that flowed into Prussian state coffers when these Nassau spas became part of Prussia in 1867 (Sarholz 260–5). Cure taxes on visitors produced further income.

The spa was a notable example of the emerging service town of the nineteenth century – in this case towns that were built, in more than one sense, on water. The most successful (Vichy, Bad Ems) managed to make their name internationally synonymous with the product. The Carlsbad Mineral Water Company had offices in Oxford Street, London and Rue du Helder, Paris.[3] Natural science played a part in this, along with publicity budgets. At the end of the century, for example, the discovery of radioactivity was quickly put to work: the French spa of La Bourboule advertised its 'arsenical and radio-active waters' (surely an unbeatable combination) (Orsenna/Terrasse 114). Auxiliary products such as lozenges, soap, salts, toothpowder and barley-sugars were developed (Kraus 29–39; Merrylees 166–9). Above all, however, spas tried to market themselves to a discriminating public – their facilities, parks, hotels and ambience. That governed the urban development of spa towns. It led to planning laws and local tax structures that encouraged the hotel industry, luxury shops and the construction of desirable residential property such as villas for summer visitors (and the wealthy retired people who settled permanently). It also meant that efforts were made to exclude undesirable human elements, an undertaking that paralleled efforts to shield visitors from threatening natural elements. One great motif of spas, from Beau Nash's eighteenth-century Bath onwards, was the energy devoted to removing vagrants. The itinerant jugglers and players still common in eighteenth-century spas also disappeared.

But what was to be done about lower-class native inhabitants? At fashionable coastal resorts, fishermen could be redefined as quaint and they served the practical function of rowing a visitor like Otto von Bismarck out into the Norderney harbour where he could shoot seals and dolphins (Kohl 15). Workers at inland spas were a different matter. Teplitz lost out in the nineteenth century to Carlsbad partly because of the brown-coal mines west of town; Aachen's reputation fell as its industrial workforce rose; Bad Cannstatt ceased to be the exclusive spa town Balzac had known when it became a Stuttgart suburb with a railway repair shop (Hahn/ Schönfels 111–12, 137; Blos, v. 2, 74). Successful places followed Wiesbaden, squeezing crafts (beginning with tanning and bleaching) out of the resort area altogther, through a mixture of proscription, purchase and planning regulations, just as they banned working animals and people who wore work clothes (Fuhs 202–6, 219–34; Sarholz 245–6, 360, 405). And all spa towns tried to make their off-duty service staffs invisible. In fact, for all the nostalgic tone of much popular writing on spas, we must surely be struck by some of their strongly contemporary features. These were sites of consumption that tried to pretend they had nothing to do with production. The spas offered an illusory world of virtual reality – Disneylands for the upper classes.[4]

The fashionable spa that emerged in the eighteenth century was something new. Late medieval and early modern European watering places, even those patronized by princes, had been less exclusive, with more social mingling, less separation between elite and popular culture. This change was one of the modern developments deplored by early twentieth-century writers on popular health and hygiene (Marcuse 81–2). One sign of it was the way that ambitious German spas created a new resort area (*Kurbezirk*) separate from the old bathing area (*Badebezirk*), something we see at Aachen, Wiesbaden and Baden-Baden. The exclusivity of the modern period was predicated on the existence of socially differentiated watering places. For the railway obviously permitted people other than the upper classes to travel, but most of them did not travel to Baden-Baden or Carlsbad. By the end of the nineteenth century, popular seaside resorts had been developed, such as Blackpool (Lancashire) and Westerland (Sylt), although the working and lower middle classes of Europe still for the most part took their waterside pleasures closer to home. They were the bathers of Seurat's *La Grande Jatte* and Heinrich Zille's similar paintings of Berlin, or the clerks in Jerome K. Jerome's *Three Men in a Boat*. There were also hundreds of spa towns across Europe that addressed the tastes and purses of the modest provincial middle classes. That was the universal pattern in Italy (with the possible exception of Montecatini Terme); it was true of the great majority of French and German spas.

Fashionable spas with an international clientele were the exception, a select group whose composition shifted over time but never numbered more than a few dozen. This was where the European crowned heads congregated, and indeed non-Europeans like the Shah of Persia, the Aga Khan and the indefatigable Don Pedro, Emperor of Brazil. These were the places like Baden-Baden, of which Sir Horace Rumbold remarked – looking back fondly on the 1850s – that one could hear 'the clatter of a thousand tongues in a dozen different languages' (Rumbold 2: 228). Even at Baden-Baden, of course, most visitors were not princes, or nobles, or cultural celebrities. They attracted disproportionate attention, but visitors' books show that most visitors to fashionable spas came from the more substantial professional and business classes (Schmid 107–10; Hüfner; Sarholz 291–2 and the works of Karl Billaudel cited there).

That raises several questions for historians. The enclosed, artificial world of the great spas (Thomas Mann's *Magic Mountain* comes to mind as a parallel) provides almost laboratory conditions for observing the intermingling of different social groups and the terms on which they met. One particular form of this has been much discussed in the historical literature on nineteenth-century Europe, namely the relationship of old social elite and bourgeoisie (Blackbourn/Eley; Wiener; Mayer). Let me make three points here. First, spa towns, taken as a whole, appear to mirror the broader bourgeois experience vis-à-vis the old elite, as manifested in spheres such as ennoblement, buying up noble estates or intermarriage with the aristocracy.

Just as most bourgeois were unaffected by these, but lived within their own world, so most went to spa towns that were not graced by the presence of nobles and princes. That was true even of Germany, for which the strongest claims about bourgeois 'imitation' of aristocratic manners have been made. The great majority of the 300 German spas operating at the end of the nineteenth century resembled Bad Berka in Thuringia or one of the solidly middle-class spas in the Black Forest more than they did Wiesbaden. Burkhard Fuhs has argued plausibly, on the basis of their official guides and advertisements, that these more modest spas went out of their way to emphasize their 'comfortable', 'intimate' and 'family' character as retreats concerned with health, not luxury (Fuhs 342–52). One might add that there was powerful middle-class support in Germany (and probably elsewhere) for the holistic medicine movement, and books advocating natural cures carried advertisements for small spa towns.[5] Second, fashionable spas always had a socially hybrid character. Their origins lay in a fusing of courtly and 'aristocratic' manners with those of an emerging and more 'bourgeois' public. In the nineteenth century there was a true intermingling of wealthy bourgeois (and later, plutocratic elements) with a noble elite. Each took some social colouring from the other as they began to merge into a new upper class, present in the spa towns in their capacity as a new leisure class (Veblen; Sombart; Campbell, chs. 3–4). Third, we can identify a group of bourgeois and indeed petty-bourgeois visitors to fashionable spas who clearly did not belong to a new upper class. Their presence is registered in the figures for one-day visitors, which rose sharply from the end of the nineteenth century and prompted recurrent attempts to maintain exclusive zones even within exclusive spas. They were spectators rather than participants in the social drama of the great spas.

The intercourse of bourgeoisie and old elite was not the only form of social encounter at fashionable spas. These were places where many different worlds came together. Goethe said of Karlsbad that it was the 'chessboard of Europe' and he put his finger on the elements of intrigue and calculation that were a major aspect of spa life (*Große Welt* 5). Aspiring writers or composers sought patrons, successful professionals or businessmen sought to gauge their standing by mixing with people from other walks of life, women sought suitable marriage-partners for their daughters, gamblers sought an edge, and everyone sought to see and to be seen – on the promenade, at the balls and receptions.[6] To use another favoured metaphor, the spa was a stage: it placed a premium on self-presentation.[7] Yet these examples also point to the fact that there was another, equally important side to this summer life-within-a-life. If the spa was frenetic in some ways, it was also a place to relax, to escape the rigours of business, or town, or court, or marriage. If women sought suitable marriage-partners for their daughters, men sought distraction in girls young enough to be their daughters – and with prostitutes, tacitly accepted at fashionable spas if they were discreet. Dress codes and etiquette, like moral codes, were less formal than in town (Lieven 151). Bad Ems was one of the few places where Wilhelm I of Prussia and Germany appeared out of uniform; rules about introductions and being 'at home' were more fluid. The spa was a place that was different from the everyday world, where one was free to play a role.

The relative anonymity and freedom to reinvent oneself also bred concern. Literary works set in spas devoted frequent attention to female infidelity, or to young women of dubious social origins and morals who looked to marry above themselves. These themes spoke to a combination of male prurience and anxiety, like the caricature genre that depicted women in bathing suits at coastal resorts. Socially, as the etiquette books warned, anonymity and the lowering of normal barriers made it more likely that one would be pressed into proximity with undesirable persons – *nouveaux riches* or social climbers, like the Spangle Lacquers invented by *Punch*, who used their access to public places 'where distinction was acquired by paying for it' as a means to advance in the private sphere (Davidoff 23–4). An extreme case of social anxiety caused by the difficulty of being able to 'place' people was the spectre of the confidence man, another familiar figure in spa literature. In short, there are many different social dynamics worth exploring in spa life, not just relations between noble and bourgeois, but between the worlds of business and culture, Gentile and Jew, men and women, and – not least – between the respectable surface of fashionable society and the anxieties that lurked beneath it.[8]

I have been writing so far as if the great spas were interchangeable, and it is true that visitors to fashionable watering places often spread their favours around, not just from one season to the next, but within the same summer. Spas competed with each other; and the forms assumed by that competition raise some interesting questions. On the one hand, the celebrity of a particular place depended heavily on what was, or was presented as, specific to it – its *genius loci*. That was one of the reasons for the carefully cultivated lore of a given spa: the visits *incognito* of crowned heads, the royal sexual indiscretions, the close association with a particular writer or composer, the legendary feats in the local casino, the stories about new fashions in clothing being set, such as Crown Prince Friedrich Wilhelm of Prussia accidentally inventing the trouser-crease at Bad Pyrmont.[9] A spa would also stress the distinctiveness of its natural setting – the mountains, lakes or waterfalls indelibly associated with that *particular* spot. And each spa advertised the unique virtues of its installations – parks, ballrooms, race-tracks.

Yet, even as the spas emphasized their distinctive histories, landscapes and facilities, they were selling dreamworlds remarkable by the late nineteenth century for their basic similarity: the same grand hotels with the same names (Park, Excelsior, Imperial, Palace), organized along the lines laid down by César Ritz (Schmitt; *Grand Hotel*); the same Escoffier cuisine (Mennell 157ff); the same sports, as tennis and golf facilities became required of any self-respecting great spa; the same eclectic, historicist architecture in large, new public rooms – a nod to classical motifs, a bit of Renaissance, a touch of First Empire, a dash of the exotic; the same eclectic musical programmes, featuring overtures and medleys (Schönherr 24–32). Even the zeal with which many spa visitors consumed the latest fashion – dances, women's clothing, the newest soprano – had a definite sameness to it. By the end of the nineteenth century we find an unmistakable homogenization of what spas offered to their visitors. Fashionable spas might be seen, in fact, as exemplars of an 'international style' of the wealthy, although an international style different from the one we associate with the birth of high modernism in architecture and culture during the years before 1914.[10]

Before 1914 – before the Great War. One tempting narrative trope is to write spa history as an elegy for the end of a serene *belle époque*.[11] There is symbolic pathos in the fact that Archduke Franz Ferdinand and his wife spent their last nights alive at the spa town of Bad Ilidze, and that the Emperor Franz Josef signed the Serbian ultimatum at Bad Ischl, before leaving his beloved residence of sixty-six summers for the last time two days later (Niel 27, 127–9). The war was undoubtedly a watershed. In the short term, service staff were called up, wounded soldiers arrived, foreign guests stayed home. And spas became one modest subject of wartime propaganda and national stereotypes. French orchestras dropped German music, German orchestras French music. In 1913, the French spa doctor Louis Lavielle had written approvingly about German spas as a model for his fellow countrymen. After the war broke out, he wrote another tract. The French, he now observed, had always known that the Germans were 'grossiers, gloutons, ivrognes, pilleurs et cruels'; their spa towns also showed that they were vain, dishonest and rapacious: they were 'réclamiers, épateurs, piaffeurs, bluffeurs, puffistes, esbroufeurs' (Orsenna/Terrasse 125–31). In the longer term, too, the war brought changes. It was not so much that the numbers of visitors failed to recover (quite the contrary in many cases), rather that fashionable spas no longer enjoyed the same social ambience.[12] Socialized medicine changed the composition of the spa clientele, and it proved hard to reconstruct the carefree world of the pre-war upper classes. To the extent that it was reconstructed, its chosen venues became more diverse, as the social elite tried to stay one jump ahead of the broader public that found its way to the spas.

However, there were signs of trouble in Paradise even before 1914. In the first place, claims to social exclusivity were already starting to ring hollow as places such as Baden-Baden and Wiesbaden saw a huge increase in the numbers of visitors, especially day-trip visitors. Even before the war, the rivieras and a variety of other venues were becoming attractive alternatives for old and new wealth alike, especially to the young. As Lady Dorothy Nevill observed in 1907, 'the life of a rich man today' was 'a sort of firework! Paris, Monte Carlo, big-game shooting in Africa, fishing in Norway, dashes to Egypt, trips to Japan' (Cannadine 384). Second, and more fundamental, the make-believe world of the spa could never entirely exclude the conflicts and crises of the larger world from which their visitors were fleeing. The financial crash of 1873, a reminder that capitalism had something in common with the roulette wheel, caused a decline in the number of guests at several Central European spas. The spas liked to offer their visitors the exotic sight of palms and pagodas, but they also treated 'colonial diseases', a reminder that the 'civilizing mission' was not without cost even for Europeans (Orsenna/Terrasse 58–61). And 1914 was not the first time war had made an impact. The Napoleonic years affected most European spas, mobilization abruptly cut short the seasons of 1866 and 1870, and the French deserted some German spas after the Franco-Prussian war (Sarholz 214–5, 280, 283; Fuhs 364, 373). Signs of nationalist bombast had also surfaced in the internecine competition between spas even before 1914. Finally, nineteenth-century spas witnessed attempts on the lives of the Emperor Ferdinand at Baden bei Wien, on Wilhelm I of Prussia at Baden-Baden and on Bismarck at Bad Kissingen, a reminder that some were fundamentally hostile to the world represented by fashionable spas.

The spa as victim, then? Not entirely. I have argued that spa life was built on illusions and suppressions. Boredom – that central motif of spa literature and memoirs – contained its own capacity for aggression.[13] It might be channelled into acceptable forms – gambling, sport, card-playing, social conquests. In the case of visitors who duelled or hunted at spas (like Franz Josef at Bad Ischl, with his lifetime bag of over 50,000 dead animals), aggression was hardly channelled at all (Wechsberg 100). In his poem *Don Juan*, Byron's indictment of 'good society' made the word 'bored' rhyme with the 'polish'd horde'.[14] In the great spas of the pre-war years, a veneer of civilization was laid on many dark instincts – exactly what the upper classes of this period complained about among the lower orders, in fact.

Let me make a final point. Nineteenth-century European political history was studded with episodes like the meeting of Napoleon III and Cavour at Plombières and Bismarck's doctoring of the Ems telegram. 'Spa diplomacy' did not end after the turbulent period that recast international politics between the 1850s and 1871. The German-Austrian alliance of 1879 was announced at Gastein; there were pre-war meetings between Edward VII, French ministers and the Russian foreign minister at Carlsbad. Policy-making on the promenade reminds us of the extent to which politics was still being conducted by dynastic rulers and a narrow political class in the era of European high capitalism. The fact that great decisions were being made between May and October at places where the harsh realities of life were systematically blocked out is worth remembering in the light of James Joll's call for us to examine the 'unspoken assumptions' of the decision-makers in 1914 (Joll).

Notes

A longer version of this article first appeared in Martin Geyer and Johannes Paulmann (eds), *The Mechanics of Internationalism* (Cambridge: Cambridge University Press, 2001).

1. The 'construction' of landscape is the subject of a sophisticated literature, such as Cosgrove and Daniels. One of the best dealing with watering places is Herbert.
2. See the articles by Bernhard and Bothe, respectively, in Bothe.
3. See the advertisement in Kraus.
4. Steinhauser refers to a 'world of illusions' 112.
5. See the advertisements for Glotterbad (Black Forest) and Bad Sommerstein (Thuringian Forest) in Bilz.
6. On the spa as marriage market, see Fuhs 232–5; Kaplan 91, 111, 126; on gambling, Barnhart.
7. On the 'stage' metaphor, see Steinhauser 112–15.
8. Spas varied in the extent to which they made Jews welcome. Some, like Bad Ems, became noted magnets for Jewish visitors. See Sarholz 292; Kaplan 124–6.
9. These stories and legends are endlessly recycled through non-scholarly works (e.g., Wechsberg).
10. A possible exception is the appearance of *art nouveau* motifs or its national equivalents (*Jugendstil, Stile Floreale*).
11. Elegy has been a widespread trope in fictional representations of spa life, from Goethe's 'Marienbader Elegie' (1823) to Alain Resnais' film *Last Year in Marienbad* (1961).
12. At Cauterets the number of visitors rose from 6,800 before 1914 to 50,000 afterwards; but it was no longer the spa of Orléans and Saxe-Cobourg-Gotha, Edward VII and Alfonso XIII of Spain (Vallas 79).
13. Lepenies identifies 'the dandy, on the model of Beau Brummell' and the *flâneur*, both classic spa types, as the successors to the court jester as dispellers of boredom, or melancholy (Lepenies 69, 87).
14. Spacks 191–2. Daniel Defoe said that Bath helped the indolent 'to commit the worst of murders – to kill time'.

3

The Culture of the Water Cure in Nineteenth-century Austria, 1800–1914

Jill Steward

Of the annual exodus to the bathing places of central Europe John MacPherson noted in 1873 that 'for German families of any means at all it is the holiday of the year which must be kept' as thousands of people travelled to lake and spa resorts to drink the waters and bathe. In the Cisleithanian territories of the Habsburg Monarchy the commercialization of health and leisure transformed traditional 'watering places' in Bohemia and the tourist areas of the alpine and sub-alpine regions into modern holiday resorts offering a wide range of spa treatments as well as recreational and sporting facilities.[1] Participants in this new travel culture still displayed the respect for the therapeutic and prophylactic uses of water that had been such an important element of sacred and secular journeys of the past. This essay examines the way in which discourses and practices associated with the systematic use of water for therapeutic purposes ('the water cure') were supportive of the emergence of the new culture of tourist travel established in Austria before World War I.

This culture had certain features in common with the travel cultures of the past, including the use of mineral springs and other water sources for salutary and pleasurable purposes. However, the growing commercialization of health and leisure was at odds with the discourses relating to health that had promoted and sustained past spa culture as well as attitudes supportive of the new health tourism replacing it. In earlier discourses the spas had been represented as places of refuge from the pressures of contemporary urban life. However, the advent of commercialized tourist cultures in many resorts led some observers to characterize them as extensions of the urban society that had brought them into being. By contrast, the ways of life associated with old-fashioned or austere water cures at other resorts still conformed in some measure to the ideals and values that had legitimated and supported spa culture in the past. This implied a criticism of a modern hedonistic culture, increasingly orientated towards individual gratification and the pleasures of consumption.

The particular forms of water therapy, or cure, practised in nineteenth-century Austria and their associated travel culture did not just represent a link between the travel cultures of the past and the tourism of the future, but were tied to important elements grounding the attitudes and expectations shaping modern tourist travel. Discussions of the latter have considered the metaphorical equivalence between tourism and pilgrimage journeys. The anthropologist Nelson Graburn, for example, compares tourism to a 'sacred journey', akin to the pilgrimages of the past, a form of 'ritualised break in routine' that defines and relieves the ordinary (Graburn19). MacCannell and others focus on the individual's search for 'authentic experience' while the Turners for whom 'a tourist is half a pilgrim, if a pilgrim is half a tourist' (Turner/Turner 20), argue that, as institutions, both pilgrimage and tourism in the modern world represent meta-social commentaries on the nature and troubles of contemporary existence (Turner/Turner 39).[2] For tourism, like pilgrimage, is a form of escape from the everyday and is therefore functionally and symbolically equivalent to other institutions that embellish and add meaning to life.

Historically the relationship between the two is more than just metaphorical, for, as Graburn remarks, the pilgrimages of traditional societies constitute the historical antecedents of modern tourism (Graburn 28–31). However, he makes a sharp distinction between the two, denied by Lepowitz in her study of southern Germany. She points to the many pilgrims of the past who travelled to shrines in the hope of a miraculous cure at a time when medicine was largely ineffective. Suggesting that their travelling behaviours were supportive of 'the cultural history of popular travel', she argues that they contributed to the 'specific expectations about travel prevalent in the general population of a given society' (Lepowitz 23–4).

These comments are pertinent to the study of tourism in nineteenth-century Austria, where similar conditions often applied and where many of the continuities between the travel culture of the past and the new culture of recreational tourism stemmed from the widespread use of water for therapeutic, prophylactic and pleasurable purposes. The practice of 'taking the cure' in a spa pertained primarily to the elite classes, but across Austria the survival at local and regional levels of pilgrimage traditions involving water indicates the retention of a widely held belief in its miraculous powers. Pilgrimage travel helped to lay the foundations for the development of tourism in the more remote areas of the region by creating an infrastructure that could accommodate visitors and was itself responsible for generating a tourist culture in places such as Mariazell, which received over 250,000 pilgrims annually (Baedeker, *South Germany* 373).

Comparisons of pilgrimage and tourist travel identify a commonality of purpose between pilgrims and latter-day tourists, articulated in their mutual wish to be transported to some kind of 'magical' place possessed of regenerative or transformative powers (Graburn 28–31). Such spaces have been conceptualized as 'liminal', 'in-between places'. The Turners draw on a concept derived from Arnold van Gennep's classic study *Rites of Passage* to represent pilgrimage as movement in and out of a discontinuity in social space (Turner/Turner 34–9). Rob Shields uses this notion in his analysis of Brighton beach in Britain to bring out the over-lapping nature of the two institutions (Shields 93–101). Here, the practice of sea bathing for reasons of health, underpinned by medical texts extolling its virtues (Floyer), had been established since the eighteenth century.[3] In his study Shields represents the beach as just such an 'in-between space', a 'goal-sacred site' where the 'Sea cure' was ritually presented to participants as a form of life-changing experience (Shields 84).

The spas and watering places of nineteenth-century Austria can be represented as similar kinds of sites where the hope of regeneration was often accompanied by the quest for pleasure. Visits to such places, particularly in the late spring, were linked to ancient times when the use of water was associated with religion and magic. Roman settlers in the region often built public baths over thermal or mineral springs previously used for religious purposes, while many Christian pilgrimage shrines (some still in use today) were established near water sources noted for their miraculous healing powers (Nolan 16). As new shrines were brought into existence during the Catholic Reformation lapsed shrines often took on a new lease of life as secular bathing places or small spas. Their baths often catered to all social classes and the bathing attendants provided one of the few available forms of basic medical care. Some spas became pleasure resorts providing the aristocracy with brief, seasonal forums for sociability: Carlsbad attracted an internationally famous clientele, including Peter the Great.

From the second half of the eighteenth century changes in spa culture led to a greater emphasis on the therapeutic value of water and, consequently, on spas as distinctive kinds of spaces (Mansén). The Habsburg government encouraged the uses of mineral water for drinking and bathing in order to improve the general health of the people and increase the population, thereby making its territories more productive. New ways of using the waters were generated by scientific interest in classifying mineral waters and identifying their medical properties. In the early modern period spa visits often entailed unlimited drinking and bathing in order to purge the body, but the new medicalized regime introduced by Dr Becher, the chief spa physician of Carlsbad, in the second half of the century emphasized discipline and restraint as improved understanding of, and respect for, the effects of the waters on the bodily system encouraged caution in the way they were used.

Becher regulated his patients' use of the waters by prescribing controlled forms of diet and exercise for them. This required the construction of colonnades and special bathing facilities as well as pavilions for drinking water directly from the spring. Patients for whom the waters were deemed unsuitable, such as those suffering from acute inflammatory disorders that the Carlsbad waters might aggravate, were often denied treatment or sent elsewhere. Repeated attempts were made to abolish bleeding, purging and other treatments beloved of traditional bathing attendants. Governmental efforts to 'police' public health meant that spa personnel had to be officially licensed and appointed: physicians had to be qualified doctors, and spa commissioners were appointed by the government's chief medical officer. Municipal cure taxes on guests were initiated in 1874 to pay for improvements, a pattern soon followed elsewhere (Mikoletsky).

In the first decades of the nineteenth-century the fashion for 'taking the waters' among the aristocracy and the influence of the Romantic taste for sublime, natural scenery encouraged the founding of spa colonies such as Marienbad that became known for their beautiful, natural settings. Others, like Carlsbad, were redeveloped and expanded to accommodate the influx of visitors. The new-found popularity of the spas was supported by particular attitudes to health and sickness and by discourses relating to health and medicine (Payer). Spa medicine formed a large part of Austria's 'medical marketplace' (Gijswijt-Hofstra, Marland and de Waardt 10–11). The medical establishment's refusal to prescribe medicines that might mask the symptoms of disease encouraged sick people left to the 'healing power of nature' to seek more positive help in the spas.

Nineteenth-century medical handbooks and spa guides reveal a continuity with ideas about health and disease promoted in the popular almanacs, manuals and articles of the previous century, such as the texts by the influential Swiss physician Samuel-August Tissot. Typically they encouraged the view that mental and physical health depended on the maintenance of a correct balance within the bodily system itself, and between the body and its natural and social environment, a principle supporting the diagnosis of conditions like poor circulation and imbalance of the nervous system. Spa medicine is still considered helpful for such complaints in many parts of central Europe (Payer). Tissot's influential *Avis au peuple* (Advice to People) attacked the deficiencies in lifestyle and environment he deemed responsible for the nervous diseases and other afflictions suffered by the social elites. He prescribed a lifestyle characterized by a Hippocratic 'moderation in all things'. Its principal features were exercise, an open-air life, early rising, early nights and attention to the excretory and respiratory processes: practices that became incorporated into the 'cure' regimes widely recommended in Austria as a remedy for the unhealthy effects of urban life.

Turner, in his study of the relation between body and society, suggested that the concept of health functions as a 'manifestation of the dialogue between order and chaos, purity and danger, responsibility and immorality' (Turner 97). Works such as C.W. Hufeland's popular *Art of Prolonging Human Life* expressed bourgeois distaste for the immorality and artificiality of modern urban life exemplified in aristocratic dissoluteness, luxurious tastes and immoderate behaviour. Such texts combined condemnation of disorder and excess with an idealization of the ordered, cleansing and disciplined life lived close to nature, as at a spa. The opposition of a healthy, purifying, natural mode of being with an unhealthy, polluting, unnatural urban lifestyle conducive to immoderation and bad character remained a feature of medical spa guides until the last two decades of the century.

Life in the spas in the first part of the nineteenth century was shaped primarily by their therapeutic function. Wealthy guests travelling to the fashionable spas observed by James Johnson, the English author of *Pilgrimages to the Spas in Pursuit of Health and Recreation*, may have differed in many respects from traditional pilgrims but, like them, they were committed to a kind of 'breaking with the world' in the hope of achieving some kind of regeneration. The change of place and lifestyle entailed by a spa visit was regarded as important elements of the treatment. So too was 'the sight of others worse off than themselves. Victims doomed to an early grave see recoveries going on all around and never despair' (Johnson 227).

The sense of transition from one mode of being to another was heightened by the ways in which the geographical space of the spa resort was distinguished physically and socially from that of the everyday world. Natural and architectural features of the site itself and the characteristic medical and social routines of spa life marked out and 'framed' the distinctive nature of the place and the experiences it offered. In Carlsbad, for example, the Sprudel constituted a dramatic sight in its own right. The prevailing sense of peacefulness was contrived and accentuated by carefully 'naturalized' and 'picturesque' landscaping, the whole usually contained within some form of park, bounded by pleasant walks and promenades. Along the walls and walks, inscriptions and tributes from grateful patients replicated those adorning pilgrimage shrines.

Spa life was defined by the medical regimes and the relatively informal, if sometimes intense, social life. Trips to the *Kurhaus* (pump room) and the baths began the daily routine while sociability centred around familiar rituals of association and display like the urban *corso* (promenade) (Kos). However, the unfamiliar environment promoted a sense of distance from normal life, accentuating the feeling of being outside normal time and encouraging informal patterns of interaction among the guests. Restoration of health was therefore not the only form of spa experience. The term 'romantic' often appeared in spa guidebooks but to readers the term often implied more than adulation of the scenery and reinforced perceptions of the liminal quality of the place. Stories of the legendary 'bathgirls' of the past evoked a time when the spas were associated with sexual licence of a kind now strongly discouraged by the authorities. Tales of the flirtatious *Kurschatten* (Cure Shadows) and *Sprudel Kavaliere* (Sprudel cavaliers) of the previous era indicated the kind of romantic, if temporary, relationships that might result from daily proximity in a strange place with time to fill. Famous examples of attachments formed while 'taking the waters' included those of the poet Goethe, the last of which took place in Marienbad when he was seventy-four.

The transformational magic of the conventional spa sometimes failed to work. Some sick people sought help from the peasant lay-healer Victor Priessnitz (1799–1851) who practised a version of the 'cold-water cure' (or hydrotherapy) in the mountain village of Gräfenberg in Austrian Silesia. Priessnitz's story was similar to other 'conversion' narratives (Gijswijt-Hofstra) associated with unorthodox lay practitioners in that he claimed to have worked out the principles of his system when treating himself and by observing injured animals: a common feature of legends associated with the discovery of healing waters. Priessnitz's view of illness was traditional, believing it to be caused by impurities and imbalances induced within the bodily system by diet, suppressed perspiration, unwholesome air and emotional distress. Treatment focused on the removal of obstructions to the circulation and the cleansing of the system through the use of bathing and sweating techniques, diet and the drinking of copious amounts of water. Patients came from across the social spectrum and included a high proportion of young men suffering from syphilis (Graham 10). Life in Gräfenberg was relatively austere, for, although the patients enjoyed fresh air, exercise and rest, the amenities were minimal, and reading, writing and intellectual effort were forbidden (Claridge 142). Publications about the place, not all of them complimentary (indeed, accusations of 'charlatanism' led to an official investigation vindicating Priessnitz's methods), contributed to widespread interest in hydrotherapy, recognized officially by the Viennese Medical School when it created a chair in the subject in 1860. The first incumbent, Wilhelm Winternitz, one of Priessnitz's leading disciples and a supporter of natural healing, opened a clinic in Kaltenleutgeben, a summer resort area outside Vienna. Although the severe regime centred around the use of cold bathing and was anything but pleasurable, it attracted an international clientele including the ailing wife of Mark Twain (Dolmetsch 221–2).

In the next decades reliance on the use of water by itself declined as doctors paid increasing attention to hygiene and climate. Tuberculosis and other pulmonary complaints began to be treated in sanatoriums located in the new *Luftorte* (air resorts) known for their 'pure air', like the Semmering in the eastern Alps or Zakopane in the Polish Tatra. The more entrepreneurial spas responded to the competition by transforming themselves into modern health resorts increasingly orientated towards recreational tourism. Most establishments offered a variety of treatments in which bathing and drinking were supplemented with 'graduated walks', fashionable diets, gymnastics, naturopathic remedies, electrical treatments, bicycling and sun, air and light baths, the latter made famous by Arnold Rikli's establishment at Veldes.

The growth of recreational tourism was relatively slow until the 1860s when the wealthy upper middle classes began to incorporate the aristocratic institution of the *Sommerfrische* (summer holiday) into their lifestyles. In the Biedermeier era they had seldom travelled far, spending summers in villas outside the town. In the second half of the century improvements in the roads and the extension of the railway networks encouraged the wealthy middle classes to travel to the spas and summer resorts. Here they put their leisure to productive use, combining the pursuit of mental and bodily health with a 'return to nature' influenced by a Romantic love of the countryside and a Rousseausque anti-urbanism.[4] However, the growing popularity of the practice encouraged the commercialization of the more popular places, initiating a conflict between the realities of resort life and the idealized view of the 'natural life' that had brought it into being.

This transformation of popular, commercially orientated spas into modern health resorts marked the emergence of a consumer culture in which travel and recreation played an increasingly important role. The discrepancy between the kinds of experience offered by life in a modern health resort and those available in relatively undeveloped, or more medically unorthodox establishments, became increasingly pronounced as the former underwent commercial development.[5] The leading resorts were distinguished from one another by the distinctive nature of their waters, size, particular location, climate and social tone. Private and municipal enterprise and investment renovated and expanded the facilities at Carlsbad, turning it into a world-renowned resort and an important model for the development of others (Mikoletsky; Steward). Pavements, cafés, theatres, shops and libraries and, by the end of the century, electric street lighting, hotel lifts and American plumbing created an urban effect offset by new parks and gardens.

Imperial patronage influenced the social tone of a spa. A visit from the Empress Elizabeth, a devotee of spa treatments, was always good publicity and often brought crowds in its wake. The number of visitors to Marienbad rapidly increased after visits from the English Prince of Wales, who liked to combine gentle mortification of the flesh with international diplomacy. Traditional spas such as Rohitsch-Sauerbrunn in Styria were still patronized primarily by the families of the lesser nobility and senior bureaucrats (Klenze 560), thereby retaining something of the select, intimate atmosphere of the resorts of the past. At the other end of the social scale the breadth of Austria's bathing culture and its link with pilgrimage traditions were indicated by the survival of tiny bathing establishments like those in the Ultental or Ratzes in the south Tyrol. These still catered primarily to local pilgrims, peasant farmers and small tradesmen and their families from nearby towns (Obertaler).

Expansion changed the atmosphere of the large spas. Some guests now found this overpowering rather than tranquil and the company often undesirable. The Bavarian poet Karl Stieler (1874) wrote of Bad Ischl, the holiday residence of the Emperor Franz Joseph, that 'the company is not entirely in unison with this youthful freshness of scenery . . . Nobility and monied aristocracy vie with each other in ostentation and the desire to obtain consideration; the hurry to shine is sometimes so boisterous that it drowns the wonderful calm that breathes inimitable among this scenery' (Stieler, 'Traun'84). Such comments indicate the hostile responses sometimes evoked by commercialization and the new types of guests it attracted. 'For these the trombones play, for these the golden rubbish of the shop is stored . . . The resident inhabitants are in some measure under the influence of these elements . . . They partake not only of the cash, but of the nature of the visitors, and so arises a sorry mixture of rural manufacturing natures, of summer industry and winter sloth' (Stieler, 'Traun' 84–5).

The mixing of social classes caused other tensions. Emily de Laszowska, the wife of an Austrian army officer, staying at Bad Ischl in 1896 noted the presence of that 'odious class – rich Jews who always run after the court like moths round a candle and who manage to infuse irritation and discomfort wherever they are' (271). The railways brought guests from all over the multi-ethnic monarchy to the largest spas. Germans from Vienna, Czechs from Bohemia, Italians from Trieste and Jews from Crakow all congregated in the pump room and mingled on the promenades of the west Bohemian spas and Meran, where there were also many foreigners. Guests in Carlsbad lamented the loss of the old intimacy as they found themselves but one 'unit of a crowd of health-seekers' (Merrylees 29). Despite the visible presence of the very sick, many of the 'vast throng' crowding the cafés and loitering in the shopping bazaars came more for the social life and recreational facilities than the medical regime and had to be constantly reminded that the 'object of all the visitors is, at least ostensibly, the restoration of health that has broken down under the stress of society functions, or political life, overwork or study, or the cares and worries inseparable from the existence of great financiers' (Palmer 127).

Those who found life in the spas too regimented, too urban or too expensive sought rest and relaxation in the more informal atmosphere of the lakeside. The Aussee in the Salzkammergut was particularly popular with writers and artists. The old pleasure resorts had once functioned as aristocratic marriage markets, and summer holidays at watering places still represented one of the few ways where young women could meet men outside their own limited circles. Karl Stieler remarked of the holiday season that '[L]ove-making is the chief occupation of tourists; it is just the time of year when a man is disposed to seal his fate, and also young ladies always play an important part during the season' (Stieler 'Tourists' 158). Boating parties on the lakes were examples of the way holiday life created opportunities for romantic attachments (Fig. 3.1). The maintenance of the relationship between watering places and romantic pleasure encouraged writers to utilize them as the *mise-en-scène* for fictitious relationships. Shlomo Aleichem's epistolary novel *Marienbad* (1911), representing romantic entanglements among a group of Polish Jews, included a marriage broker among its characters. Arthur Schnitzler drew on his own experiences of resort life by the Aussee in his writing as did Felix Sacher-Masoch, who used a small Galician spa as a setting for his novel, *Venus in Furs* (1870), reputedly based on a relationship initiated in Baden.

Figure 3.1   A. von Ramberg, Boating *(Schmid/Stieler 163) Courtesy of the Literary and Philosophical Society, Newcastle upon Tyne*

   In the last two decades of the nineteenth century the urge to participate in the 'return to nature' symbolized by a spa visit or a sojourn by a lake was reinforced by anxieties about the effects of modern urban life on mental and physical health. The writer Max Nordau declared the 'inhabitant of a large town ... continually exposed to unfavourable influences which diminish his vital powers far more than what is inevitable. He breathes an air charged with organic detritus, he eats stale, contaminated, adulterated food; he feels himself in a state of constant nervous excitement' (Nordan 35). Unfortunately, the growth of tourism meant that it was often impossible to avoid the contaminating and debilitating effects of civilization even when on holiday. Mark Twain described the Hallstättersee as a '[B]eautiful lake in a cup of precipices' but its 'surface [was] littered with refuse and sewer contributions [despite which] men swim in it' (cited in Dolmetsch 105).

If 'retreating to nature' was increasingly difficult to achieve, the ability of many people to retain their belief in 'nature's healing power' was exemplified by the cult of Kneippism. This was a version of hydrotherapy that combined religion with cure and turned the Bavarian village of Wörishofen into a medical shrine. Father Sebastian Kneipp's (1821–1897) philosophy and methods, as they were described in 1886 in *Meine Wasserkur (My Water Cure)*, combined the principles of cold-water therapy with the use of herbal remedies. Like Priessnitz, Kneipp, drawing on his own experiences, claimed to have cured his youthful consumption by following the advice of a book on cold bathing (Hahn). He declared that water, if 'properly applied' was 'capable of curing every curable disease . . . which mostly proceeds from insufficient hardening and bracing of a system' (9). Techniques focused on wrapping and bathing to purify the system and on the application of water to particular body parts, often using a watering-can.

Wörishofen attracted many invalid priests and monks, who mingled with the rich and famous, including Crown Prince Joseph of Austria, as they hardened their systems by walking barefoot on 'dewy grass' or new-fallen snow (de Ferro xxxii). The distinctive nature of the place was enhanced by the dripping sheets, towels and bedding hung up to dry everywhere (xix). Resisting derision from orthodox practitioners, Austrian disciples spread the message of Kneipp's 1889 book *So sollt Ihr leben* (Thus Shalt Thou Live) by establishing *Kneippvereine,* the members of which offered holistic treatment for body, mind and spirit. The Vienna section made weekly outings into the countryside equipped with sandals and watering-cans (Nowotny 551–2).

Important factors in Kneipp's success were his charismatic presence (de Ferro xx) and a growing interest in body culture and life reform shared by people from across the social and political spectrum, including the Empress Elizabeth, who was known for her obsession with slimming, sport and gymnastics. Kneipp himself was highly critical of fashionable and constraining clothing, a point of view supportive of *Reformkleider* (free-flowing female garments worn without corsets as their foundation). Equally important were the *Pfarrer*'s writings, which reinstated the relationship between morality and health and invoked puritanical values of temperance and asceticism, as did the cheap, simple and democratic nature of life in Wörishofen. This contrasted markedly with the hedonist tone of advertising for the new health resorts by warm Italian lakes or the sunny Adriatic which were driven by commercial enterprise. Even the humble *Pfarrer* was subjected to the same entrepreneurial forces. Not only did he appear on postcards (Fig. 3.2), but as de Ferro noted, his 'name has become a household word throughout Germany and Austria: his photograph is displayed in every shop-window; and "Pfarrer

Figure 3.2 'Gruss aus Wörishofen'. Postcard. Author's collection

Kneipp" bread, coffee and linen are everywhere advertised by wide awake specul-
ators who seek to make capital out of his popularity' (de Ferro xvi).

Kneipp's emphasis on 'hardening the system' was particularly in tune with contemporary anxieties about masculinity, most keenly felt by members of the elite
and educated classes and expressed in contemporary medical, psychological and
sociological texts dealing with 'degeneration' and its symptoms. Kneipp himself
commented that 'the effeminacy and degeneration of men have reached a very high
pitch. Weakened and weaklings, bloodless and nervous individuals, sufferers from
the heart or digestion are now almost the rule; the strong and vigorous have become
the exception' (Kneipp, *Water* 9–10). 'Effeminacy' was the theme of Max Nordau's
popular book, *Entartung* (Degeneration, 1892), the success of which indicated the
extent of such concerns.

Nordau reiterated the ideas of earlier texts as he wrote about the enervating
psychological and physical consequences on the upper classes of ill-disciplined
urban lifestyles oriented towards self-gratification (Söder). 'The effect of a large
town on the human organism offers the closest analogy to that of the *Maremma*,
and its population falls victim to the same fatality of degeneracy and destruction
as the victims of malaria' (Nordau 35). Many of the symptoms of degeneration
that he listed – 'nervous irritability', 'sexual psychopathy', 'neurasthenia' and
'hysteria' – he claimed to observe in those frequenting 'the highways of fashionable
watering places' (7), men as well as women. This was unsurprising for, variously

defined, these were all central elements in the discourses of the period (Steiner) and were complaints for which a *Badekur* was often the standard treatment (P. Berger).

Contemporary concerns of this kind were bound up with anxieties not just about the nature of masculinity and femininity, but also class and race (Mosse 81; Gilman). One writer who was particularly sensitive to both the gender and racial implications of the rhetoric of degeneration, expressed most clearly in Otto Weininger's *Geschlecht und Charakter* (Sex and Character, 1903), was the consumptive Jewish writer Franz Kafka, who was deeply influenced by the *Naturheilkunde* movement and made persistent attempts to harden his body. His friend Max Brod recalled their youthful pilgrimages into the forests around Prague, where they tried to unite themselves with nature by swimming 'in the forest streams, for Kafka and I lived then in the strange belief that we hadn't possessed a countryside until a nearly physical bond had been forged by swimming in its living, streaming waters' (cited in M. Anderson 76). This practice was expressive of the complex and symbolic function which water continued to play in the collective psyche. Kafka himself visited a number of spas for pleasure during his life only to find that, diagnosed as tubercular, he was to be numbered among those to whom no hope of salvation could be offered.

At the beginning of the twenty-first century, it is possible to look back on the developments discussed in this chapter and see them as analogous with our own situation. For then, as now, the concern with health can be read for its symbolic value and as a comment on the complexities and troubles of the age (Sontag). At the end of the nineteenth century contact with water still remained a symbol of hope for many sick people, but advances in medicine and the advent of recreational tourism meant that its value was now associated less with bodily renewal than with mental regeneration and general physical well-being. In our own time the new health tourism catering for people stressed out by the demands of modern life is an expanding component of the contemporary leisure tourism industry, manifested in the proliferation of luxurious spa establishments and the New Age therapies and holistic philosophies with which they are associated. Now, as then, cultural, anxieties and conflict between the consumer culture, exemplified by the new health resorts, and the materialism of the contemporary world sustaining them indicate that the focus on health and 'return to nature' in the new leisure culture represent not just a strand in medical or tourist history but a critique of 'civilization and its discontents'.

Notes

1. In 1867 these included Bohemia and Moravia, Polish Galicia and the Alto Aldige.

2. Criticism has pointed to the emphasis they placed on the search for 'communitas'. By contrast Eade and Sallnow view pilgrimage sites as arenas for the expression of competing religious and secular discourses, while Smith argues for the changing and multiple motives of travellers. Reader and Walter focus on the current use of the word pilgrimage in broad and secular contexts.

3. Translated into German in 1749, these ideas influenced a number of doctors including J. S. Hahn, who promoted cold water as a cure for cholera.

4. The philosophy of moderation justifying spa life harmonized with the *bürgerliche* virtues of reverence, discipline, simplicity and the avoidance of excess that had characterized Biedermeier Austria (Waissenberger 87; Sperber).

5. For comprehensive statistics relating to the development of spa tourism (Leonardi).

4

The Waters of San Sebastián: Therapy, Health, Pleasure and Identity, 1840–1936

John K. Walton

Perhaps the most potent linkages between water and recreation can be sought in those leisure environments that base themselves on the enjoyment and exploitation of water: the spa and, quintessentially, the seaside resort. This essay looks at relationships between water, enjoyment, amenity and conflict. By going beyond the obvious liminalities of shoreline and sea, it examines the roles of fresh as well as salt water in providing comfort and reassurance, cleanliness and security, as well as pleasure and excitement. It considers the relationships between water(s) and place identity in a distinctive resort environment, that of San Sebastián, the first and most successful seaside resort of pre-Civil War Spain, and presents approaches to an urban cultural and environmental history of water and its meanings and significances. It seeks a deeper understanding of urban pleasures and processes through a case study which should prove to have wider resonance. We begin by introducing water as a motif of tourism in modern Europe (see Shields; Luckin; Walton, 'Tradition and Tourism').

Water, Therapy and Tourism

Waters with allegedly therapeutic properties were central to the origins of modern tourism. As medical entrepreneurs provided ostensibly scientific rationales for the health-giving properties ascribed to holy wells and mineral springs, the waters became channelled, controlled and commodified. 'Taking the waters' became assimilated into fashionable rituals and practices, and certain spas attracted free-spending visitors from beyond the local area and invested in accommodation and entertainment. Across Europe Spa, Carlsbad and Bath were by the early eighteenth century among the beneficiaries of this trend, which induced crowned heads, aristocrats and representatives of newer or aspiring kinds of wealth to travel in pursuit of display, status, enjoyment and sexual adventure as well as the cure or alleviation of ailments (Towner ch. 4 and bib.). Central to the promenading and cultural rituals of spa society, however, was taking the waters, underpinned by the new mystique of chemical analysis. But surroundings and company were also part of the therapy, and the trade in bottled or even artificially simulated spa waters was recognized to offer a poor substitute for residence, and access to expertise, on the spot.[1] Water without amenities availed little, but medical enthusiasm and promotion encouraged investment in the other essentials.

The sea was more difficult to subjugate to this regime of 'taking the waters'. It had, where accessible, to overcome a set of prejudicial assumptions which regarded it as dangerous, turbulent and uncontrollable, and its environs as marshy, miasmatic and mosquito-laden. Corbin has illustrated the sea-change in medical fashions and elite attitudes, which converted deserted shores and decaying fishing villages into both therapeutic environments and fashionably desirable destinations, as a new maritime aesthetic was incorporated into the emergent cults of the picturesque and the sublime from the mid-eighteenth century. At the same time, the sea came to be seen as fecund, life-giving and evocative of creation and antiquity (Corbin). Building on popular traditions of much greater antiquity, English medicine's 'discovery' of the seaside had already begun by the early eighteenth century, before the new aesthetic of the seaside had really taken hold. But this was to be a pan-European phenomenon, and the revolution in sensibilities and tastes that Corbin chronicles helped to develop English sea bathing as well as to spread the vogue elsewhere (Walton, 'Seaside' 125–47). Sea bathing was a more 'open' phenomenon than taking the waters at a spa: beaches were open to public access as well as to the elements, although they could be 'zoned' by space and time, rule and convention. The polite society of opulent bathers could be concentrated into a bathing establishment or 'casino' to which access could be restricted by subscription, dress code and social acceptability (Gil de Arriba). The seaside was potentially a more democratic space than the spa, even though the spas in their turn might be capable of making room for impecunious health-seekers, often funded by public charities or the state (Bennett-Ruete). The differences were significant.

San Sebastián

San Sebastián became the most important Spanish sea-bathing resort, beginning in the late 1820s with French aristocrats and the Spanish royal family, nearly a century after the seaside became a commercial proposition in England. By the 1840s, long before the arrival of the railway in 1864, hundreds of Madrid families were braving the two-day journey by creaking diligence through the mountain passes (Luengo 34–5; Walton/Smith 35–61). The northern Atlantic coast was attractive for its climate, the character of the sea and complementary spa therapies nearby. This was, emphatically, water-based tourism.

Medical orthodoxies about sea bathing prescribed immersion in cold, invigorating northern seas, according to regulatory regimes which specified the length and rhythm of exposure to the waves and the precautionary measures which should be taken before and after. The Mediterranean was dangerously enervating, undermining both the physical and the moral constitution, and potentially malarial (Corbin; see also Pemble). Spain's aspiring sea-bathers were directed northwards, where the summer climate also offered relief from the stifling August heat of the capital, the central provinces and the south. Refugees from the disease-threatened furnace of a mid-July Madrid greeted the moderate temperatures and refreshing rainfall with delight.[2] The Basque coastline was the most accessible. It also had the advantages of attractive scenery (on newly fashionable criteria involving mountains and greenery), together with the distinctive language and culture of the Basques (romanticized for the consumption of tourists) and the locals' reputation for honesty and hospitality (Walton in Kirk 87–108). There were also established aristocratic spas in the hills, from which visitors descended in the summer for a complementary course of sea bathing (Urquia). San Sebastián, an established town with urban amenities and lodgings, and rebuilt since 1813, was the obvious place for bathers to congregate. Natural attributes were also important: the principal bathing beach, La Concha, a curving bay shielded by an island from the full force of the Atlantic waves (enabling bathing to take place when it was suspended elsewhere), was safe, sandy, accessible, clear, tranquil, comfortable and scenically attractive. Without this particular feature, San Sebastián would not have dominated the developing Spanish market for seaside holidays during the century between the Carlist Wars of the 1830s and the Civil War, which began in July 1936.[3]

The railway from Madrid, coupled with the long-desired demolition of the town walls and the beginnings of planned urban expansion across the plain and marshland to the south, gave a great boost to the tourist economy from the 1860s (Calvo Sánchez). Urban government set out to create and sustain a desirable environment for the Madrid-based aristocrats, civil servants and merchants who formed most of the early visitors, although as early as the 1870s they were augmented by more marginal holidaymakers who came for a week or a fortnight on special cheap trains from the capital. By the turn of the century middle-class visitors were drawn from all the Spanish provinces. There was also an international presence, especially from France. San Sebastián's status as a meeting-point for cosmopolitan high society reached a peak during World War I, when it benefited from Spain's neutrality. This fashionable edge was lost in the 1920s, especially when the dictatorship of Primo de Rivera closed down the gambling casinos in 1924 and subsequent regimes failed to reopen them; but visitor numbers and entertainment spending remained buoyant. The winter population grew steadily

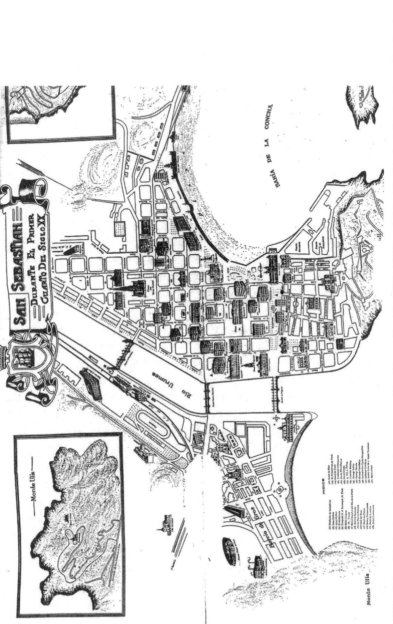

Figure 4.1 Map of San Sebastián in the early twentieth century (Anabitarte Gestión 1901–1925, published in this form by the Grupo Dr Camino de Historia Donostiarra in San Sebastián in 1971)

from just over 16,000 in 1868 to more than 78,000 in 1930 (Walton/Smith). The latter figure confirmed the town's status among a prosperous second tier of European resorts, below Brighton or Nice but among the top twenty on this one-dimensional but still telling measure (Walton, 'Seaside' 36–56).

The therapeutic, prophylactic and recreative qualities of the sea, and the desirable aesthetic qualities of a maritime environment, remained at the core of San Sebastián's appeal. In 1911, Alfredo de Laffitte articulated the 'commonsense' view on the value of sea water for various corporeal purposes, including its role as beauty treatment. He cited the admirably modelled feet of the sea-nymph Thetis, the story that Venus was born of sea-spray, and other classical allusions; but in more down-to-earth fashion he also asserted that,

Everybody knows, without needing an understanding of chemistry, that owing to the salts and organic materials which sea water contains in solution, to the aeration derived from the movement of the waves, and to the exercise which they impose on the bather, these baths produce a special tonic action which is much more energetic than those taken in fresh water. (*PV* 3 Jul 1911)

More worldly considerations were articulated by another columnist in 1920, who claimed that 'eighty per cent of bathers do so in order to fill the requirements of the highest level of the social system. It is necessary to go sea bathing in Biarritz or San Sebastián just as it is essential to take tea with pastries, or to wear a pleated skirt'. Another 10 per cent did have genuine health reasons. The rest allegedly used their seaside visit for an annual wash. The columnist emphasized that most bathers took no notice of detailed medical advice on the timing and duration of bathing, spending up to an hour and a half in undisciplined use of beach and sea. He concluded by suggesting that children's health was often an excuse for mothers to enjoy a fashionable seaside summer (*PV* 22 Aug 1920; 20 Jul 1922). The assumption that the Spanish seaside holiday was often the product of female manipulation of unwilling husbands was a newspaper commonplace.[4]

In the competitive world of fashionable resorts, maritime attributes had to be augmented by artificial and sociable attractions, on land and indoors as well as on and around the beach itself, and set in a comfortable, attractive and well-serviced urban environment. Royal patronage was important: after occasional royal visits in earlier years, Queen María Cristina summered there almost every year between 1887 and 1928. From 1893 onwards her Miramar Palace affected the use and social organization of the shoreline, and in her train came diplomats and politicians whose summer intrigues added political spice to the resort's allure. This remained so even when her son, King Alfonso XIII, came of age and was less in evidence. Casino gambling profits helped to underwrite high-class music, dancing and theatre, and later to subsidize fashionable sports such as horse-racing, motor-racing and golf, while other enterprises provided impressive bullfights and sustained theatre, cabarets, cafés and later cinema and open-air amusement parks. Local government also subsidized sport and entertainment, while policing the development of the fashionable parts of the new town and looking after the comfort and security of the visitors, not least by poor relief programmes. These helped to justify the hard line towards begging in public places (Walton/Smith). Water was thus part of a much bigger story, especially as elite enjoyments broadened to take in hills and countryside as well as central entertainments and promenades, and automobile excursions became fashionable. But, in its various guises, water was still the essential lubricant of San Sebastián's competitive success.

The Basque Sea

The sea was central to San Sebastián's identity and economic health. It involved both of the town's core identities: its Basque incarnation as the alternatively named Donostia, associated especially with the Basque-speaking Old Town and fishing quarter, and its Spanish and international roles as garrison town, centre of provincial administration, and (increasingly) gathering-place for high society and the comfortably-off from right across Spain and as far afield as pre-revolutionary Russia and the Americas. This latter guise overlapped with the Basque one: Basque virtues of hospitality, politeness, honesty, placidity and friendliness were among San Sebastián's advertised attractions (Luengo 100–10).

Basque maritime identity claimed deeper roots than the cosmopolitan one. Its relations with the sea had little to do with bathing: the Basque tradition of dancing in the Atlantic rollers in Biarritz seems to have had no counterpart in San Sebastián (Corbin 262–3). Basque seafaring traditions had strong local roots, however, in terms of whaling, fishing for cod (involving pretensions to the 'discovery' of 'America'), international commerce and a particularly demanding (in the famously storm-tossed Bay of Biscay) incarnation of inshore fisheries.[5] The fishing quarter, on the harbour side of the Old Town, was often presented as a repository of Basqueness, with local festivals appropriated from time to time, at least on the surface, for political purposes. Tourism remained peripheral here. What did become a tourist attraction was the regatta for *traineras*, or ocean-going rowing-boats, in September, but the crowds were overwhelmingly local, coming in from the neighbouring fishing villages. The municipality acknowledged this as a Basque festival, supporting it as such, as well as an opportunity to promote tourism (*Voz* 8 Sep 1918; *PV* 11 Sep 1928). Similar negotiations between tourism and Basque maritime identity could be found in (for example) the commemoration of the medieval whale-fishers' vantage-point, the *Pena de los Balleneros*, on Monte Ulía;

the monumental fish market on the edge of the Old Town, with its Basque fishwives, which was always highlighted in guidebooks; the fishing and naval museum; and the prominent statue of the explorer Admiral Elcano on the west bank of the river. Meanwhile, fishermen made money by offering boat-trips to the island and taking visitors out on fishing expeditions. Here the working and exploited sea of the Basque speakers met the Spanish and international visitors and accommodated their requirements.[6]

The Basque lower orders were discouraged from enjoying their own beaches. Right through from the 1880s to the 1930s a theme in the local press was the problem of nude or otherwise unacceptable public bathing by boys and youths, above all in the river estuary opposite the station, where they formed an undesirable spectacle to greet new arrivals. The harbour area, where those visitors who penetrated the Basque-speaking fastness sometimes encouraged boys to dive for coins (raising an ambiguity between the notions of civilized decency propagated by the press and a tendency among some visitors to seek entertainment in the 'otherness' of the local poor), was another point of tension. The problem was intensified because La Concha itself was increasingly out of bounds, as bathing regulations and the cost of meeting them made it exclusive, and the dangerous beach at Gros, on the unfashionable eastern side of the river, was reduced to a remnant by building development in 1923. Bathing here was forbidden soon afterwards. The problem of the effective exclusion of the locals from their own beaches gave rise to some anguished discussion in the 1920s and 1930s, but nothing was actually done about it.[7]

If the constraints, controls and commercialization of the cosmopolitan sea drove out the poorer locals, the quislings in this transaction might be identified as the *bañeros*, the proprietors of cabins and bathing machines (wheeled wooden sheds drawn to the water's edge by oxen, for modest undressing and shelter). Themselves Basques, they made a living by enforcing bathing controls and charging for their services. They had created a property in regulated access to the sea, dipping timid bathers themselves, from the 1830s. The municipal corporation looked after their interests when a new bathing establishment opened on La Concha in 1869 and also when the transition was made from bathing machines to cabins in 1926. The *bañeros* also hired out the awnings under which families and conversation parties gathered in the shade, and the seats on which they sat. It was never clear whether the summer made them enough to last the year or whether they reverted to fishing out of season; but, famous for their taciturnity, they were fiercely self-interested guardians of the proprieties of the beach against any form of bathing which evaded the hire of their premises. Here was a small group of Basques of both sexes who became fully co-opted into the service of the polite conventions of the beach and built up regular customers across the generations.[8]

John Walton

The Cosmopolitan Sea

Although Basque maritime traditions contributed to San Sebastián's attractions as a resort, it based its tourist prosperity on the positive perceptions of the sea that had permeated European polite society and on the fashionable accoutrements of the bathing season. San Sebastián between July and September came to be regarded as a northern Madrid, as the capital was denuded of 'good society'. Its bathing waters were important to dynastic politics: summers in San Sebastián were seen to be vital to the delicate health of the infant king at the end of the nineteenth century, and with it the initially fragile Restoration settlement of 1876 and the political stability of the country. Royal visits also provided an opportunity for the ruling family to build bridges towards the Basques, who had lost important traditional privileges in the Restoration settlement, and María Cristina embraced these opportunities. In terms of the local economy, however, what mattered was a formal use of the sea, which might have local idiosyncrasies, but matched international expectations.[9]

From the earliest days of commercial sea bathing, La Concha was regulated through the required use of bathing machines and neck-to-ankle bathing-dress. Civilization and constraint were imposed on nature and the liminality of the shoreline: immersion was to be rationed and endured under conditions tightly prescribed by medicine and morality, and a grid of prices, codes and boundaries covered the use of beach and sea. The spontaneity of Basque bathers in the estuary was deemed barbarous and threatening. Much of this was only a veneer, and policing (by a special force of *celadores de la playa*) was relaxed outside fashionable bathing hours; but the cosmopolitan sea was experienced very differently from the Basque one.[10]

Beach customs became more recreational and relaxed over time. Around 1900 families began to stay on the beach for extended periods, as children played in the sand and sea bathing became enjoyable as well as therapeutic. New technologies of pleasure were applied to beach and sea: a floating platform with gymnastic apparatus, races with rubber 'horses' (*caballos de goma*) and canoes. By 1928 the ability to swim was a fashionable necessity. Visitors gazed appreciatively on the sea where previously they had preferred to face inland. But their gaze was directed at Nature tamed, framed and dominated, in keeping with the widespread adaptation, across the western world, of the picturesque to the collective version of the tourist gaze. Alongside the elite yacht clubs there emerged, by the 1920s, a fashion for speedboat racing which, like the canoes and the growth of beach football, generated demands for restraint on peace and safety grounds. In 1931, but only briefly, recorded music was broadcast through loudspeakers. Beach and bay had become playgrounds for the comfortably-off. As part of this process the bathing establishment *La Perla*, remodelled in the early 1930s, became as important as a rendezvous for cocktails and dancing as for bathing.[11]

Figure 4.2 *'San Sebastián: beach scene (postcard view of La Concha beach in the 1920s)' (Sada/Hernandez)*

By World War I the fashionable beach was drawing increasingly critical fire from strict Catholics and cultural and political Basque nationalists. The vogue for sunbathing was beginning: men were frolicking and showing off their bodies in ways that disturbed moralists, who saw beach and sea as revolving around health rather than hedonism. When, by the mid-1920s, the combination of skimpy bathing costumes and flirtation on the beach and in the sea spread to young women, a fierce polemic developed. By the 1930s a Catholic campaign against immodesty on the beach was reaching a climax. 'Acción Católica de la Mujer en Guipúzcoa', a Catholic women's action group, lobbied local and provincial government in attempts to get their approved neck-to-ankle bathing dress made compulsory and tried to keep parts of the beach safe for like-minded people by hiring blocks of bathing-cabins. Here, however, they ran up against the traditional loyalties of bathers to particular cabin proprietors, and youthful fashions proved too powerful for them. The campaign was a noisy fiasco, and it took the outcome of the Civil War to reinstate (or indeed introduce) the Catholic campaigners' preferred bathing regime.[12]

The local authority continued to police morality on the beach, but at a much lower intensity than the campaigners demanded. Its dilemma (to allow enjoyment but not licence, in a setting where one seemed to elide easily into the other) reflected the perceived dualities of water: pure but easily polluted, moral but corruptible, health-giving but life-threatening. The beach brought all this into sharp focus, but related issues emerged elsewhere (compare Shields ch. 2; Walton, 'Popular' 170–88).

The Water of Life

To sustain their mystique, resorts also needed more mundane aquatic attributes, including reliable supplies of fresh water for drinking, domestic and public uses, and sources and storage systems that were above suspicion. Where the visiting season coincided with low precipitation and high evaporation, any problems were magnified, and this applied to San Sebastián, despite an annual rainfall which, on late twentieth-century statistics, made it the second wettest European city with over 100,000 inhabitants. But the water supply was an enduring preoccupation: as a local historian remarked in 1916, it was vital, not only to make the streets and promenades look attractive, but also 'to resolve issues intimately connected with public cleanliness, general hygiene and a multiplicity of needs felt by all classes of people'.[13]

Despite municipal investment in water supplies in the mid-1860s and early 1870s, problems were already arising in dry summers a decade later.[14] Short-term improvements were mere palliatives, and in 1891 the Queen's own water supply was delivered by train from Madrid. Municipal self-esteem was at issue, and in 1895, after a long parliamentary struggle, access to new supplies was granted. This was greeted with elaborate civic ceremony and public rejoicing, which were eclipsed only by the opening ceremony four years later. The town's needs, as calculated for the campaign, included water for 500 baths, 3,000 'English water-closets' and the washing of 400 carriages. Public fountains accounted for more than twice as much as all these requirements put together. Water was more than just a public health issue, and the town's needs continued to outpace its sources.[15]

Not until the early 1920s was the corporation able to buy a source and catchment area, which guaranteed a copious supply of pure water, and combine this with a hydroelectric scheme. This not only enabled the town's street lighting to be updated, silencing its critics, but also liberated the gasworks from the need to illuminate the outlying streets, enabling it to cope with expanding residential demand. Thus the water supply was directly linked with the bright lights that were necessary to prolong the tourists' pleasures (and to show that the town had nothing to hide), although in some eyes the pristine purity of the drinking water might be compromised by prior use, as the water which powered the turbines later emerged through the taps. Here was a triumph of modernity and rational economy, founded in the domination and harnessing of nature, and duly celebrated as such.[16] The weather was beyond control, and from time to time unexpected storms were damaging rather than refreshing, while sustained spells of bad weather in late August and early September might bring the season to a premature end. But here, too, water was essential to San Sebastián's attractions, especially for those who made the pilgrimage from the hot aridity of a central Spanish August. Controlling the weather might be out of reach, but policing water quality was a different matter. It is instructive to see what was done and what was neglected here, where the concern with drinking-water quality was not matched by awareness of damage to the marine environment. Fortunately for the tourist industry, the visitors were even less aware of the issues than were the municipal managers (*VG* 1 Sep 1893; 17 Jul 1912).

Pollution and Control

Basque and fashionable maritime ideals depended on the purity of the waters that were being consumed, but the growing numbers of permanent and seasonal residents, together with the industrialization of San Sebastián's hinterland, made it impossible to rely on nature to cleanse itself. Intervention to remove or minimize evidence of marine pollution eventually became a concern of municipal government, although (as in other bathing resorts) investment and technical success were less convincingly apparent than in other technologies of presentation, pleasure and comfort. The first concern was to get an effective sewering system in place. This outweighed all but the most obvious and direct considerations of marine pollution. As a journalist remarked in 1884, it was vital to 'avoid as far as possible the nauseating smell emitted by the sewers in most of the streets', which threatened the town's reputation for good urban management as well as for its public health (*Urumea* 17 Sep 1884). The improvements to sewer gradients and flushing procedures, which gradually resolved this problem (relying in turn on expanded water supplies), also served to transfer the sewage more rapidly and efficiently into the sea. The local authorities were well aware of the threat this posed in specific settings. When the Queen and infant King began their San Sebastián bathing regime in 1887, the royal bathing machine was placed closer to the centre of La Concha beach than would have been ideal, because in the western corner of the beach a small sewer ran into the sea, and the Queen refused to bathe any closer to it (*Epoca* 17 Aug 1887).

Direct sewage pollution causing visible turbidity and smell was dealt with swiftly, and sewer outfalls were kept well away from La Concha. The interplay of prevailing winds and currents in the bay was not understood, although studies in the mid-1970s were to show that a disturbing number of cards placed in the water at the sewer outfalls found their way to the beaches of Gros (especially), Ondarreta and to a lesser extent La Concha itself, with corresponding levels of bacterial pollution (Contreras Poza 76–87). Worries about invisible pollution, with possible public health consequences, were of long standing. One of the arguments in favour of a proposed sea-wall and causeway linking the western side of the bay with the island of Santa Clara was that a new sewer outfall could be placed on its seaward side. Deposited pollution was sometimes tangible: as an environmental health researcher put it, 'on the famous and aristocratic Ondarreta beach . . . children spent time playing in the sand among large pieces of excrement', although this made no discernible impact on disease statistics. But the acknowledged lack of understanding of currents and beach formation, and a strong sense of the vulnerability of La Concha to interference, inhibited a sequence of such projects, especially when, in the late nineteenth century, they came from proponents of sea-port development in this area, which foundered when it became clear that they were incompatible with the bathing season. Tangible short-term damage caused by quarrying and sand abstraction offered warning lights, which were heeded more readily as the importance of beach tourism to the local economy continued to grow (de Izaguirre 71–109; Contreras Poza 90).

Treating the sewage, which was mooted in the 1890s, was rejected as too expensive and complicated, and municipal officials continued to assume the sea's efficacy as a purifying agent. Reactive intervention in response to specific, visible problems left the larger, hidden agenda untouched. Away from La Concha, the less fashionable beach of the Zurriola was not only polluted by the Urumea estuary, but also suffered from rubbish dumping which, in 1894, included the corpses of horses killed in the bullfights (*UV* 3 Aug 1894). Not until the mid-1930s was systematic palliative action begun, as complaints about unpleasant smells from decomposing materials in the harbour (which reached the noses of strolling visitors) and from the river estuary at low tide were followed up by the local authority (*PV* 19 Jul 1934). At the start of the 1935 season a net was placed at the harbour entrance to prevent refuse from reaching La Concha, and the corporation was disinfecting the beach itself every afternoon with a chemical product, as doubts began to be aired about the salubrity of this symbolic core of the resort's identity (*PV* 14, 28 Jul 1935). Before this could go any further, the Civil War intervened. Assumptions about the pristine state of the Basque and cosmopolitan sea remained almost unchallenged. San Sebastián's river was another matter.

Pollution problems in the Urumea came to a head in the mid-1920s, when the corporation developed schemes to exploit the channelled and controlled river as a tourist attraction, with boat trips and an aristocratic club at the mouth of the estuary. The clerical traditionalist newspaper *La Constancia* objected to this in principle, as an extension of profit-driven worldliness into new areas, using a scheme that might damage the lands of virtuous Basque farmers higher up the river. In support of this political agenda it provided detailed evidence on the pollution, which would undermine the plan, pointing out that the city itself, and a string of smaller settlements upstream, voided their waste into the hapless river, which had become an open sewer. This was apparent to all who used the evidence of their eyes and nose. 'This cannot be tolerated in the name of hygiene, nor of public health, nor of the beauty of Donostia, nor even the reputation of the Urumea, which, despite its present ugliness and all that goes with it, is to be changed into something even worse and dirtier'. Common sense should have told the corporation not to impede the flow of these waters and that the river must be cleaned up before it could be exploited in the proposed ways. Here principled opposition to development was able to draw on a sense of the defiled sacredness of Donostia's Basque river in order to advocate the pursuit of practical remedies. But these were to take a long time in arriving.[17]

A key element in the concept of pollution is that of matter out of place (Douglas). San Sebastián's politics of water focused on sustaining the illusion that the sea, at least, was free of such misallocated material, and that it constituted a safe recreational and indeed a therapeutic environment. La Concha was especially sacrosanct. But water itself was perfectly capable of getting out of place and posing problems for an orderly municipality, and this constitutes a further theme in the relationship between water, therapy, enjoyment and the civic identity of San Sebastián/Donostia.

Keeping Water in Its Place

The concern to contain and control unruly water worked at several levels, from the very general macro-level concern to reclaim land from its dominion, by draining and levelling marshland for building, to the micro level at which personal hygiene had to be regulated, while the watering of plants on balconies was constrained as a private process, contained within the household, rather than an invasion of the public street. Marsh drainage and containment of watercourses were central to San Sebastián's urban expansion, which extended over a peninsula whose dunes and reed-beds had to give way to streets and building plots, and whose stagnant and often polluted waters had to be made safe and healthy. This theme ran through the period, climaxing impressively with the completion of the Old Town's eastern extension in the late nineteenth century, which involved building a sea-wall, whose cost and upkeep generated dispute between developers and municipality; and the Kursaal development east of the river in the early 1920s, shortly after the building of a carriage drive that subjugated the rocks around Monte Urgull, the fortified central hill behind which the Old Town nestled. Thus was the domination of Nature, particularly the containment and observation of the sea, a prominent aspect of San Sebastián's development, and one in which its propagandists took public pride (Izaguirre; Calvo Sánchez). Once rendered almost impotent (except when its sudden rage put bathers to flight and smashed bathing-vans), the angry sea became an object of fascinated contemplation, especially when huge waves smashed against the viewing-platform of the *rompeolas* on the western estuary or made the carriage drive impassable. Occasionally those who played with the waves got a good soaking, but the pleasure taken in the spectacle of wild seas (especially among visitors from central Spain) was predicated on its containment, the technology of which also assisted in its presentation as spectacle.[18]

The containment of potentially contaminating personal fluids was also a concern of local government. The regulation of sexual behaviour (as opposed to bodily display in and around the sea) is a step beyond the themes of this chapter. San Sebastián was furtive about its record here.[19] Its public urinals, an essential aspect of civilizing the streets by containing and directing problematic liquids, were another matter: here civic pride was ostentatious to a striking degree. As part of San Sebastián's claim to be a model local corporation in 1884, its urinals were singled out for their daily disinfection and careful cleaning. Improvements were made in 1891, and from 1906 the older lavatories were replaced by new under-ground conveniences, the first of their kind in Spain. The most prominent of these occupied 'perhaps the most attractive site in San Sebastián' and featured promin-ently alongside more conventional architectural features in a map of 'monumental San Sebastián' published shortly afterwards. Such facilities removed all trace of legitimacy from urination in the street, although they did not prevent it from happening.[20]

The streets, assiduously watered by the local authority to lay the dust, which symbolized local government failings elsewhere in Spain, were protected from the random and damaging consequences of the balcony gardening that added to the town's attractions. A theme running through from the 1870s is the regular prosecution of householders for watering their pot-plants onto the heads of passers-by: a telling illustration of the attention to detail that the local authority applied to every aspect of the preservation of order and the containment of potential sources of disamenity and nuisance, liquid or otherwise.[21]

Water, Technology and the Ordered City

As a beach resort, San Sebastián continued to depend on the reputation and amen-ities of La Concha (and, after 1925, Ondarreta) even as visitor tastes changed and other attractions multiplied in the first decades of the twentieth century. After Primo de Rivera's closure in 1924 of the roulette tables at the two casinos (the Gran Casino of 1887 and the Kursaal of 1922), which in addition to being attractions in themselves had subsidized a wide range of other fashionable entertainments, contemporary commentators tended to reiterate the importance of the beach, with extravagant praise for its pleasures, comforts and picturesque appeal. The municipality was urged to offer more amusements on the beach, for children and adults alike, and from the mid-1920s onwards it duly did so, while it negotiated with difficulty the conflicts over changing fashions in bathing dress (including the appearance of 'beach pyjamas' for women in 1931) and sunbathing (always associated with proximity to the sea). The reinvention of *La Perla* as a seaside dancing, drinking and entertainment centre is symptomatic here. But a key part of San Sebastián's identity, its Basque incarnation as Donostia, entailed an alternative (if overlapping) array of perceptions of the sea, and of water, which was often in tension with the resort's cosmopolitan face.[22]

The organization and control of water-based recreation thus remained central to San Sebastián's fortunes as a resort, in a fiercely competitive international environment. The pursuit of consensus, or at least of ways of managing the beach that satisfied most of the visitors most of the time and minimized overt conflict between contending activities and cultures, was a high priority for an increasingly strife-torn local authority, especially as San Sebastián embraced the Second Republic in 1931 with an enthusiasm not shared by many of its elite visitors (Rodríguez Ranz). But this chapter also draws attention to the other roles of water, and the social tensions surrounding its supply, quality, containment, control and enjoyment, in this setting. Holidaymakers (and residents) drank and washed in water as well as bathing in it, enjoying aquatic sports and contemplating it (and its denizens, in the popular local Aquarium). Water ran through the veins of the city, so often personalized by contemporaries. The equation between water and health was particularly important, and its resolution demanding, in a setting where a healthy image was an essential advertisement. The pleasures of the holiday were predicated on a sense of security about health and amenities, in which water played an essential part, and the building development of the town depended on containing water that had been newly defined as out of place through drainage and public works. A full analysis of the relationships between water and recreation in an urban resort context necessitates that all these themes, and the relationships between them, be contextualized and worked through. That is what this chapter, in limited compass, has attempted to do.

Notes

1. *La Epoca* 30 Jul 1872, advertisement for 'baños de mar en casa'.
2. For example, *La Epoca* 21 July 1870; 15 July 1872.
3. For example, *El Pueblo Vasco* (hereafter *PV*) 13 Aug 1911.

51

4. For example, *El Diario de San Sebastián* (hereafter *DSS*) 3 Jul 1881; *La Epoca* 10 Jul 1885.

5. Kurlansky ch. 3; see also Archivo General de Gipuzkoa, Tolosa, SM ISM 24/2 (*El Sol*, 1919) and 24/19, Múgica proofs, on Basque fisherfolk.

6. *La Unión Vascongada* (hereafter *UV*) 16 Jul 1892;1 Aug 1898.

7. *La Voz de Guipuzcoa* (hereafter *VG*) 8 Jul 1886; 7, 11 July 1891; *UV* 15, 29 Jul.1892; and subsequently; Contreras Poza 93 shows a contemporary painting (1888) of children diving for coins in the harbour.

8. AGG, DM IDM SS 67; *PV* 11 Sep 1924; 6 July 1926; 3 August 1928; 15 August 1930; *VG* 8–15 Aug 1931.

9. See the eulogistic obituary of María Cristina in *VG* 30 Jan 1929; this was San Sebastián's Republican journal.

10. Walton, 'Consuming'; Archivo Municipal de San Sebastián (AMSS), A, 10, I, 69, 6, Reglas para bañistas, 1905.

11. *PV* 27 Aug 1922; 22 July; 28, 31 August 1928; 5 July 1930; *VG* 20 Jul 1891; 11, 30 July, 1, 9, 15 August 1931; 9 July 1933.

12. Koldo Mitxelena J.U. 5280, Acción Católica de la Mujer en Guipúzcoa July 1934, 5–7; Aug 1934, 5; May 1936, 9–10; *La Constancia* 24 Jul 1934; *PV* 2 Jul 1934; *La Cruz* 28 Apr 1935 and passim.

13. AGG, SM ISM 24/8, proofs of Múgica's history of Guipúzcoa 13.

14. Larrinaga 49–50; AGG, SM ISM SS 22, history of San Sebastián's water supply; *DSS* 28 Jul and 10 Aug 1881.

15. Anabitarte 63–87; AMSS, B,10, I, 392, 12; VG 18 Jul 1891.

16. AGG, SM ISM SS 22, cuttings from *PV* 22 Mar 1922; *VG*, undated, c. 1923.

17. *La Constancia* 25 Jan 1924, in AGG, SM ISM SS 22.

18. *El Urumea* 27 Aug 1884; *UV* 9 Jul 1892, 17 Aug 1894; *VG* 14 Sep 1918.

19. *La Constancia* was the only local newspaper to discuss the subject openly; see Graves 47–8.

20. *El Urumea* 12 Aug 1884; Anabitarte 78–9; AGG, SM ISM 25.III 7/1, map of 'San Sebastián monumental'.

21. DSS 10 Jun 1876; PV 9 Jul 1915 and 29 July 1919; Walton et al., 'Crime, Migration' 103–4.

22. *PV* 15 Jul 1925; 30 Apr 1927; 4 Sep 1928; 5–20 Jul 1930; 7 Jul 1931; *VG* 2 Sep 1931.

5

The Thrill of Frozen Water: Class, Gender and Ice-skating in The Netherlands, 1600–1900

Jan Hein Furnée

From the earliest dykes and the United East India Company onwards, water has been viewed as a main source of Dutch identity in terms of political culture and economic success. As a place for leisure pursuits, however, it has been frozen – rather than fluid – water that has substantially marked Dutch identities and experiences for more than four centuries. In 1841 a national typology of the Dutch reflected this long tradition by suggesting that the Dutch 'come into their own' only during those relatively scarce moments when canals, ponds, rivers and lakes are covered with a thick layer of ice, offering an exceptional stage for ice-skating:

> Hardly has all of nature come to rest, hardly has the earth covered its nose and ears with a woollen blanket of snow, hardly has the stream lain down to sleep in its bed, than the Dutchman defrosts and changes his temperament in the opposite order. He burns and boils like the Hekla under the snow. The time has finally come! The ice is still weak and scarcely three florins thick . . . But on ice he is a daredevil . . . Everything indicates where he is going. Not only his duffel coat, his red muffler, the burnished skates in his hand, but his whole appearance, the bloom on his face, the gleam in his eyes . . . the thrift and impatience that his posture bespeaks . . . With cold and zealous fingers he fastens his skates. He is ready. One-two! three-four! five-six! There he floats like a bird on its wings . . . His sense of himself is an enviable mix of consciousness of strength and enjoyment of movement. As long as he has his skates under his feet, the skater is the happiest of all people. (Hasebroek 86)

In Dutch cultural imagination, frozen water not only transforms individual moods but also sets a fascinating scene for ice-skating practices that temporarily intensify and transform social experiences. Evaluating these practices and experiences in terms of class, gender and, to a lesser extent, age, this essay introduces the seventeenth-century 'canonical' Dutch skating culture, discusses the emergence of new competitive skating practices in the nineteenth century and analyses the resulting mixture of skating patterns as exemplified by the late-nineteenth-century Dutch residential capital The Hague. In this way, the essay will show that, especially in the last decades of the nineteenth century, the thrill of frozen water was invested with a wide, complex and often conflicting range of meanings, which both reflected and contributed to genuine shifts in urban social and political relations.

The Carnivalesque Tradition of Ice-Skating in the Seventeenth Century

Although ice-skating practices find their origins in the Middle Ages, their abundant representation in seventeenth-century visual arts and literature – collected in nineteenth- and twentieth-century folkloristic accounts and anecdotal anthologies (ter Gouw 580–92; Wichers; Meijerman) – marks their significance at that time and shows that they had already developed into a coherent skating culture. In an urban society characterized by increasing social divisions, the crucial motif in both the famous winter landscapes of painters like Hendrick Avercamp and the so-called literary 'ice-pieces' (*ijsstukjes*) by writers such as Bredero reflected the notion that skating momentarily softened, dissolved or even overturned existing social differences and hierarchies of class, gender and age.

So when, for example, Bredero in his 'Moortje' described the culture of ice-skating in early seventeenth-century Amsterdam, he emphasized that, during the periods when the river Amstel was covered with ice, one could discern how both 'flaxworkers' and 'the most splendid youth' – representing in his view two of the most extreme positions in the city's social hierarchy – were equally engaged in the pleasures of ice-skating (ter Gouw 584). A lesser known writer, Godewijck, alluding to the model of a three-layered society, stressed the same democratizing capacity of ice-skating on the canals of Dordrecht, where it 'swarmed of gentlemen's sons and daughters, mixed with burghers (*burgers*) and the poor' (ter Gouw 584). Visual and literary representations also emphasized how ice-skating attracted to the same extent people of all ages, e.g., toddlers, marriageable youth, adults and even the aged. In some cases, hierarchies of age were overturned as the elderly were represented as the best skaters of all (Meijerman 92–5). Finally, ice-skating culture was also perceived as a main leisure pursuit equally accessible to women and men. After having pointed out the elderly, Six van Chandelier summed up the presence of women ice-skaters in one breath, making special reference to their 'respectability' and suggesting that this unconstrained female access was some-thing quite exceptional and in need of legitimization (Wichers 115). By having social indicators of class and gender intersect, representations of ice-skating revealed a particular fascination with the participation of upper-class women, who skated so graciously and freely amongst what was defined as 'the public'.

Figure 5.1   Hendrick Avercamp, Winter scene with a frozen canal, c. 1620. Panel,
36.8 × 65 cm. (From the private collection of Mr and Mrs Edward William
Carter, Los Angeles, California; in Sutton, plate 10)

Overturning the usual hierarchy between the sexes, some writers did not hesitate
to portray them as 'great mistresses on ice' (the Dutch *bazin* being the feminine
equivalent of *baas*, 'master', without the romantic-erotic connotations of the
English 'mistress').

Skating on frozen canals, ponds, rivers and lakes did not merely attract persons
of different classes, gender and age, it also intensified their mutual social relations.
The informal and intimate custom of skating in rows (*aan een lijntje*) materialized,
or as one might argue, embodied social relations between individuals who did not
socialize in other areas of urban life. Representing the skating rinks as the
'shuffling lane (*sullebaan*) of love', the poet and historian P.C. Hooft, like most
of his contemporary writers and painters, highlighted how ice-skating offered
young men and women an exceptional opportunity for acquaintance and intimate
contact (ter Gouw 586). As another poet wrote approvingly, the act of ice-skating
even dissolved boundaries dividing young men and women from different classes
(and of different ages): 'Here one does not ask of class, / here one is frank and
free. / Here a farmer's maiden has a nobleman at her side, / there one sees a
farmer's son skating at the head of a row of some damsels, / over there one sees a
courtly chap leading a female burgher (*burgeres*)' (Meijerman 59).

In his illuminating article on the cultural meanings of ice-skating, the Dutch
anthropologist Eric Venbrux recently argued that the temporary softening,
dissolving and overturning of social boundaries in ice-skating should be understood primarily in terms of the liminal position of frozen water, both in its temporal

and spatial dimensions.[1] In his view, periods when waters freeze over mark the climax of the winter season and announce a new cycle of seasons, making them especially suited for so-called '*rites de passage*'. During these rites of passage a society turns reflective, challenging its main organizing principles of class, gender and age. Yet it does so without posing a structural threat to these existing social orders. In the case of skating, periods of frost were highly unpredictable and mostly short-lived (even during the so-called 'Little Ice Age' between 1550 and 1850), while the quality of the ice was always variable and an easy prey to snow-fall. The challenge of the temporarily intermixed social orders on ice could not represent, therefore, a structural form of social protest but, by its extraordinary character, contributed to the general consensus that beyond the skating season the existing social relations were to be perceived as 'normal'.

The spatial qualities of frozen water also enhanced the ritual capabilities of skating. Its ambivalent, hybrid status – not land, not water – made it an exceptional type of space where existing social differences and hierarchies could be challenged and negotiated more freely than on more 'stable' surfaces. According to Venbrux, the very act of skating itself – moving from land to water and shifting the usual correlations between one's body, time and space by way of accelerated speed – makes it a transgressive ritual. In analogy to its temporal exceptionality, the unusual spatial phenomenon of frozen water defined, in a way, the rigid social status quo beyond its banks.

Seventeenth-century ice-skating obtained much of its ritual character and meanings from the representation and canonization of the above-mentioned democratic motifs in literature and the visual arts. Appropriating various elements from the carnivalesque culture of urban fairs, the practice and performance of skating itself, however, contributed to its ritualization. The so-called 'ice-fairs' represented the climax and main point of reference of early modern Dutch skating culture (Ter Gouw 585–8). In the harshest winters, when even the broadest rivers such as the Amstel in Amsterdam and the Maas running through Rotterdam froze over, various performers, varying from conjurers and tightrope walkers to male and female dancers on skates, gathered on the ice. Loud bands, the sound of trumpets, Turkish drums and spectacular fireworks defined the fair as a rite of passage and legitimized the excessive and sociable consumption of jenever, cognac, pancakes and waffles at a multitude of refreshment stalls (the so-called *koek-en-zopies*). The ice also attracted animal sports, target shooting and even, as a result of its legally ambivalent status, gambling. This competitive culture – with its ingredients of transgression, spectacle and commercialization – extensively affected the practice of skating itself. Publicans organized speed-skating compet-itions for fat geese or trophies of silver and gold. Both farmers and aristocrats organized horse-drawn-sledge races, and fishermen competed in ice-boats. To underline the exceptional nature of the ice fairs, a range of stalls offered memorabilia, such as prints and curiosities, thereby imprinting these fairs on frozen rivers as crucial sites in the collective memory.

The ice-fairs, just like skating in general, created occasions during which the organization of society became an object of self-reflection. Dominant ways of social organization could be criticized and alternative social arrangements temporarily performed. On the other hand, one might argue that these intense experiences of an alternative society contributed much to the continuity of existing social orders. The extraordinary character of the fairs assumed that both the existing hierarchies between classes and the ruling ideas about the unequal relations between the sexes were 'normal' and 'natural'. Ice-fairs offered times when social discontent could be temporarily relieved rather than challenged. The repeatedly stressed fact that intimate contacts between men and women were free of obligations suggested that the unhampered warmth and freedom offered by frozen water did not threaten existing conventions on stable ground (Venbrux 276). In addition, the social cohesion performed in ice-skating – contrasted to models of society consisting of two or three sharply divided classes – was not so much framed by a democratic idea of egalitarianism as it was by an aristocratic perception of a society consisting of a God-given chain of closely connected, yet unequal ranks and individuals. The custom of people from different classes skating in a row, therefore, symbolized an aristocratic rather than a democratic worldview. The participation of local mayors in ice-skating, a fact described repeatedly, was not a democratic gesture but primarily a political statement of their aristocratic supremacy. Indeed, Bredero praised the intense sociability on ice, yet kept a keen eye on the way Amsterdam aristocrats distinguished themselves from the public by overtly showing off the richness and beauty of their winter coats (Wichers 118).

The Nineteenth Century: The Emergence of Speed-Skating

The seventeenth-century carnivalesque tradition of ice-skating established a canonical set of practices and meanings that have framed Dutch attitudes towards frozen water until the present day. Nevertheless, from the eighteenth century onwards, and especially in the first half of the nineteenth century, processes of decreasing social cohesion between classes, the increasing cultivation of 'separate spheres' between the sexes, climatological changes and the emergence of new skating practices considerably shifted the ways in which skating was performed and experienced.

As early as 1776, the first Dutch folklorist Le Franc van Berkhey observed that within upper-class circles, and even among women in general, the appeal of ice-skating was already decreasing substantially (Wichers 134). On the other hand, in 1770 a French diplomat remarked that ladies and gentlemen in The Hague were still skating before dinner to increase their appetite (Meijerman 62), and in 1809 a chronicler from Amsterdam stressed the unconstrained continuity of early modern skating culture. He described how 'not only the mob, but also the bourgeois (*burgerlieden*), yes even *petit maîtres* and so-called *elegans*, and often women of all ranks, enjoy themselves on the canals' (Wichers 180–3). Even the ice-fairs on the Amstel were still popular, 'a sort of Carnival, where all is joined: sledges and carriages, pubs and waffle stands, tightrope walkers and music . . . as if one were engaged in celebrating a public feast to which the whole city was invited'. In the same manner, 'equality reigned' during the 1838 ice-fair on the Maas in Rotterdam, where 'the velvet greets the serge amicably, and duffel and fur skate together', and in 1855 a Rotterdam minister thanked the broad river again for having created a 'colourful mix of classes, sexes and ages': 'Its even path levels the inequalities of life', so that 'the skating rink establishes a conciliation of ranks like a mirror of refined communism, a conciliation which cannot be obtained by any other egalitarian system' (Bogaers; Ridder 20).

By 1850, however, many of the key elements of early modern skating culture had lost much of their self-evident vitality. In his folkloristic study on Dutch popular recreations, Jan ter Gouw in 1871 confirmed that 'in this century skating rinks have become unfashionable in the eyes of "distinguished" persons and those who seek to emulate them, so that the unconstrained cheerfulness and familiarity, the freedom, equality and brotherhood of earlier times are lost, and one skates in the skating rink as if one were alone in one's own company, without looking at anybody or engaging with others' (ter Gouw 583, 591–2). Nineteenth-century skating discourses such as the above offered not so much actual descriptions as they attempted to revitalize the ice-fairs as rituals of social cohesion in destabilized urban societies and as respectable alternatives to the increasingly disputed urban fairs. But the climate did not co-operate. After the end of the 'Little Ice Age', Dutch winters by the 1850s were generally too mild for broad rivers to freeze over (de Jong 25–7).

The decreasing occurrence of ice-fairs and the declining popularity of active skating among the upper classes, and among women in general, was also a result of the rise of a new skating culture constructed around speed-skating competitions. Originating in the northern province of Friesland, these competitions appropriated key elements from the early modern tradition, yet changed ice-skating practices considerably. Organized by publicans, speed-skating competitions had always been a part of Dutch skating culture (ter Gouw 592–3). But not until the first decades of the nineteenth century, when small committees of Frisian notables initiated speed-skating matches as well – first by using subscription lists and later by establishing local skating clubs – were they transformed into major landmarks of popular culture, frequently attracting thousands of spectators (Bijlsma). Increasingly standardized as short-track matches of 150 metres, the competitions shifted

*Figure 5.2   J.C. Greive jr, Speed-skating match on the Amstel river, 19 January 1864.
Drawing on wood (From* Nederlandsch Magazijn*)*

the focus of ice-skating from active recreation to spectator sport. No longer the act of skating itself but the collective act of watching the skaters structured experiences of social cohesion.

To a certain extent, speed-skating matches, more than ice-fairs, challenged and even overturned existing social hierarchies (Venbrux 277). The most active competitors came from the lower-class circles of fishermen, small farmers and labourers. Their physical achievements embodied the idea that, instead of birth and occupation, now talent and physical strength defined the local hierarchy of public esteem. This idea of transgression was reinforced by popular costumed speed-skating matches, which filled the skating rinks with farmers and fishermen in the historic clothes of noblemen (ter Gouw 594). Because the social elites who organized speed-skating competitions did not participate themselves in active speed-skating, arguing that accepting prize money would be unrespectable, one might maintain that the competitions and their implicit element of gift-giving mainly underlined upper-class authority (Venbrux 285). The famous story of the Frisian governor Baron Van Sytzama, participating as 'Jan Sytsma' and success-fully competing against the local favourite Hantje Speerstra, suggested that, even if social elites did not withdraw, they would reinforce their authority on the basis of physical superiority (Meijerman 63). Nevertheless, the most successful lower-class speed-skaters effectively resisted these hegemonic implications of skating

competitions by making secret, mutual agreements as to where they would compete
and who was going to win. From a long-term perspective, the professionalized
corps of lower-class speed-skaters thus structured the further institutionalization
of speed-skating. After all, the relatively elitist Frisian League of Ice Clubs, dating
from 1919, though preceded since 1859 by many earlier initiatives, was established
specifically to put an end to this phenomenon of lower-class 'cartel' formation
(Bijlsma, *Yn streken* 11–15).

Interestingly, lower-class women actively engaged in speed-skating competitions. On 1 February 1805, about 130 women, from 14 to 51 years old, each
hoping to win the promised golden cap brooch, subscribed to the first speed-
skating match for women in the Frisian capital of Leeuwarden (ter Gouw 592–3;
Van Schuppen 12–4; Steendijk-Kuipers 120–1). The match attracted an enormous
number of visitors, from ten to twelve thousand, and was, just like the ice-fairs,
imprinted in the collective memory in a fine print. During the next harsh winter of
1809, after women's speed-skating had spread beyond Leeuwarden to the other
northern regional capital, Groningen, commentators and authorities began to
dispute whether the phenomenon of women skating in their underpants, scarf,
bonnet and undershirt was 'a natural proof of female beauty' or a 'moral shock'
(Wichers 179–80; Van der Woude 10–13). Both the positive and negative reception
of their skating implied a sexual commodification of the female body – a fact most
unashamedly affirmed by a Frisian farmer poet who enjoyed how the 'natural
qualities' of the women skaters shocked his 'cuddling rod' (Bijlsma, *Yn streken*
18). During the rest of the century speed-skating matches exclusively for women
remained rather exceptional and were, until the twentieth century, sometimes even
forbidden by local and regional authorities. Still, the fact that skating-club archives
contain documentation on various prizewinning women suggests in the very least
the widespread introduction of mixed matches (Van der Woude 15–27). By 1850
many skating clubs started their seasons with a male-only competition and then
followed it with matches for mixed pairs skating in rows, but captained by men
(Wichers 212–13). The discussion of women's speed-skating added much to the
mid-century problematization of the respectability of women's skating in general
and appears to have contributed particularly to the withdrawal of upper-class
women from active participation. By 1880, as will be shown below, the institutionalization of ice-skating, originating from the speed-skating culture, also paved the
way for their comeback.

The Frisian committees of notables, the skating clubs and their supporting local
elites promoted speed-skating as a respectable popular recreation (ter Gouw 592–
3; Venbrux 288–90). Newspaper accounts more than once stressed the regularity
and orderliness of the crowds, which were often under police supervision. Headed
by commissioners, followed by participants and accompanied by music bands, a
ritual procession from the local pub to the skating rink frequently preceded

competitions, whereas during the matches commissioners made themselves noticeable by their garb and 'medieval' lances. After the competition they again preceded the prizewinners in the procession to the pub, where awards were handed out. The well-to-do members of the skating clubs distinguished themselves from the rest of the public by wearing membership buttons and sitting on special bleachers in front of the skating rinks.

Speed-skating competitions not only created social events in which local hierarchies were made visible, they also placed the meanings of popular recreational activities within the framework of national and monarchic discourses and practices. Initially, speed-skating represented a typically Frisian skating culture in contrast to figure skating, characteristic of the coastal province of Holland (ter Gouw 590–1). Nevertheless, national flags often surrounded the shiny provincial rinks, while bands alternated national and regional hymns, thus reconciling the contemporary process of regional identity-building in Friesland with the emerging integration of the Netherlands as a nation-state. In 1860, the aristocratic commissioners of the Leeuwarder skating club successfully attracted as an honourable member the twenty-year-old Dutch Prince of Orange, a passionate skater. By supplying the club's material prizes, he expressed his traditional aristocratic commitment to skating as a ritual that cohered society and at the same time symbolized the integration of the Dutch nation-state (Kruisinga/De Groot 23–8).

The Local Construction of Skating Culture: The Hague, 1880

In the second half of the nineteenth century the declining occurrence of ice-fairs and the spread of speed-skating competitions and skating clubs beyond Friesland did not result in the construction of a new, uniform national skating culture. Rather it gave rise to a proliferation of local skating cultures in which elements from these different traditions were appropriated in different ways. In Amsterdam, for example, a skating club, established as early as 1864, organized speed-skating matches 'completely in the Frisian way'. But instead of excluding upper-class men and women from active skating, the club successfully reconciled its members' roles as both spectator and participant. By 1880 the club adapted the coastal tradition of figure skating into the Frisian competitive format of speed-skating, while at the same time reorienting itself towards the tradition of ice-fairs by reintroducing the famous *koek-en-zoopies* (refreshment stalls).[2]

In the residential capital The Hague, notorious for its obsessive class distinctions, the transformation of local skating culture followed quite a different path, which, to the outrage of many, blatantly challenged the quintessence of the Dutch skating tradition itself. Accordingly, The Hague offers perhaps the best example of how, in the last decades of the nineteenth century, Dutch frozen water gave rise to various conflicting practices and meanings, which reflected and contributed to different changing local social and political orders.

Since the 1850s The Hague's fashionable bourgeoisie – consisting mainly of court officials, diplomats, politicians, civil, legal and military servants, professionals, bankers and persons of independent means – had experienced how its traditional hegemonic position in urban society, from the field of politics to leisure activities, had increasingly been contested by the 'middle-class' bourgeoisie of manufacturers, dealers and shopkeepers. By 1880, the successful advances of these occupational groups resulted in a rather assertive tendency of fashionable bourgeois towards distinctive organization and display. At the same time, conflicts within The Hague's upper and middle strata were, however, alleviated in a joint civilizing offensive towards the urban lower classes, resulting, e.g., in the abolishment of the local May Fair in 1885. Upper- and middle-class women, having gradually lost in the previous decades much of their free access to public space, took advantage of the growing bourgeois monopolization and reconstruction of this space to expand again their public access and autonomy, especially in places where a high level of class homogeneity was promoted (Furnée).

In January 1880, The Hague's most prominent doctor, two members of parliament, a banker, a notary, a judge and a person of independent means announced in the newspaper their wish to establish an ice-skating club, which the city, unlike Amsterdam and Rotterdam, still lacked.[3] Although they declared that the club would create work for the unemployed by hiring them to sweep the rinks, the hundred people who attended the first afternoon meeting – in one of The Hague's most fashionable public locations – instantly agreed that the club would be primarily directed towards providing recreational skating for its members only. And, unlike other skating clubs, they would not be involved in organizing any speed-skating competitions whatsoever. Even though the new self-appointed members agreed that the club would promote, 'as much as possible', skating opportunities for 'the great public', they decided that membership would be exclusive and subject to balloting by the board of commissioners, adding that they would not be obliged to account for rejections.

From the seventeenth century onwards, ice-skating in The Hague had been centred on the so-called 'Hofvijver', the 'court' pond adjacent to the parliamentary and main government buildings and in front of the aristocratic quarters. In the urban imagination, the Hofvijver represented *the* centre of The Hague and, attracting 'skaters and spectators from all ranks and classes', it still functioned in the 1860s as a main site for local rituals of social cohesion. The most obvious example of the overtly hegemonic and even class-antagonistic character of the new skating club was its request of the local authorities to grant its members, the city's elite, the exclusive privilege for skating on this exact location. Despite its personal ties to the skating club, the council, comprehending the symbolic implications of permitting the skating club to monopolize such a significant public site, did not, however, concede. The King's sister Sophie, the grand duchess of Saxen-Weimar, overlooking royal interests in the socially cohering capacities of ice-skating, showed fewer scruples and offered the club the exclusive right to skate on the ponds on her well-known estate, Zorgvliet.

The skating club's exclusive character was such a flagrant offence against Dutch skating tradition that embarrassed newspaper correspondents initially gave it the benefit of the doubt. One correspondent presumed, for example, that the skating club was established to ensure the sweeping of public rinks, while its members would distinguish themselves only by wearing club insignias. Another journalist, referring to the class conflict between The Hague's fashionable bourgeoisie and upwardly mobile shopkeepers and dealers, somewhat ironically warned 'one should recall that on the ice there are no aristocratic bourgeois or shopping quarters'. Only at the end of January, when the exclusive skating ponds at Zorgvliet were inaugurated, did journalists realize that The Hague's skating club indeed represented no less than an 'unfortunate novelty on ice'. Irony quickly changed to sarcasm and cynicism: 'Instead of practising ice-communism and skating in a row with his caretaker, smith and baker, one can now practise the cherished national "system of fences and enclosures". Now, one remains in his own sphere and needs no longer to fear contact with people who, on skates, might behave more familiarly than on the solid ground'. Consequently, rumours that the skating club would organize a popular feast, modelled after the traditional ice-fairs, soon appeared groundless.

Notably, the club's manifest break with the democratic tradition of skating paralleled and supported upper-class women's emancipation. In Amsterdam, the local skating club had strongly promoted a revival of active skating among 'respectable' middle- and upper-class women by offering many recreational activities besides speed-skating competitions. In The Hague, women's emancipation in ice-skating adopted an even more political stance. In their first advertisement, the club's initiators emphatically invited 'the ladies' to attend the inaugural meeting. And, as if to underline the extraordinary phenomenon of women's participation in the establishment of leisure clubs, all newspaper reports made special note of the fact that at the first meeting forty out of the hundred attendants were women. Within the traditionally transgressive context of ice-skating, however, gender hierarchies did not just simply dissolve. After all, the provisional chairman, referring to the 'extraordinary attractiveness' of the women, proposed they adopt the status of 'extraordinary members'. He argued that if women could become common members, they could also serve on the board of commissioners and as a result would at times have to oversee the ice-sweepers early in the morning, 'so that milady would not be with her husband at breakfast and could not take care of her children' (and, instead, would be alone in the company of lower-class men).

To his surprise, the women attendees did not accept his argument, but demanded and received common membership – 'as it did not count for political rights'. Consequently, they also elected the daughter of an ex-Minister and one of the club's founding members to the board of commissioners, an honour she, however, declined, as the city's main newspaper wrote approvingly.

The Hague's skating club also affected contemporary definitions of age. Various newspapers, for instance, mentioned how a young lady had objected to the provisional article that offered members the opportunity, for higher dues, to extend membership to their children, up to 18 years of age. She had argued that persons from 16 to 18 years of age hardly deserved the designation 'children' and, even more importantly, should be able to become members in their own right. As the votes were equally divided, her proposal failed, although the term 'children' was replaced with 'sons and daughters'. Nevertheless, the traditional idea that ice-skating offered a legitimate occasion for young men and women to get acquainted provided a strong argument in the generational conflict of the 1880s, in which young upper-class people claimed the right to a self-conscious, free choice of marriage partners – especially within the 'safe' class boundaries of The Hague's skating club.

In the winter of 1880–1, the club's second season, The Hague's elite experienced its first evening feast on ice. Bengal fire, burning tar casks and skaters equipped with 'giorno'-illumination spread a fantastic glow onto the rinks. The third regiment of the Hussards played cheerful tunes, and the newly built wooden stall offered refreshments and some warmth. Clearly, the evening party recalled the former ice-fairs – except for the fact that now it was for members only. The old Dutch proverb 'On the ice everyone is equal; he who has no maiden avails himself of one' still prevailed, but now within the social boundaries of the club: 'The Hague's damsels make intense use of it and often tumble in order to offer a chivalrous *cavalier* the opportunity to do them a good turn'.

Diversification and Integration, 1880–1900

The Hague's elitist skating club strongly contributed to the growing cultural and spatial distance between different layers of urban society in the 1880s, a development that the abolition of the May Fair in 1885 rigorously reflected.[4] Although sanctioned by the frequent presence of The Hague's new mayor – who, as a member of parliament, had been one of the club's founders in 1880 – and by the fascination of the young Princess of Orange, the skating club evoked resistance not only from circles of, for instance, petit bourgeois, but also from leading aristocrats such as the well-known Baron Van Hogendorp:

Figure 5.3   *W.B. Tholen,* Schaatsenrijden in het Haagse bos *(Skating in The Hague Woods), c. 1900. Oil on canvas, 99 × 132.5 cm. (Collection Gemeentemuseum Den Haag, 2001 c/o Beeldrecht Amstelveen)*

Until now we had two free days a year: one in the winter on the ice, and one in springtime during the May Fair. At those moments various classes fraternized by celebrating a joint feast. And believe me, these feasts aroused feelings of mutual regard, notwithstanding various inequalities. Has one thought about the ways that a somewhat more relaxed manner and more accessibility might upset the applecart of the Social Democrats? Has one forgotten that in our glorious seventeenth century the highest ranks were friendly towards the lowest middle-man?

The Hague's skating club challenged but did not, however, eliminate the city's traditional democratic skating culture. In the course of the 1880s, the town accom- modated an increasingly varied range of continuing, reintroduced and newly invented skating practices and meanings. In 1885 ice-skating in the local woods still offered experiences where social boundaries became more fluid and, as a journalist wrote approvingly, where 'communism reigned'. By 1887 – after some winters in which the local authorities, apparently for safety's sake, had the ice on the Hofvijver broken up each time it had frozen over – a local councillor success- fully defended and re-established the tradition of skating in the city's symbolical centre as compensation for having abolished the May Fair. In the same winter of 1886–7 a new limited liability company established a skating rink in a farmer's field. Its director organized speed-skating competitions with horses and sledges, which were accompanied by traditional music and electric lights, and established both *koek-en-zopie* stalls and a photography stand, where family memories could be imprinted. Thus he constructed a curious spectacle that ingeniously mixed nostalgic and modern skating experiences.

The elitist position of The Hague's skating club, however, remained highly contested. In January 1890, the club, in order to enhance skating opportunities during mild winters, built an extra, artificial skating rink by constructing a pair of dykes and by using modern pump pistons. Just before the first evening party some unidentified people, however, demolished the dykes and flooded the area, thus ruining the skating rink. An act of class-antagonistic sabotage? In spite of severe financial damage, the club expanded its activities in the next season of 1890–1. Because, on a national level, amateur speed-skating had increasingly dissociated itself from professional speed-skating, the club felt legitimated in setting aside its initial prejudices against competitive skating and introduced its first amateur speed-skating matches for members. In children's (i.e. boys') matches prizes of 'taste and art', such as golden watches and binoculars, were awarded instead of undignified money. Mixing the speed-skating tradition with the tradition of ice-fairs, the club subsequently organized a skating costume party. But despite these successes the club did not survive long. In November 1890 King William III died. When his sister the Grand Duchess – residing in Weimar – was informed that members of the skating club, at a time of mourning, were amusing themselves on her property by playing loud music, dancing and skating all night long, she immediately withdrew the club's permission to use her ponds. In the following years, the club did not succeed in finding other persons or institutions prepared to lend land for members' exclusive skating. In 1896 the club disbanded, handing over the remaining cash money to a local orphanage.

In the end, The Hague's democratic tradition of skating prevailed (at least until 1906, when a new exclusive skating club was established). In February 1891 some notables took the initiative and established a provincial skating association that was to keep public skating paths in good condition within and beyond the city. Its bylaws explicitly defined equal membership for men and women, promoted skating 'without distinction of class', and concluded: 'Members commit themselves tacitly to the promotion of a helpful, companionable, cheerful and charitable spirit on ice, spreading, each within his own social circle, the broad conception and good intentions of the association, which can be achieved only through mutual co-operation'. In return for a very modest contribution, the club organized the sweeping of skating lanes by the unemployed who were associated with a local philanthropic league. Through newspaper advertisements the club informed the public of ice conditions around the city and supported, by producing regional skating maps, the possibilities of long-distance treks throughout the province. Despite the permanent lack of financial support the provincial skating association thus (re)constructed a local skating culture that both crossed boundaries of class, gender and age, and successfully integrated The Hague into an ever-increasing regional and national recreational skating culture.

Conclusion

In the Dutch cultural imagination the phenomenon of frozen water is inextricably linked to practices and experiences of ice-skating. Its history reveals how these practices and experiences have mirrored social relations and hierarchies and especially how skating has contributed to the construction of new social formations. In the case of the seventeenth century we have seen how the transgressive character of skating both challenged and reinforced dominant class and gender hierarchies. By 1850, the decreasing occurrence of ice-fairs and the emergence of speed-skating competitions reflected at first sight general patterns of increasing class and gender divisions in contemporary Dutch society. But at the same time the interaction of these phenomena resulted in a proliferation of local skating cultures in which elements from different skating traditions were appropriated, often self-consciously, in reaction to specific local situations and developments.

In The Hague, the establishment of an elitist skating club in 1880 represented and directed the assertive reorganization of the fashionable bourgeoisie, as distinct from the lower classes, as well as from the rising manufacturers, dealers and shopkeepers. At the same time, the skating club contributed to the bourgeois mono-polization of public space and to the gradual re-empowerment of bourgeois women in public space and the public sphere. Likewise, the continuous skating activities on the ponds in The Hague's woods, the re-invention of skating on the Hofvijver, the commercial skating rink and the establishment of the democratic provincial skating association in the following years affected urban society beyond the mere pleasures of moving on skates. These activities contested the hegemonic implic-ations of the elitist disruption of public culture and promoted a public culture in which elite participation became less essential, men and women could move more freely, local horizons widened and, in general, freedom of choice increased.

And what about today? Ice-skating is still one of the favourite Dutch spectator and recreational sports. As I write these lines, television newscasts have just broadcast enthusiastic reports of the first skating matches on natural ice, employing a patriotic discourse that seems hardly appropriate in any other context. More than 800 skating clubs are awakening from their 'summer sleep', and 234 skating routes, with *koek-en-zopies*, are being arranged. A new literary journal on skating has been founded. Schoolchildren look forward to their teachers' giving them a traditional day off to go skating. And the province of Friesland is – as always – preparing for the so-called 'Elfstedentocht', a legendary long-distance race past the region's eleven cities. The race, organized in the severest winters, is definitely one of the most emotional nationwide happenings in the Netherlands, comparable only to world-championship matches. Frozen water – dividing and cohering people – is still a boundless cultural source.

Notes

I would like to thank Kiene Brillenburg Wurth and Wessel Krul for their stimulating support in this project.

1. Venbrux; his article ('On the meaning of skating') offers the first theory-informed synthesis of the broad yield of anecdotal, folkloristic and commemorative accounts on ice-skating. Elaborating on the same kind of issues as addressed in the first two paragraphs of this essay, its main focus is systematic rather than historical.

2. Balbian Verster; *AmsC* 17 February 1864; *AH,* 1 February 1871; *Amsterdam en de Amsterdammers,* 106; *AmsC* 23/24 January 1876; *AH* 17 December 1879, 4 February 1880, 23 January 1881; *NRC* 28 January 1885; 'Brieven uit de hoofdstad', *AC* 26 January 1885; 'Amsterdamsche brieven', *DZHS* 27/28 December 1891.

3. For the analysis from here to the end of this section, see: Gemeentearchief 's Gravenhage (City Archive of The Hague) [GAG], Archief gemeentebestuur (Local Council Archive) [AG], inv. nr. 823, Agendastukken 1880, no. 245; *DZHS,* 13 January 1880; *VL,* 13 January 1880; *DZHS,* 18/19 January 1880; *VL,* 19 January 1880; *DZHS,* 7 January 1864; *VL,* 27 January 1880; 'Haagsche kout', *PGC,* 26 January 1880; 'Uit de residentie', *UPSD,* 26 January 1880; 'Haagsche kout', *PGC,* 2 February 1880; *DZHS,* 28 January 1881; *VL,* 28 January 1881; 'Uit de residentie', *UPSD,* 30 January 1881; 'Brieven uit de hofstad', *AC,* 31 January 1881.

4. This section is based on: *HC,* 27 January 1885; Damas 33–34; 'Haagsche kroniek', *AH,* 28 January 1885; GAG, *Handelingen van de Gemeenteraad van 's Gravenhage* (Local Council Minutes), 11 January 1887; GAG, AG, Agendastukken 1886 no. 2471; *VL,* 18 January 1887; *DZHS,* 18 January 1887; *DZHS,* 5/6 January 1890; 'Haagsche sprokkelingen', *UPSD,* 6 January 1890; *DZHS,* 19, 21, 24, 28 and 30 December 1890, 4/5 and 17 January 1891; 'Haagsche sprokkelingen', *UPSD,* 25 January 1892; *DZHS,* 20 November 1895; 'Haagsche sprokkelingen', *UPSD,* 25 November 1895; GAG, Library F f 12, Brochure for a new skating club; GAG, AG, Agendastukken 1896 no. 152; 'Haagsche sprokkelingen', *UPSD,* 23 November 1896; Algemeen Rijksarchief Den Haag (State archives), Centraal Archief Vereenigingen 1874–1976, inv.nr. 2985, Statuten Zuid-hollandsche IJsvereeniging; *DZHS,* 13 February 1891; GAG, AG, Agendastukken 1891 no. 7955; *DZHS,* 24 and 25 December 1891; 'Haagsche sprokkelingen', *UPSD,* 28 December 1891; *DZHS,* 20 January 1892; 'Haagsche sprokkelingen', *UPSD,* 25 January 1892; *DZHS,*

1, 5, 6 and 7 January 1893; 'Haagsche sprokkelingen', *UPSD*, 9 and 23 January 1893; *DZHS*, 3/4 February 1895; 'Haagsche sprokkelingen', *UPSD*, 16 April and 30 December 1895.

5. A concluding note: in March 2001, after the completion of this essay, the Dutch Prince of Orange Willem Alexander announced his engagement to his Argentine girlfriend, Máxima Zorreguieta. In interviews the young couple recalled how the prince had proposed to her during one of the highlights of her 'crash course' on Dutch culture: on the frozen pond in The Hague's woods, a stone's throw from the Queen's private palace, while catching their breath from their first joint skating experience . . .

6

The Finnish Sauna and Its Finnishness

Pekka Leimu

The sauna is generally regarded as a Finnish phenomenon both within and outside Finland. However, other forms of sauna bathing have been practised widely throughout the northern Eurasian coniferous zone. The sauna experience was also known in Central Europe during the Middle Ages. Even today Estonians and Russians have their own traditional sauna culture. And in the USA, where some indigenous peoples had sweat lodges, Finnish-style sauna bathing is gaining in popularity in mainstream society. Furthermore, according to information from the International Sauna Society, whose headquarters are in Helsinki, there are at present more than five million people in Germany and twelve million in Japan who take the sauna regularly, each country having more sauna bathers than the total population of Finland (five million). Nevertheless, in relation to the number of sauna bathers per capita, the Finns are the real sauna people. Unlike the inhabitants of other countries, almost all Finns take the sauna.

The model for these foreign saunas is the Finnish sauna, though a Finn visiting one would hardly recognize the connection. While family saunas predominate in Finland, saunas outside Finland are usually club or business enterprises, where club members or paying customers bathe. Western Central Europe is a case in point.[1] Having lost its sauna tradition after the Middle Ages, the inhabitants of this area are now embracing the Finnish sauna but modifying it for business. Western Central European saunas often do not segregate by sex, unlike either Finnish public saunas, which are becoming less common, or Finnish saunas in public swimming halls. Many owners of Western Central European saunas argue that the practice of joint sauna bathing for both sexes and for all ages is necessary to deter any kind of sexual encounter. However, the strangest thing for Finns about such saunas is the prevalence of strict norms and rules for bathing. For instance, temperature, humidity and sauna time are precisely defined. In addition, a sauna attendant throws a specified amount of water on the stove at stated intervals, a practice bathers are prohibited from doing. The reason is that bathers, as non-Finns, are not expected to know how to throw the water or judge the temperature, etc. So as not to harm themselves, bathers require clear guidelines. Even if these Western Central European saunas operate differently from Finnish saunas, their rules and regulations show, in my judgement, that the Finnish sauna nonetheless serves as a model.

The widespread use of the Finnish word *sauna* offers further proof that the world regards sauna bathing as Finnish.[2] Yet, some other cultures do have expressions for it in their own language. The Russians, for example, use *banya* and the Scandinavians *bastu*. While these terms can also refer to the room where one does any kind of bathing, only the Finnish *sauna* connotes in one word both the specific type of bath known as 'sauna' and the experience of taking the sauna.

However, despite the general opinion that the sauna is a Finnish phenomenon, very little scholarly research has been done on it, especially in Finland. Finns have always viewed the sauna as self-evident. Each Finn believes he or she is an expert on it, but this is a perception rather than fact. This essay adds to the scant scholarly research on the Finnish sauna by describing the results of a recent survey on it among Finns. It then presents a brief history of sauna use in Finland. After connecting changes in sauna practices to modernizing impulses and the development of a nationalist sentiment, the essay concludes with several suggestions as to why the sauna has evolved into a Finnish national symbol. But first a general description of the sauna experience will set the stage.

The Sauna Bath

Bathing in the sauna, or, as popularly expressed, 'taking the sauna', involves undressing, going into the sauna room, sitting on a bench and beginning to sweat. The temperature is between 65 and 100°C depending on the size of the sauna room and the level of humidity. Nevertheless, the heat is dry, but just in the beginning, and turns damp as soon as water is thrown on the hot stones of the sauna stove, a process which produces steam and makes those taking the sauna sweat even more. Throwing water on the stove also makes the air in the sauna feel hotter; the more water thrown, the hotter it feels. However, the actual temperature does not change, only the humidity. When the air does not feel hot any more, more water is thrown. This is repeated for five to ten minutes. When those taking the sauna have sweated enough, they leave the room to cool down, originally going outside into the open air – even in winter – for as long as needed. Then they return to the sauna room and repeat the procedure. If going outside into the open air is not possible, a cool room beside the sauna room will do. In modern saunas the possibility of taking a cool shower in a separate room or sometimes of even swimming in a swimming pool exists, but neither belong to the old sauna tradition. In the summer, swimming in the sea, a lake or a river is another way to cool off, but this does not belong to the old sauna tradition, either. In the winter, people using country saunas cool off by dipping into the sea or a lake through a hole in the ice, but even this does not belong to the old sauna tradition. Rolling in the snow is also unusual and, as with jumping into cold water, may pose a health risk due to the stress caused by such a sudden great change in body temperature. However, the purpose of cooling down is to have a break before re-entering the sauna. The whole process is repeated up to as many as three to five times in an hour or an hour and a half. The goal is to enjoy cooling down even more than sweating, but both are essential.

Whether or not they are dirty before the sauna, people always wash afterwards. In the sauna room there were originally wooden barrels of hot and cold water, which could be mixed in a basin until it was suitably warm. In place of soap, sauna bathers used birch whisks, even while sweating in the sauna room. Nowadays, they use whisks to improve the effect of steam on the skin, not as a means for cleansing. Before beating oneself with the whisk, bathers should dip it into the cool water. Since the introduction of soap, bath brushes, sponges, shampoos, etc. have also come into use. In the old types of saunas people washed in the sauna room proper, but nowadays there is usually a separate washing room with one or more showers. After washing people sit for a while and drink something cold, like water, juice or beer. Because sweating causes thirst, they can also drink during the cooling-down periods. After the sauna, bathers are relaxed and soon ready to eat, because taking the sauna should be done on an empty stomach. In old Finnish rural communities the sauna was the only means people had to wash properly, and this is the case even today for people on holiday at their summer cottage. In modern urban communities there are bathrooms, showers and tubs. However, city dwellers still use the sauna, but just for fun and relaxation.

The Finnish Sauna and Sauna Research

Although there are numerous popular publications on various aspects of the sauna, few important scholarly studies on it exist. These have appeared either outside Finland or in languages other than Finnish. As a result, they have had limited reception in Finland. Only two deal with the sauna from an ethnological approach. The more comprehensive is the doctoral thesis, *Bastu och torkhus i Nordosteuropa* (The Sauna and the Drying House in Northeastern Europe), by the refugee Estonian ethnologist Ilmar Talve, which he defended in Stockholm in 1960. He later became Professor of Ethnology at the University of Turku, Finland. His thesis was published in Swedish but never translated into Finnish. Based mainly on archival material and mainstream ideas from 1950s European ethnology, the study emphasizes sauna buildings, not their use, and therefore does not give clear explanations of the issues presented above. Another important study on the Finnish sauna, the Master's thesis by Canadian anthropologist Lisa Marlene Edelsward, was conducted in Finland but published in English in the USA. It appeared in 1991 under the title *Sauna as Symbol: Society and Culture in Finland*. The book is based on interviews and questionnaire materials collected in Finland in the late 1980s as well as on a broad knowledge of Finnish scholarship on the topic. Edelsward's work is comprehensive, and she addresses most of the issues mentioned above. Her explanations do not, however, give the whole story.

In 1993 the Department of Ethnology at the University of Turku, in cooperation with the Finnish Sauna Society in Helsinki, distributed in Finland its own questionnaire 'Miten minut opetettiin saunomaan?' and 'Hur fick jag lära mig att bada bastu?' ('How did I learn to take the sauna?'). The first version was in Finnish and the second in Swedish.[3] Local radio stations publicized the questionnaire throughout the country and included instructions on how to obtain it. The only question revealed through the broadcasts was that of the title. In other words, the department aimed to collect information about childhood experiences of sauna bathing and gave respondents the freedom to describe them in their own words. There were only a few questions concerning the respondents' background. A total of 1,040 responses, of various length and quality, from all over the country were received. Both sexes and all possible age groups responded, but only very few were Swedish speakers. Unless mentioned otherwise, my conclusions here are based on the results of this questionnaire.

In addition, a student in the Department of Ethnology at the University of Turku, Tapio Laaksonen, completed in 1994, under my supervision, an unpublished Master's thesis mainly on this material. Laaksonen's thesis, 'Yhteissaunominen Suomessa' ('The Joint Sauna Bath [of Both Sexes] in Finland'), analysed an additional questionnaire he had distributed with the cooperation of the National Board of Antiquities in Helsinki. Before this study, the history and tradition of the joint sauna bath had been quite a riddle, but Laaksonen solved it completely, as will be discussed below.

Descriptions of the Finnish Sauna in the Nineteenth Century

The young Italian explorer Giuseppe Acerbi travelled in 1799 through Sweden and Finland. He published his experiences in 1802 in London in the book *Travels through Sweden, Finland, and Lappland, to the North Cape, in the Years 1798 and 1799*. Acerbi's book was reprinted several times and was translated into German, French, Dutch and, as a shorter version, into Italian and Danish. It introduced Finland to Europe and at the same time made it known as the homeland of the sauna, in spite of living sauna traditions in some other countries, because it contained both a description and the first published picture of the Finnish sauna. The picture showed both sexes taking the sauna together and gave the impression that the practice was common to all Finns. But as a matter of fact, Acerbi's description concerned just one sauna and one sauna bath on the northwestern coast of Finland in 1799 (Acerbi 297–8; Leimu 'Acerbi'). Only recently has research ascertained how

*Figure 6.1   The Finnish sauna according to Giuseppe Acerbi (1802), who can be seen
here left of the door peeping into the sauna*

widespread this practice was in Finland and when it ceased. Although Acerbi
established the sauna as a Finnish phenomenon, he is not the only one to whom
Finns owe this reputation (Leimu 'Acerbi').

Acerbi's book soon lost its relevance, because Finland was separated from
Sweden already in 1809 and was incorporated as an autonomous grand duchy into
the Russian Empire. During the Russian rule, until 1917, a national movement
arose in Finland as it did in many other European countries. The popular slogan
in Finland at the time was: 'Since we are not Swedes and do not want to be
Russians, let us just be Finns!' In this new geopolitical situation, Finns had to build
a new national identity. According to Edelsward, the most important elements of
this new Finnish national identity were the Finnish language, the national epos
Kalevala and the sauna – all consciously constructed as national symbols. The
sauna, in Edelsward's opinion, had always been a regular part of Finnish culture,
but only as a triviality. In other words, the Finns saw nothing special about it.
However, as Edelsward further maintains, the Swedish-speaking intelligentsia
adopted into the nationalist movement the Finnish language and the sauna, both
of which they had abandoned generations ago when they had attained their higher
social status. In the nineteenth century, they eagerly began to learn Finnish and go

to the sauna, and, she claims, began to use the latter as a subject in paintings, poetry, literature etc. (Edelsward 185–9). The situation, however, was not as simple as she contends. For instance, the sauna was not really a popular image in nineteenth-century Finnish paintings. There are, in fact, only two more or less well-known paintings that include a sauna, one by R.W. Ekman, 'Morsiussauna' ('The bridal sauna'), from 1861, and the other by Axel Gallen-Kallela, 'Saunassa' ('In the sauna'), from 1887 (Ilmonen 25–7). Only the latter represents a proper depiction of the sauna. In the former case, the figure of a naked woman, rather than the sauna, is foregrounded. The model was Milo's Venus statue, because Finnish morality at the time prohibited using naked women as models. At present, the sauna is without doubt the Finnish national symbol, but how did this really come about?

The Development of the Finnish Sauna from the Beginning of the Twentieth Century

The questionnaire's respondents who were born in the two first decades of the twentieth century remembered well their childhood saunas. Their recollections were similar to Acerbi's description from more than a century before. They remembered the smoke sauna. Having no chimney, the stove filled the room with smoke, which dissipated through an open door. Of course, this kind of sauna first had to be heated and could be used only after the fire had died down and all the smoke had dissipated. The floor of the sauna was merely the bare ground. Water for bathing was heated by lifting hot stones from the stove and placing them into handmade, wooden barrels. These barrels reflected the self-sufficiency of the old agrarian economy at the beginning of the twentieth century. Iron pots, made by a smith would have been too costly for these country people. Later, iron pots replaced the barrels, and wooden floors replaced the bare ground. As soap was not yet in use, sauna switches from birch trees were employed instead. Finns regard this kind of smoke sauna as the best. Many of them still remain in Finland, and new ones are still being built.

The technical development of the Finnish sauna progressed rapidly during the last century, and Edelsward gives a comprehensive report of it in her book. No such research is available in Finnish. In my opinion, this rapid development alone justifies the label of Finland as the homeland of the sauna. First, the sauna with a chimney was introduced, but it still had to be heated before bathing. The next invention was a sauna that could be heated while bathing, thus requiring much less wood. This is the only stage in the overall development that Edelsward overlooks. The reduction in the use of wood was, however, important to Finland's national economy at a time when exports were based almost solely on forest and paper industries. Later, when townspeople began to take the sauna, gas, oil and finally

KARTTA 1.
PERINTEINEN YHTEISSAUNOMINEN MAASEUDULLA

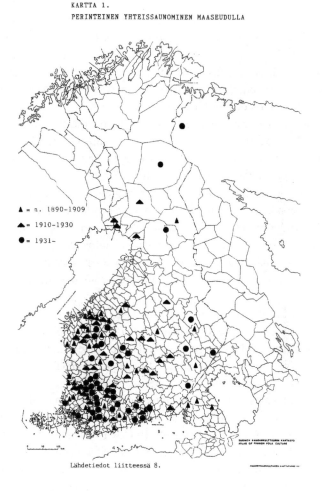

▲ = n. 1890–1909
▲ = 1910–1930
● = 1931–

Lähdetiedot liitteessä 8.

*Figure 6.2   Map of Finland showing areas of concentration of joint sauna bathing
practices in rural communities according to T. Laaksonen*

Karelia, the southeastern part of Finland, but the inhabitants were evacuated and
placed in different areas all over the country.) They had long since abandoned the
old ways of joint sauna bathing, and their disapproval of it influenced the local
people to give up the practice (Laaksonen 26ff.). How can we explain such a
development? Why did both sexes bathe together, and why did they stop? Why
did they stop first in eastern but only later in western Finland?

   The crucial point here is exactly how we define the groups who took the sauna
together. They were from old rural communities, in some cases from within one

household or farm made up perhaps of several generations and servants (Laaksonen 26ff.). In other cases, even the whole population of a small village took the sauna jointly (Laaksonen 40–3). In large country manor houses, all workers took the sauna together (Laaksonen 47–50), and the same was true for small industrial communities (Laaksonen 56ff.). Later, there were also public saunas for both sexes even in larger towns, but this was during the phase when the whole phenomenon had already started to decline (Laaksonen 65–9).

How do we define these sauna get-togethers; what did they have in common? First of all, these people knew each other very well. In large farmhouses they worked, ate around the same table and even slept together in the same large main room, and, of course, they spent most of their free time together, too, including bathing in the sauna (Edelsward 147–8). In manors and industrial communities they did not sleep in the same main room, but the conditions were otherwise quite similar. The origins of these sauna traditions derived, however, from rural farming communities before the beginning of industrialization. So the circumstances in manors and industrial communities should be considered secondary or temporary compared to those in farmhouses. As is commonly said, they were all like one big family. Whether these were blood-related families in the ethnological or social-scientific concept of family, much less nuclear families, is not relevant here, because a family or household was always much larger. This expanded family's collective participation in all aspects of daily life is the origin of the joint sauna bath (Leimu 'Finnish Sauna Tradition', 'finnische sauna-Tradition'), though it should not be viewed as a family sauna per se.

Social control was always in force in the community, and there was no risk of immorality. Likewise, in public joint saunas in larger towns, members of the sauna party knew each other more or less well. But, as I have already pointed out, by this time the whole phenomenon was temporary and in decline. In larger villages and towns public saunas for both sexes – and later on the separate ones segregated by sex – served an additional purpose. Saunas were like the village tavern or English pub where people from a village or a part of a town could get together and exchange news (Edelsward 146). Bathers often drank alcoholic beverages, which was officially forbidden, but they usually did so only in the dressing room and not in the sauna room proper. The essential point again is that these people knew each other (Leimu 'Finnish Sauna Tradition', 'finnische sauna-Tradition'). The old farmhouse or small village saunas, in contrast, often had no dressing rooms; no alcohol was used; and there was no news to exchange since bathers were already aware of all the goings on.

In western Finland the population was denser, and farmhouses, villages and saunas were larger than in eastern Finland. Eventually, western Finland had more and larger manor houses, iron works and industrial communities and towns than eastern Finland. Western Finnish communities in general were also more stable than eastern communities. The settlements and culture were more community-centred in the west, which is why the joint sauna bath for both sexes continued longer there. However, the questions remain, why did it cease there at all and how did it cease? This most likely happened in conjunction with a change in the concept of family. During the modernization of Finnish society the notion of the nuclear family grew in importance with the rise of the bourgeois or middle class. The typical, agrarian family of several generations and households, also including the servants, decreased in number and normative function. This gave rise to a new model of the family, one consisting of parents and children only. Just as the concept of family became more narrowly defined, so did the notion of the joint sauna. Thus, the sauna bath for both sexes never really disappeared but continued within the nuclear family, and still continues today (Leimu 'Finnish Sauna Tradition', 'finnische sauna-Tradition').

Some Finnish sauna enthusiasts have at times recommended that the old tradition of the joint sauna bath be revitalized. They have even experimented to some extent (see, for instance, Laaksonen 71–5). However, in view of the reconceptualization described above, this is impossible. Their idea of the joint sauna bath belongs to a society and to communities that no longer exist. Thus, revitalizing the joint sauna bath would mean reintroducing an older concept of family. This could connect with the current rise in alternative socio-political ideologies, such as that of green ideology. However, in Finland joint sauna bathing is not part of this movement. Yet, the situation with regard to Western Central European saunas for both sexes mentioned above is, in my opinion, connected to green values. The proprietors of these saunas have profited from green ideology by selling natural products, such as juices and herbs.

The Sauna Moves to Town

In the wake of rapid class mobility during the modernization, industrialization (since the 1870s) and urbanization of Finnish society, new problems in connection with sauna traditions arose when Finnish-speaking Finns began to move into towns. For instance, the Swedish-speaking upper classes, whose traditions did not include the sauna or the Finnish language, mostly planned and built the more expensive apartment houses in town for the wealthy. Thus, they were better equipped with amenities such as bathrooms than were the suburban workers' quarters and houses for the poor. As mentioned above, the Swedish-speaking intelligentsia adopted the Finnish language during the nineteenth-century national movement, but their embrace of Finnish culture did not extend to the sauna. This contradicts Edelsward's claim that the intelligentsia made the sauna into a symbol of Finnish identity. The Finnish-speaking people took the sauna tradition with them to the towns. But the apartment houses into which the wealthy moved had no saunas, only bathrooms and tubs, their model being from Scandinavia and the European continent. Finnish-speaking Finns were not, however, used to bathing in bathtubs in their own 'dirty' water. The solution was to install a common sauna for the whole apartment house, and each family took turns using it once a week. This worked well as long as taking the sauna once a week was sufficient. In time, Finnish-speaking Finns learned to use the shower between weekly saunas, and some even threw the tub away (Leimu 'Finnish Sauna Tradition', 'finnische sauna-Tradition').

Recently, apartment dwellers have learned to install their own small saunas in place of the old bathrooms (Edelsward 166–8). In addition, there are now businesses that build saunas made to fit into the bathrooms of old apartment houses. These kinds of prefabricated saunas are not very expensive. Nowadays, new apartment houses – not to mention terraced and detached houses – are always constructed from plans that include saunas. New apartment houses usually have an additional common sauna for company, and some also have a swimming pool in connection with the sauna. However, as noted above, swimming is not, and has never been, obligatory within the sauna bath tradition. The sauna is still an essential part of the Finnish way of life. But even this does not explain Finland's international reputation as the homeland of the sauna.

Conclusion: Finland as Homeland of the Sauna

Although Edelsward argues that nineteenth-century Finnish intelligentsia made the sauna into the nationalistic symbol of Finnishness and Finland into the homeland of the sauna, her arguments do not present the whole picture. Based on my investigations, there are at least six other factors. First, average Finns, who did not want to abandon the sauna when they moved into towns during industrialization, took the tradition with them and later built saunas by or in their summer cottages. Second, Finnish engineers and architects played a central role in the development of the sauna to suit the demands of modern Finnish society. These first two factors have solidified the sauna as a Finnish phenomenon, as no other culture has so maintained and developed it. These factors are, however, only domestic and would not necessarily have influenced the sauna's international reputation.

The following four factors also provide explanation for why non-Finns and Finns alike view the sauna as Finnish. In fact, Finns know that the rest of the world associates the sauna with Finland and that this is perhaps the only thing for which they are known. The first of these factors has not been investigated yet, but can be inferred. German and Austrian soldiers, fighting in northern Finland during World War II, became acquainted with the sauna because in these circumstances they had no other means to wash. They then brought their sauna experiences home with them and some even built their own sauna in their home countries. Next, according to the information of the International Sauna Society, Finnish Olympic athletes require the sauna in their accommodations at the games. This partly explains why the sauna expanded to Germany and Japan several decades ago, because the Olympic games took place in Berlin in 1936 and in Tokyo in 1964. Another factor, based on the results of a 1993 survey conducted in cooperation with the Department of Ethnology of the University of Turku and the Finnish Sauna Society, is that Finnish United Nations peacekeeping soldiers took the sauna with them to all the places they served, from Suez and Sinai in 1956 to the Balkans of today. As a matter of fact, inhabitants of the countries in which the peacekeeping operations took place did not adopt the sauna tradition. Instead, fellow peacekeepers brought it home with them after Finnish soldiers had invited them to sauna bathe with them (Leimu 1986). The last factor involves foreign explorers, travellers, and researchers who have become acquainted with the Finnish sauna, have written about it and made it known elsewhere. Giuseppe Acerbi was the first, and there have been several others after him. L. M. Edelsward was until now the latest.

Notes

1. By Western Central Europe I mean the transition area between Northern and Southern Europe, to the west of Eastern Europe; thus the Netherlands and Germany belong to Western Central Europe; Scandinavia and the European Mediterranean countries do not. My knowledge about Western Central European saunas is based on papers presented at international sauna congresses in Piestany, Czechoslovakia (1981), Utrecht, Netherlands (1986), Kyoto, Japan (1991) and Helsinki, Finland (1994). The Japan Sauna Society published abstracts of the following before the Kyoto conference: Rolf-Andreas Pieper (Germany), 'The Development of Sauna Facilities in Germany and their Visitors'; Walter Brenneis (Austria): 'Development of Sauna and its Habits in Middle Europe'; Willy Messmer (Switzerland): 'Practical Uses and Usages of Sauna in Switzerland'; Heinz Steinfeld (Germany): 'Education and Training of *Sauna-Meister* – Experience and Practice.' Although the titles are in English, the abstracts and papers are in Japanese and German. For more information about Central European saunas, see the Web site of the International Sauna Society.

2. The Estonian word is also sauna, but the sauna is not regarded as an Estonian phenomenon.

3. Swedish speakers make up only about 6% of the Finnish population, but they are an important minority we did not want to neglect.

Part II

Aesthetics and Ideology

7

Seaside Visitors: Idlers, Thinkers and Patriots in Mid-nineteenth-century Britain

Christiana Payne

The seaside holiday is generally regarded as a typically British – or, at least, English – invention. By the mid-nineteenth century, the custom of spending weeks or days each summer by the coast was well established: resorts were growing rapidly, and with the coming of the railways, middle-class prosperity and more paid holiday, the experience of the sea was being extended a long way down the social scale. Sea bathing, initially recommended by Dr Richard Russell in the mid-eighteenth century as a cure for invalids, was now being enjoyed for its own sake, and the beach was increasingly becoming a playground for children. Social historians have noted that amongst all social groups, there was a growing emphasis on pleasure, rather than health, and that guidebooks were stressing the climate of a resort, rather than the quality of its seawater, as the health-giving properties of sea air came to be more highly valued.[1]

The mid-nineteenth century was also the period when the seaside began to appear in high art, as opposed to satirical illustration. In the 1850s and 1860s, memorable paintings of the beach and its inhabitants were being exhibited. This article looks at a selected number of these paintings, along with a sculpture and a satirical cartoon, against the background of contemporary attitudes to the seaside and its perceived role in the formation of national character. Whilst some writers and artists dwelt on the frivolous aspects of the theme, they often did so with a moral purpose. Other voices emphasized the deeper and more solemn meanings of the seaside, thereby drawing attention to the opportunities for the study of natural history and to the military and economic significance of the coast as well as encouraging seaside visitors to breathe in religion and patriotism along with the bracing sea air. As Alain Corbin has recently demonstrated, the seaside was a focus for philosophical, religious and political meditation in eighteenth- and nineteenth-century Europe, not merely a site of consumption and pleasure (Corbin).

The very idea of leisure was inimical to the work ethic of the early Victorians, and visual and written descriptions of the seaside often take the opportunity to castigate the stereotypical 'idler' – usually thought of as a bored-looking man with moustache and cigar. In 1855, Charles Kingsley began his book *Glaucus; or the Wonders of the Shore* with a rhetorical address to the London merchant, setting off for a seaside holiday:

> You are going down, perhaps, by railway, to pass your usual six weeks at some watering-place along the coast, and as you roll along think more than once, and that not over-cheerfully, of what you shall do when you get there. You are half-tired, half-ashamed, of making one more in the 'ignoble army of idlers', who saunter about the cliffs, and sands, and quays; to whom every wharf is but a 'wharf of Lethe', by which they rot 'dull as the oozy weed'. You foreknow your doom by sad experience. A great deal of dressing, a lounge in the club-room, a stare out of the window with a telescope, an attempt to take a bad sketch, a walk up one parade and down another, interminable reading of the silliest of novels, over which you fall asleep in the sun, and probably have your umbrella stolen; a purposeless fine-weather sail in a yacht, accompanied by ineffectual attempts to catch a mackerel, and the consumption of many cigars . . . and after all, and worst of all, at night a soulless *rechauffé* of third-rate London frivolity; this is the life-in-death in which thousands spend the golden weeks of summer, and in which you confess with a sigh that you are going to spend them. (Kingsley, *Glaucus* 1–2)

Kingsley's passage epitomizes the negative view of the seaside in the 1850s, as a parody of the worst kind of urban living, a place of boredom, vanity and trivial pursuits, where art and literature are used only to while away the time and the masculine virtues are neglected, the wealthy shown up as useless, unable even to catch a mackerel. In Christian tradition, sloth is one of the seven deadly sins, and the commercial society of mid-nineteenth century Britain, dominated as it was by Protestant values, put a strong emphasis on industriousness. Kingsley's answer to the boredom of the seaside holiday was to take up the study of natural history, which would lead to a strengthening of faith and reverence for the Creator; as we shall see, he was not alone in offering wholesome and productive pursuits for the seaside visitor, as an antidote to soul-destroying, time-wasting leisure.

Kingsley's book makes no mention at all of one of the main activities of the seaside holiday, sea bathing. Bathing was a focus for amusement, embarrassment and censure in early Victorian Britain. In the resorts, areas of the beach were set aside for bathing and scrupulously segregated, with separate areas for male and female bathers; the use of bathing machines, carriages in which bathers could undress before being pulled out to sea, ensured that bathers would not need to walk from the beach into the sea in a naked or semi-undressed state. Bathers were assisted in the sea by 'bathing women', who were generally of advanced age and

Figure 7.1   William Powell Frith, Ramsgate Sands: 'Life at the Seaside', *1854. Oil on canvas, 76.8 × 154.9 cm. (The Royal Collection © 2000, Her Majesty Queen Elizabeth II)*

masculine appearance. The men usually swam naked, although moralists tried to enforce the use of trunks, but the women wore voluminous shifts, which clung revealingly to the body when wet. In the 1850s there was much concern expressed in the newspapers about the impropriety of sea bathing in crowded resorts, such as Ramsgate, where bathers could be seen from the beach and spectators even used telescopes to get a better look (Arscott, 'Modern' 41–66; Walvin 69–72). In a society where nudity was taboo, sea bathing was not a suitable subject for depiction in painting, although it could be shown in satirical cartoons and also in sculpture, where bathing figures, usually children, seem to have been fairly common. (Fig. 7.2). The shifts worn by bathing women suited the aesthetics of sculpture, with its allusions to classical precedents, and, as the sculptor of *The Young Naturalist* (Fig. 7.5), Henry Weekes, argued, 'Absence of colour from statue removes it so entirely from common Nature that the most vulgarly constituted mind may contemplate it without its causing any feeling of a sensuous kind'.[2]

Weekes' sculpture was shown at the Royal Academy in 1854, the year that William Powell Frith's painting, *Ramsgate Sands* (Fig. 7.1) was exhibited. This painting has become very familiar as an image of the early Victorian seaside: people are, to modern eyes, fantastically overdressed, with bonnets and parasols to protect fair skins from any hint of unfashionable sunburn. No bathers are shown in the painting, but, as research by Caroline Arscott has established, contemporary viewers would have been aware of bathers' proximity to the section of beach depicted. On the far right of the painting, two men look with interest towards bathers, and on the far left, an elderly man and a child point their telescopes in the same direction (Arscott, '*Ramsgate*' 162). Clustered together on the beach, people look as if they are in a city rather than in the open air, and, indeed, Frith went on to paint scenes of crowded city life such as *Derby Day* (1858; Tate Gallery, London) and *The Railway Station* (1862; Royal Holloway College, Egham). Frith's painting established a fashion for beach scenes in which the subject becomes a sub-category of urban genre: it became widely known through engraving, and was bought by Queen Victoria, who hung it in her seaside home, Osborne House on the Isle of Wight.

Ramsgate Sands transferred to high art a theme that was already familiar from satirical illustration. Leisure activities on the beach had been the target of satirists, both artists and writers, since the late eighteenth century. Jane Austen's unfinished novel, *Sanditon* (1825), and Charles Dickens's short story, 'The Tuggses at Ramsgate' (1836), are particularly well-known examples of written satires on seaside behaviour. In the early part of the nineteenth century visual representations could be explicit about the nudity and voyeurism of the seaside. In 'Summer Amusements at Margate' (1813), for example, Thomas Rowlandson depicted a group of men with spyglasses leering at naked women frolicking in the water.[3] In the mid-nineteenth century, the cartoonist John Leech produced many illustrations of the seaside for the well-known satirical magazine, *Punch*, which poke fun at certain stock characters, including ugly bathing women and middle-aged spinsters, impressionable young ladies who are susceptible to the flirting of cigar-smoking 'swells', and the harassed 'paterfamilias' who has taken his large family to the seaside.

In keeping with the stricter taboos of his period, Leech is subtle and restrained in his references to the erotic pleasures of the beach. Tantalizing glimpses of female bodies are offered by windy walks on the sands, or by characteristic activities that involve bending over, such as shell-collecting. *Capillary Attractions* (Fig. 7.2), published in *Punch* on 31 July 1858, shows female bathers in their shifts next to bathing machines in the background, but the group in the foreground are fully dressed. However, the women have let their hair down to dry. This was evidently a subject of great fascination: in 1858 Leech produced several cartoons on this theme. In one of them Mr Punch, holding a pair of scissors, comes up behind a woman; she sits on a rock with a comb and mirror hanging from her waist, looking like a mermaid, and, indeed, a fish's tail can be seen protruding from her dress (*Punch*, 7 August 1858, 52). The joke in Fig. 7.2 is the vanity of the plump older woman, with sparse hair, who assumes that she is the object of masculine desire, rather than the two beautiful young women who sit on the sand in front of her. In polite society of this period, adult women wore their hair down only in very informal situations (such as on retiring to bed), and the sight of loose hair on the beach evidently did cause some excitement. Paintings in the 1850s and 1860s depict long, flowing hair as a signifier of sexual availability, either in representations of modern 'fallen' women such as Holman Hunt's *The Awakening Conscience*

Miss Stout "The worst of letting one's Back Hair down is, that it makes the Young Men stare so!"

Figure 7.2   John Leech, Miss Stout. 'The worst of letting one's back hair down is, that it makes the young men stare so!' *(illustration in* Punch, *No. XXXV, July–December 1858, July 31ˢᵗ, 1858)*

(1853–4; Tate Britain, London) or in literary evocations of *femmes fatales* such as Dante Gabriel Rossetti's *The Blue Bower* (1865; Barber Institute of Fine Arts, University of Birmingham). In Leech's cartoon, too, there is a man lying in a very informal attitude close to the ladies and reading a book, a detail suggestive of the opportunities offered by the seaside for flirtation away from the restraint and convention of inland society.

There are no women with let-down hair in Frith's *Ramsgate Sands,* but he draws, nevertheless, on the satirical tradition, giving his viewers types that they could easily understand. The painting had its origins in studies made by Frith on the beach on his own seaside holiday in Ramsgate in September 1851, but, not surprisingly, his knowledge of earlier art governed his selection of suitable groups to sketch from life. He includes some of the stock characters that also appear in Leech's cartoons, such as the stony-faced old woman under a parasol on the left, the paterfamilias with his newspaper and his pretty young daughters, the idle swell with his cane, and, on the far right, the frightening bathing woman from whom the child shrinks away in terror. The painting also includes the entertainers and vendors who were seen as a nuisance by some of the more sedate visitors to the seaside. Leech was a friend of Frith (indeed, Frith wrote a biography of him in the 1890s) and he visited Frith while he was at work on the painting, and said it would be 'a great hit' (Frith I: 247).

However, Frith's painting also illustrates serious and more positive aspects of the seaside holiday. The beach was a place where different social classes could mix freely, and Frith shows them coexisting happily. He also puts the emphasis on children and families. There is a family group right at the centre of the painting, consisting of father, mother and three grown-up daughters; in the foreground, children are prominent, engaged in a variety of different activities, paddling tentatively in the sea, digging in the sand, looking through a telescope, or hiding in mother's skirts when confronted by the bathing woman. The painting's buyer, Queen Victoria, would presumably have appreciated these details.[4] The early 1850s was a time of national relief and self-congratulation after Britain, unlike her continental neighbours, had come through the revolutionary activity of the late 1840s without serious disruption. It was also a period of fears of invasion, especially after the coup d'etat of Louis Napoleon in 1851. The setting of Frith's painting, Ramsgate, is, significantly, a port that faces the Channel. Indeed, it was regarded in 1838 as a suitable place for the embarkation of troops in the event of a continental war.[5] Frith, in his autobiography, quotes Douglas Jerrold's remark that 'the liberty of England was preserved in brine – the brine being the British Channel' and emphasizes the value of '"the silver streak" that separates happy England from Continental strife'.[6] In the painting, then, the sea is not just a place for bathing but also a protective barrier, behind which the inhabitants of Britain can enjoy their happiness and liberty. Critics noted that the crescents behind the beach bore the names of Nelson and Wellington, two great heroes of the successful war against the first Napoleon (Arscott, '*Ramsgate*' 163). The picture's twin emphases on social harmony and defensive topography are reminiscent of Alfred Tennyson's dedication to his first book of poems as Poet Laureate (1851). He praised Queen Victoria's wise rule, which kept her throne unshaken, 'Broad-based upon the people's will, / And compassed by the inviolate sea'.[7]

In reviews of British art in the 1850s and 1860s, it was common for critics to praise the artists' reverence for home, family, landscape and truth, and to see all these as representative of the national character. In 1865, for example, in a review of the Royal Academy exhibition, the *Art Journal* declared:

> British Art is like the island that gave it birth . . . Its range . . . is as varied as our inland valleys, our woodland streams, and our sea-girt coasts, peopled by a peaceful peasantry and girded by the gallant mariner . . . Happy the land that finds in nature a benignant providence; and blessed the people that makes its truth-seeking Art the expression of the joys of domestic life and the reflection of a nation's greatness. (*Art Journal* 161)

Frith's painting was able to touch on two important areas – the family, regarded as the heart of British life, and national power for which the family was seen as

new developments produced steam-powered screw-battleships, at first still made of wood, but then, from 1859, of iron. The warship in Brown's painting is a wooden one, but it has funnels, and therefore it must be one of the new screw-battleships, powered by steam. The first iron-hulled ships, the *Warrior* and the *Black Prince,* had been ordered only months before the picture was painted (Hamilton 89 and *passim*). Brown would have been very aware of the significance of the features he points out to his wife and child; like other artists, he had joined a volunteer corps in 1859. To a generation reared on stories of Horatio Nelson's heroism in the victory at Trafalgar over the French and Spanish fleets, the wooden warships had enormous significance. John Ruskin in *The Harbours of England* (1856) writes of his time as 'the exact period when the nation had done its utmost in the wooden and woven strength of ships' and he goes into capitals to state what he considers to be the greatest achievement of the nineteenth century: 'THEY BUILT SHIPS OF THE LINE' (that is, ships of the line of battle) (Ruskin 28, 47). Charles Kingsley, in his very successful novel, *Westward Ho!*, published in 1855, writes of the pride felt by those who had watched 'the great screw-liners turning within their own length by force invisible' in the previous summer at Plymouth harbour (Kingsley, *Westward* 577). At the same time, the wooden ship was a reminder of Britain's naval heritage and of the role of the sea in the growth of trade and empire. Kingsley's novel was set in Elizabethan times, and his hero, Amyas Leigh, is described as 'a symbol . . . of brave young England longing to wing its way out of its island prison, to discover and to traffic, to colonise and to civilise, until no wind can sweep the earth which does not bear the echoes of an English voice' (Kingsley, *Westward* 19).

In his painting (sold, appropriately, to his friend Major Gillum), Brown presents his own family as thoughtful patriots, far removed from the empty-headed pleasure seekers of popular satire. His choice of resort is significant too: Walton-on-the-Naze was a tiny resort, with a population of only 729 in 1851 (compared to Ramsgate's 14,853) (Walton, *English* 53). Those who thought of themselves as discerning were avoiding the big resorts and sought out smaller places, where there was less urban social life but more opportunity to pursue quieter interests, such as natural history. There was a tremendous enthusiasm for natural history in early Victorian Britain, and the seaside offered particularly good opportunities for collecting and examining specimens. The interest in natural history at the seaside blossomed from the 1820s onwards, reaching a peak in the mid-1850s with the craze for the marine aquarium. Shells, seaweeds, pebbles and marine flora and fauna were eagerly studied, with the help of both specialist and popular books. The best-known writer of such texts was Philip Gosse, father of Edmund, but he was only one of a host of authors. Indeed, it is possible that some of the books that appear in paintings of the seaside are not novels at all, but more serious guides to natural history, which had a very wide circulation in the 1850s and 1860s. The writer of one of these, W. H. Harvey, stressed that there was no excuse for boredom on a seaside holiday: 'There is no need to import the winter resources of cities – balls, parties, and theatrical representations – to a watering-place . . . There is so much to be enjoyed on the sea-shore when the mind is once opened to the pleasure afforded by the study of Natural History, that no other stimulus is wanted to keep the interest of the visitor constantly awake'. In the same book he declares that there are nearly 400 different types of seaweed alone (more than 500 if the microscopic species are included).[8] In 1859, J.G.Francis, author of a work on seaside pebbles, says that only inveterate sportsmen can find a seaside stroll monotonous: 'others, who are better informed and more awake to what lies around them, will be cheerfully employed in kindred pursuits at the foot of the cliff, or away on the beach, or far out, at low tide, among the weedy rocks and sand. Here they hunt the cockle and the razor-shell, collect bright algae and marvellous zoophytes, or search for agates and fossils among the endless heaps of shingle' (Francis 3).

Social histories of the nineteenth-century seaside often mention the craze for natural history, but they tend to see it as a symptom of the Victorian 'collecting mania' and ignore its religious motivation. However, this was of immense import-ance. Philip Gosse, for example, was a deeply religious man, some of whose books on the seaside were published by the Society for Promoting Christian Knowledge; Kingsley was a Church of England vicar, typical of many who combined pastoral work in their parishes with studies of the natural world. Gosse and other writers emphasized the value of natural history in bringing the observer closer to God. In his preface to *The Ocean* (1849) Gosse describes his aim as 'especially to lead youthful readers to associate with the phenomena of nature, habitual thoughts of God'. Harvey declared that the study of natural history would furnish 'innumerable proofs of the care of Providence over his creatures', and, if pursued in the right spirit, 'proofs of the *personality* of God'. Above all, the evidence would show that 'The same skill and care is employed (sic) in the formation and adaptation of the minutest animal or plant as in that of the largest . . . In nature everything displays the same evidence of greatness of design' (Gosse, *Ocean* iii; Harvey 15, 20, 7). The intricacy, beauty and endless variety of marine life were widely seen as convincing proof of the existence of God. Even though the scientific status of this mode of reasoning, the so-called Argument from Design, was doomed by Darwin's discoveries, published as *The Origin of Species* in 1859, it continued to have many adherents, and its emotional appeal survived.

Henry Weekes' sculpture *The Young Naturalist*, first exhibited in 1854, (Fig. 7.5) draws directly on this widespread interest in the natural history of the seashore. It was very popular and exists in several versions: there are marble versions in Leeds, Dublin and a private collection in Scotland, as well as reduced copies in bronze.[9] The pose alludes to the classical types of the crouching Venus and the Venus Pudica, but the model is a child of the 1850s, wearing a garment similar to a bathing shift,

Figure 7.5   Henry Weekes, The Young Naturalist, *1870 (replica of sculpture exhibited in 1854). Marble, 145 cm. high. (Leeds Museums & Galleries (Lotherton Hall). Photograph: Photographic Survey, Courtauld Institute of Art)*

engaged in the popular hobby of examining sea-creatures and standing on seaweed and holding a live starfish against her knee. The verses chosen by the artist for the Academy catalogue (source unknown) make it clear that such activities are meant to involve profound philosophical reflection:

Alone, upon the wild sea-shore she stands,
While dance the breezes in her golden hair,
Gathering odd things, and strange fantastic shapes
From 'mid the rocks that half embedded lie
In the soft sand and tangled weed beneath;
Her young mind marvels much, why such exist,
If aught of purpose their creation show,
Or if but the sparks that glittering fly
From Nature's anvil, as she hammers out
Mightier forms in her great Foundry, the Deep,
Where heave those giant throes that make vibrate
Old ocean with the echo of their force,
And to its verge convey that never-ceasing splash
That notes on Nature's dial the moments of Eternity.

(Royal Academy, no.1370)

One may suspect that the grace and beauty of the sculpture, and the way the thin material clings to the girl's developing body, made it popular, rather than the profundity of its theme. Nevertheless, one reviewer was keen to take the opportunity to display his own knowledge of natural history specimens and methods in his comments on the sculpture: 'The earnest student of nature here represented has chosen a windy day to add to her collection: perhaps "after a storm" would be the more appropriate time to add to her stock of corallines and confervae' (*Art Journal*, 1 June 1854, 172).

Modern social historians tend to ignore, or to make light of, poetic approaches to the seaside, which were, indeed, often the objects of satire at the time. However, the great abundance of nineteenth-century English verse that considers the sea and the shore in terms of profound symbolic meaning indicates that, for many, the feelings of sublimity and religious awe induced by the sight of the sea were perfectly sincere. Poetry was frequently quoted, both in the naturalist handbooks and in Royal Academy catalogues. Often its sources are the well-known poets, particularly Wordsworth and Tennyson, but there was also a vast amount of ephemeral verse written and published in this period. A study of the symbolism of the sea in English poetry by John Bourke, which draws heavily on the nineteenth century, identifies three main symbolic uses of the sea. It stands for freedom, because it is boundless, and represents the defence of the island as well as the defence of British political liberty; the tides, storms and harbours are symbols of the fluctuation of human fortune and the voyage of life; and finally, the sea is a symbol of eternity and infinity, hence of God (Bourke). In prose, too, the very topography of the seashore had religious connotations. J. G. Francis, in his book on collecting pebbles, wrote:

Figure 7.6   William Dyce, Pegwell Bay, Kent – a Recollection of October 5th 1858
c.1858–60. Oil on canvas, 63.5 × 88.9 cm. (© Tate 2000, London)

here, better, we think, than in any inland scenery, man can muse and meditate. That ever-varying curved line of moisture on the shore depicts the fluctuating changes which momentarily visit his 'little day'; the tide running in is the flood of his early life; the tide running out is the ebb of his declining years; the vast sweep of the coast, backed by the upland ranges and everlasting hills, and itself only lost to sight in the far horizon, tells of a steadfast future, an immutable eternity. (Francis 97–8)

Poems by Wordsworth and Tennyson are frequently cited, both in books on natural history and in Royal Academy catalogues, to emphasize the divine workmanship of a shell or the significance of the sea as a symbol of death and eternal life.

William Dyce's *Pegwell Bay, Kent: A Recollection of October 5th, 1858* (Fig. 7.6) is the pictorial equivalent of this scientific and religious approach to the seaside. Like the paintings by Houghton and Brown, it has strong personal significance, showing the artist with his family – his wife, son, and two sisters-in-law. Pegwell Bay, near Ramsgate, was famous for its tea garden and donkey rides. Dickens's family, the Tuggses, go there in his well-known short story: after having lunch in the tea-garden, 'they went down the steep wooden steps a little further on, which led to the bottom of the cliff; and looked at the crabs, and the seaweed, and the eels, till it was more than fully time to go back to Ramsgate again' (Dickens, 'Tuggses' 339).

But the Tuggses were foolish and easily duped; it is unlikely that they would have seen any deeper meaning in the marine flora and fauna. Dyce and his family were much more learned. There is no trace of the tea-garden in the painting: the figures, staring out to sea or up at the sky, are face to face with the elemental coast. Dyce himself, holding his sketching materials, looks at the comet while his family collects shells; the tide is out and, out amongst the rocks, there are other figures holding the nets that indicate that they are naturalists. The painting displays the different elements in the seaside which appealed to the naturalist – from the seaweeds, shells and pebbles in the foreground, through the rock pools in the middle distance, to the crumbling cliffs behind, whose layers show the stages in geological time. The meticulous detail with which they are painted invites the observer to examine the painting in the same way as the naturalist was meant to look at nature. All the figures, in their different ways, are reading the 'book of nature', looking through nature, up to nature's God.

Pegwell Bay has been interpreted as a commentary on the meaninglessness of human activity in the face of the threats posed to religious faith by the discoveries of astronomy and geology – threats of which Dyce, as a man of strong scientific interests, would have been well aware (Pointon, 'Representation'). However, it seems more likely that it is an affirmation of the artist's faith, which most people in 1860 would have considered to be perfectly compatible with scientific interests. Dyce was a religious man, and there is no evidence that he ever lost his faith. In the following year, 1861, he painted a picture of George Herbert in his garden – a seventeenth-century divine reading from his 'book of nature' (Pointon, *Dyce* 175 [Guildhall Art Gallery, plate 112]). As recent writers have pointed out, there was potentially great religious symbolism in Dyce's coast scene. St Augustine had landed near Pegwell Bay on his mission to convert the English in 597 – an event Dyce knew well, having painted a mural of Augustine baptizing King Ethelbert of Kent. The comet could be read as an echo of the star of Bethlehem, leading the three kings to Christ just as Dyce's study of nature brings him closer to God (Warner 108; Barringer 79–81). The small boy, looking out to sea, is reminiscent of Sir Isaac Newton's description of himself in Brewster's biography, recently republished, as being 'like a boy playing on the seashore, and diverting myself in now and then finding a smoother pebble or a prettier shell than ordinary, while the great ocean of truth lay all undiscovered before me' (Brewster II: 407). The religious symbolism would explain the solemnity of mood in the painting, which is far removed from the frivolity of paintings like Frith's *Ramsgate Sands*.

As Dyce's painting shows, the seaside could be the setting for industriousness on the part of its visitors. As well as natural history, there was much serious artistic activity going on in coastal towns and villages: not just the watercolours of the amateur but pioneering work by photographers and artists.[10] The seaside could also be a place where the industry of others was studied and admired. Many writers comment on the activities of fishermen, coastguards and lifeboatmen. Their exploits were becoming more prominent, too, as subjects for artists. Ruskin, Kingsley, Dickens and Tennyson all wrote eloquently about such people. Kingsley's poem, *The Three Fishers*, written in 1851, emphasizes the bravery of fishermen, the dangers of their lives, and the stoicism of their families. Its most famous line, 'But men must work, and women must weep', is often quoted by painters in Royal Academy catalogues. Dickens, in the same year, wrote eloquently about the boatmen of Broadstairs: 'These are among the bravest and most skilful mariners that exist. Let a gale arise and swell into a storm . . . or let them hear through an angry roar the signal-guns of a ship in distress, and these men spring up into activity so dauntless, so valiant, and heroic, that the world cannot surpass it'.[11]

Thomas Falcon Marshall's painting *Seaside Visitors – Story of the Wreck* (Fig. 7.7) juxtaposes the wealthy holidaymakers with poor fisherfolk, whose story brings them up against the less benevolent side of nature. It was exhibited with an extract from a poem, the source of which is not given:

- - - - - - - - - - - thou treacherous sea!
Now, slumb'ring peaceful on the rocky bed,
And luring to thy borders on the pebbled strand
The beautiful, the delicate, the gay: – and then,
Forth from the caverns of the mighty deep,
In storm or tempest roaming for thy prey;
. . .
Thou makest widows weep, and children are left fatherless.

Figure 7.7   Thomas Falcon Marshall, Seaside Visitors – Story of the Wreck, *1861. Oil on canvas, 92.5 × 153 cm. (Private Collection. Photograph courtesy of Sotheby's)*

101

The central group, one of whom has loose hair, implying that she has been bathing, listens to the story told by the boy holding a boat. The age of the man mending nets on the right suggest that this is a family which has lost its father. The woman on the right reaches into her purse, but it is not clear whether she plans to buy a shell from the girl in the foreground or to give charitable help to the fisherman's family. Irrespective of the exact details of the narrative, the composition makes the point that visitors to the seaside are led to serious reflection by their contacts with its working inhabitants: life at the seaside is not just one round of frivolity and vanity. Behind and to the left, a woman pauses from her sketching to have a conversation with a fisherman; thus she, too, is presumably using her leisure productively.

Depictions of the seaside illustrate aspects of life that would have been seen, in the mid-nineteenth century, as emblematic of British national identity. Although the seaside was the site for satirical observation of ogling, flirtation and idling, it could also exhibit much more positive values. The devotion of the middle class to family life is stressed in the paintings by Frith, Houghton, Brown and Dyce; indeed, three of these artists painted their own families by the seaside. A child is the subject of Weekes' sculpture; she is learning from her study of the starfish and seaweed, just as naturalist handbooks of the period emphasized the role of natural history in the education of children. The mixture of social groups at the seaside, an area where there were no boundaries, no divisions of property, could be seen as proof of the cohesion of British society, a society in which gradual reform replaced the cataclysmic upheavals experienced by Britain's continental neighbours, most notably in 1848.

The coast was a reminder of protection from foreign invasion, as well as from revolution, a theme that is made explicit in Brown's painting with its warship; pride in the navy was matched by pride in the bravery of the fishermen and lifeboatmen around the shores. The latter were a reminder of the spirit of brave adventure which was regarded as responsible for the growth of Britain's trade and empire. Finally, the emphasis on natural history evoked two areas of British life where there were grounds for national pride: firstly, the British reputation for empirical science, from Newton's discoveries in the seventeenth century to Darwin's in the nineteenth; and secondly, and closely allied to science, the place of religion in British life. The symbolism of the sea in poetry of the period reinforced the tendency for contemplation of the seashore to lead naturally to thoughts of faith in eternal life.

In the 1850s and 1860s, then, paintings and sculptures, poems and prose emphasize the advantages of the seaside holiday as nourishment for the soul and the mind, not just for the body. The activities depicted represent facets of what was considered to be the national character. In their relationships with one another, the people on the shore displayed family affection and social cohesion; in their response to the wonders of the natural world, they reflected the British tradition of empirical science as well as the belief that the nation was fundamentally Christian. Coastal scenes were a reminder of the security and freedom of an island 'compassed by the inviolate sea' and yet whose citizens were willing to venture out upon it 'to discover and to traffic, to colonise and to civilise.' Many early Victorians would have agreed with Dickens's conclusion to his article, 'Our Watering Place' (1851), 'We have a fine sea, wholesome for all people; profitable for the body, profitable for the mind' (Dickens 17).

Notes

The author would like to acknowledge the financial support given by the Arts and Humanities Research Board towards the research upon which this article is based.

1. For the social history of the seaside holiday, see Pimlott; Howell; Walvin; and Walton. Specific remarks on the shift from health to pleasure are in Walton, *English* 41; and on the growing interest in climate, Walvin 66–7. As the titles of the books by Pimlott and Walton indicate, the emphasis in such works is on England, rather than Scotland and Wales. There was little development in Scotland, for reasons of climate, although there were notable resorts in Wales, such as Llandudno and Rhyl. However, in painting and in literature the fashionable resorts of the southeast, which were frequented by Londoners, attracted much more attention: in cultural productions which were disseminated in other parts of the island, the activities and attributes displayed in this limited geographical area could stand for the 'national' virtues in general.

2. Henry Weekes, *Lectures on Art, with a Short Sketch of the Author's Life*, London 1880, quoted in Read 200.

3. Private collection, illustrated in Pimlott, plate 10. A related drawing of *Dr Syntax and the Bathers* (Dr Syntax looking at nude women bathing, through a telescope) is illustrated Paulson, plate 53.

4. Millar 74–5. J.K.Walton writes: 'perhaps the most important function of the seaside holiday was to display the stability and affluence of the Victorian middle-class family' (Walton, *English* 41.)

5. Finden 122. On the invasion fears of the early 1850s and their impact on art, see Ribner.

6. Frith II: 28. The occasion for his comment was a visit to Paris in 1871, where he witnessed the effects of the Franco-Prussian war and the Commune.

7. Tennyson, *To the Queen*, published as dedication of *Poems*, 7th edition, 1851: Ricks, no.299: 992.

8. Allen 108–125; Gosse, *The Ocean, Sea-side Pleasures,* and many other works; the quotation is from Harvey 8–9, 13.

9. The Witt Library, Courtauld Institute, has photographs of a 19-inch bronze in a private collection, as well as marble versions at Lotherton Hall, Leeds, in a private collection in Scotland and in the Royal Dublin Society.

10. There is no space here to examine the pioneering efforts of Victorian photographers at the seaside, but the calotypes of David Octavius Hill and Robert Adamson, of fishermen of the Firth of Forth (1840s), and the photographs of waves breaking taken by John Dillwyn Llewelyn in the 1850s are two important examples. (Stevenson; Titterington).

11. Dickens, 'Watering' 15; see also Ruskin 27, and Tennyson's poem *Enoch Arden* (1864) which was a great popular success in its time (Ricks, no.330: 1129–52).

8

A Sound Mind in a Sound Body: Bathing in Sweden

Michelle Facos

Bathing escalated steadily in Sweden during the course of the nineteenth century, rising dramatically in popularity in the first decades of the twentieth. All varieties of bathing were practised – indoor and outdoor, costumed and nude, hygienic and recreational. A Romantic appreciation for nature, combined with an impetus to define national identity as well as with a more scientific understanding of health and disease, transformed bathing from a rare luxury to a popular commonplace within the course of several decades. The grand era of sea resorts as the exclusive domain of the well-heeled coincided with the summer residence of King Oscar II on Marstrand from the mid-1880s until his death in 1907. Subsequently, a new kind of life began to emerge along Sweden's coasts, as summer vacations away from the city became a reality for the middle and working classes. The fact that vacationers chose to engage in sea bathing, as well as other outdoor activities such as hiking, mountain climbing and boating, attested to the success of bureaucrats and intellectuals in indoctrinating Swedes with the conviction that proximity to nature was a fundamental component of their identity.

Attitudes toward nature are cultural phenomena. They, along with outdoor activities, are acquired in a complex process of socialization. Thus, the outdoor tradition of Sweden is encoded with a variety of values, ancient as well as modern. In this regard, significance is often attributed to the facts that Swedes have lived in Sweden for more than ten thousand years and that the Scandinavian countries are an atypical corner of Europe because of their general lack of a feudal system. This absence had crucial implications for the relationship between the people and nature. Because feudal land ownership was virtually non-existent, except in southern Sweden and Denmark, social relations were less hierarchical, and land rights for the populace were historically quite different from those on the continent. Among the rights Swedes have enjoyed is the Right of Public Access (*allemansrätt*), a customary law still viable today, which allows for the use of land, public or private, without leaving a human trace. It includes the right to make fire, travel by boat, temporarily camp, hunt, pick wild berries and plants and bathe wherever one chooses, without disturbing the landowners. The Right of Public Access fostered a belief in the importance of an unmediated, interdependent relationship between people and nature, and formed the basis for modern Swedish attitudes. The principle of equal access for all, while rooted in the tribal origins of Swedish society with its strong collective ethos, harmonized with the values of modern social democracy. Sweden's Social Democratic Party, established in 1889, took as its motto the French Republican slogan 'freedom, equality, solidarity' (*liberté, égalité, fraternité*), and the ancient Right of Public Access seemed to legitimate historically these goals as an authentic and integral dimension of Swedish social relations. Thus, at the end of the nineteenth century, intellectuals and politicians asserted the interconnectedness of people in nature as an essential aspect of Swedish identity.

According to historian Sverker Sörlin, the investigations of Karl Linnaeus (1707–78) constituted the watershed in the Swedish awareness of nature (Sörlin/ Sandell 20). The Swedish botanist travelled throughout the country describing with precision the flora, fauna and geography of the country's twenty-four provinces. His findings were of immediate interest and relevance to other scientists, but his convivial, journalistic style soon attracted the attention of writers, artists, intellectuals and bureaucrats. Linneaus's writings demonstrated that the careful observation of nature yielded pleasure beyond the intellectual and they inspired others to look more closely at the landscape they inhabited.

In the eighteenth century there was a revival of bathing culture in Sweden, on both a popular and an aristocratic level. Indoor bathing has a long history in Sweden, dating from the Middle Ages. Traders brought the tradition from Russia, Finland and Persia, and Persian traders travelled with luxury goods in the tenth century to the Swedish Hanseatic town of Visby, on the island of Gotland, where they established baths. Public baths existed as early as the fourteenth century in Kalmar, on the island of Öland, and on the island of Helgeandsholmen, in Stockholm, situated on the spot where the parliament building now stands. By the sixteenth century, most villages, which had a rich tradition of shared services such as laundries and bake houses, also possessed a communal bathhouse (Curman, *Bad* 32–3). These bathhouses were saunas, where the bather sweated out bodily poisons before cleansing the skin's surface by scraping or washing. Wealthy farmers and aristocrats often built private, and sometimes quite lavish, bathhouses for themselves. For instance, Linneaus described in his *Journey to West Gothland* (*Westgötharesa*), the private bathhouse of Count Bengt Gabrielsson Oxenstjerna as 'a masterpiece and the most beautiful I have seen in the province of Väster-götland' (Curman, *Bad* 34). This tradition of bathing, which was prevalent among the whole of the Swedish population, was gradually abandoned beginning in the sixteenth century, so that by the end of the eighteenth century most Swedes avoided water touching their bodies, with the exception of hands and face, from cradle to grave. This seems directly attributable to two causes: the taboos about the body promulgated by conservative Lutherans following the Reformation and the Swedish aristocracy's eschewing of bathing as provincial once they were exposed to the lifestyle of the French nobility. The Lutheran Church successfully discouraged a variety of activities they considered morally suspect, including dancing and drinking alcohol. Exposing the body, especially in a public venue, was a practice they opposed.

Beginning with the reign of Queen Kristina (1632–54), French culture furnished the model first for the Swedish aristocracy and eventually for the affluent middle classes who followed their lead. Kristina was deeply attracted to French culture and brought the philosopher René Descartes to her court in the winter of 1649. (Four months later, he died in Stockholm of pneumonia.) From that point onward, the French aristocracy set the standard for Swedish high culture, a trend that continued until the late nineteenth century. In France, as elsewhere in Europe, bathing was considered unhealthy; as a result it gradually fell into disfavour in much of Sweden as well. However, the sauna tradition did survive north of Stockholm, especially in the provinces of Dalarna and Lapland. The Finns never relinquished sauna bathing, and the Eastern part of Finland was part of Sweden from 1200 until 1809. In the sixteenth century, several thousand Finns were settled in the province of Lapland in order to retain Swedish control of the region over the native Sami people. In the central Swedish province of Dalarna, whose fiercely independent peasantry never abandoned their communal services despite pressure from state and church, sauna bathing also survived intact into the twentieth century.[1]

Following a period of general neglect, saunas throughout much of Sweden were by 1750 in a state of dilapidation, and hygienic standards were at a low ebb (Bortas). This situation soon changed with the emergence of an aristocratic bathing and spa culture in Sweden in the late eighteenth century. Influenced by Enlightenment ideas regarding health and hygiene as well as by the psychologically and physiologically salubrious benefits of immersion in nature, a new interest in bathing emerged, but this time in the form of specialized locales for a medically supervised cleansing experience. The first resorts were in Borgholm, a town on the island of Öland, situated off Sweden's southeast coast, and in Gustavsberg, located in the province of Bohuslän, on the west coast. Elegant inns and hotels opened to accommodate guests, who came to drink the restorative spring water, inhale the fresh sea air, and, above all, socialize. French ideas continued to influence the values and behaviour of Sweden's aristocracy, and the widely read writings of Jean-Jacques Rousseau now provided endorsement for the benefits of close contact with nature, particularly in the case of women and children, whose constitutions were considered more fragile and in need of the restorative power of nature. For Rousseau and others, distance from urban centres was equated with increased healthfulness. As a result, the villages of Sandhamn and Dalarö in Stockholm's outer archipelago and Strömstad, on the northernmost reach of

Sweden's west coast, began attracting guests, who came to drink their mineral-rich water in the 1780s. British author Mary Wollstonecraft was among the visitors coming to Strömstad in 1794, an indication of the international status Swedish resorts attained in the late eighteenth century (Mattson 187).

After 1800, the value placed on nature in Romantic art and literature led to an increasing demand for spas and resorts, which began to dot the Swedish coast, especially near Stockholm and Göteborg, Scandinavia's two largest towns. Gustavsberg (unrelated to the centre of porcelain manufacture near Stockholm) escalated in popularity when Crown Prince Gustaf began visiting it in 1804 in order to improve his health. As a result, it became a summer magnet for the Swedish nobility. By the 1850s seaside resorts had proliferated and were well established in Sweden, so much so that there was a ready market among Sweden's growing bourgeoisie for the guidebook published in 1858 by J. Wallin, entitled *Handbook for Bathing Guests* (*Handbok för badgäster*). In it, Wallin described in romantic terms the appearance of, and activities at, coastal resorts – the endless vista of the sea, the sublime power of nature. Dozens of towns were included, thereby providing readers with an ample selection depending on the facilities they preferred. By 1900 there was a vast array of bathing resorts, fresh and salt water, by the sea and in the mountains, which offered a wide variety of temperature, humidity, mineral content in water and oxygen content in the air. Climatologists analysed the minutiae of conditions in Sweden's bathing resorts as a guide for doctors who sought the right combination of factors for their patients.

Carl Curman, Sweden's best known balneologist, wrote extensively on the optimal conditions for curing various kinds of ailments. In a 1901 article he noted that 'if the Nordic doctor acquaints himself properly with the numerous and varied health resorts offered within our own countries, he will have to admit that only in a very few instances will he have to suggest, at least in the summertime, that our sick need to travel to more southerly sanatoria on the continent' (Curman, 'Betraktelser' 3). Indeed the second edition of Dr. Alfred Levertin's guidebook, *Swedish Springs and Baths* (*Svenska Brunnar och Bad*), published in 1892, describes twenty-two mineral springs resorts, twenty-three sea resorts, eight cold-water spas and seven mountain sanatoria.

Despite the distance and the fact that Stockholm also had a rugged archipelago, Stockholmers and the aristocracy tended to frequent west coast resorts. Until the 1850s, Gustavsberg was most popular with the aristocracy, but this changed when the trend-setting Duke of Dalarna began spending a portion of his summers on the west coast island of Marstrand. In characteristic fashion, other members of the nobility followed suit. In fact, counts and barons comprised more than half of the guests in Marstrand during the late 1850s (Krantz 266).

A full schedule characterized sea resort life from the 1850s to the early 1900s, and daily activities were fairly routinized. Evenings generally preserved a degree of urban formality, with elegantly dressed guests dining and attending concerts and dances. Guests were frequently acquainted with each other, and stays were extended – the summer season was divided into two terms of approximately one month each, with guests staying for one complete term, if not both. Guests subscribed to a strict regimen that included diet, water drinking, exercise and mud bathing, a staple of most spa programs. Most guests, at least initially, enrolled at the suggestion of their physicians, and an extensive medical staff attended to their well-being. Cold-water (sea) bathing was prescribed in some cases, but not all visitors were considered hardy enough to withstand the rigours of the sea. One bathed only with a physician's endorsement, and such bathing consisted of a quick dip, followed by some sort of strengthening activity such as gymnastics or a glass of port (Krantz 269). Bathing took place within the confines of a fenced area constructed in the sea as a barrier to the assault of waves. This seems a somewhat unnecessary precaution considering that waves are minimal and there are not so much as tides along the Swedish coast. Until the 1890s, men and women bathed in separate facilities because it was considered immoral to place them in too close a proximity. And it was not until the 1920s that sea bathing beyond the confines of the swimming basin became common.

Within this context, the bathing pictures of Anders Zorn appear radical. Executed outdoors in a style influenced by Impressionism, Zorn depicted in the 1880s nude women bathing in a landscape seemingly remote from the boardwalks and bathing basins associated with coastal resorts. Zorn, a peasant from Dalarna, and his well-to-do wife, Emma Lamm, belonged to the coterie of Stockholm artists, intellectuals and bourgeoisie inhabiting Dalarö during the summers of the mid-1880s to early 1890s. At that time, Dalarö had a vibrant resort life in which the Zorns participated, but significantly, the artist eschewed this familiar aspect in his paintings in favour of a more private, yet ideologically freighted, subject matter. He painted a series of bathing pictures of which *Out of Doors in Dalarö* is typical (Fig. 8.1). Here, three young women sit on a rock outcropping in Stockholm's archipelago. Their means of transportation, a rowing boat, is moored nearby. Two of the women, their hair pinned up in order to avoid soaking it in the salty Baltic, inch their way toward the unquestionably frigid water, while a third disrobes in the left foreground. The artist/viewer is either standing or seated on a higher rock, perhaps also in the process of disrobing. The facts that the artist has included us in the fictional space of the painting and that the women ignore our presence suggests our familiarity, if not our participation.

While to modern viewers, especially Swedish ones, this scene may appear natural, it did not to Zorn's contemporaries. Not only do these women bathe in the wild, away from the safety and sanction of resort bathing basins, but women, particularly young women, were discouraged from cold-water bathing because of its allegedly adverse effect on female fertility. That *Out of Doors in Dalarö* would have

Figure 8.1   Anders Zorn, Out of Doors in Dalarö, *1888. Oil on canvas, 133 × 197.5 cm. (Göteborgs Konstmuseum, Sweden)*

appeared contrived to Swedish audiences in the 1880s suggests that the image represented something other than a summer idyll. Part of its unusual character stems from the fact that Zorn did not eroticize his subject. Female bathers were a common trope in nineteenth-century European painting, and they were uniformly conceived for the delectation of male viewers. Sometimes they were engaged in blatantly artificial and erotic poses, as in Pierre Auguste Renoir's *Large Bathers* (1887, Philadelphia Museum of Art), or surprised in their solitude like Venus at her bath, as in Karl Blechen's *Bathers in the Park at Terni* (1831, Charlottenburg Museum, Berlin). Zorn's bathers are not displayed in an erotic manner, they are not bathing where they should be, they are naked, and women of that age should not be bathing in any event. What then, does this painting mean?

Zorn was a member of the national Romantic generation of artists and intellectuals, who promoted a generic Swedish identity beginning in the late 1880s, based on a love of indigenous nature and the preservation of architecture and traditional culture. Zorn was himself deeply engaged in this crusade in his native province of Dalarna. His efforts to further folk culture included his sponsoring of annual fiddle and dance competitions and the establishment of a folk high school in his hometown of Mora, which specialized in native arts and crafts. Many of his paintings from the late 1880s and 1890s focus on the interdependent relationship between people and nature, and his first works in this mode were women bathing nude in the Stockholm archipelago. Zorn's paintings reflected a shift in attitude toward the sea, from a sublime and powerful devourer of fishermen, boats and coastal settlements, to a benign object of affection and communion.

Among the first to articulate a sense of joy before the sea was Fredrika Bremer, the pioneer Swedish feminist, whose 1849 visit to the west coast inspired her novel *Shining Lighthouse* (*Blänkfyren*). In it, she confesses her love of the sea in a national Romantic mode that was decades ahead of its time. The craggy coastline and expansive sea fill her not only with a love of nature but of Sweden. This patriotic response to Swedish nature anticipated a bureaucratic imperative initiated in the 1860s, by which the Swedish government sought to promulgate a generic national identity among its citizenry. It wisely targeted Sweden's youth who, since 1842, were required to attend school for a minimum of seven years. Government officials recognized the potential provided by the schools to transform a conglomeration of vastly different regions, unacquainted with one another's culture, geography and history, into a unified nation.

The 'know-your-land' initiative was an essential aspect of the government's plan for Swedes to embrace a generic national identity. It was resoundingly successful, spreading quickly in schools and a variety of organizations dedicated to health (such as the gymnastic associations), nature and tourism. A member of the Swedish Tourist Association wrote in its 1886 yearbook that 'if love of native land (*foster-landskärlek*) cannot be ignited in someone who has the opportunity to travel around and see with his own eyes our wonderful native land, if this feeling cannot be awakened, then this man or woman is not worth calling **Swedish**' (original emphasis) (Svenvonius 84). This patriotic attitude was reflected a generation earlier, in the first edition (1868) of the official Swedish schoolbook, *Läsebok för folkskolan*. It included a section devoted to Sweden's geography, a kind of armchair tour through a geographically and culturally diverse country. The *Läsebok* contained a dramatic description of Bohuslän, the province where most of Sweden's bathing resorts were situated:

> The view of the archipelago during a western storm is incredibly beautiful. It is, during such times, a single, enormous breaker. Along the band of the archipelago a wall of foam rises, and the wild waves break against the cliffs, throwing themselves in the air as high as a tower, frothy columns of water, which with a terrifying din disintegrate, in order to make room for the others. The sailor who finds himself carried here discovers, without hope of rescue, his grave. (Holmberg 196)

This description of a violent and unforgiving sea emphasizes the very real dangers encountered by fishermen and focuses on the romantic titillation engendered by sublime experiences. However, it seems somehow inimical to the objective of promoting sea bathing and a beneficial interrelationship with nature. Nowhere in the article is there a mention of the burgeoning number of bathing resorts in Bohuslän, despite the fact that they played an increasingly significant role in the coastal economy and social life.

By mid-century, Swedish bureaucrats were convinced of the beneficial effects of nature and its utility as an instrument of individual and social health. In 1866, a governmental committee noted that 'Large cities foster physical and moral ruin. This affliction then spreads in the general social body . . . Through parks, the populace will partake in the restorative effects of rural nature' (quoted in Wiklund 209). Such ideas spread quickly both in schools and in popular publications. For instance, an article in a turn-of-the-century issue of the *Friluftsfrämjandet* (Promoting the Outdoors) yearbook, the leading organization for the promotion of outdoor life, asserted that 'a healthy and hardy sportive life beginning in earliest childhood is undoubtedly one of the most crucial aspects of one's upbringing. It strengthens the life force of the nation and enhances its ability to defend itself . . . Let [children] follow their instinctive urge for athletics and outdoor activity and teach them to love our Nordic nature . . .' (Sörlin/Sandell 35). National Romantics fused a Rousseauian belief in the salubrious effects of immersion in nature with the imperative to establish a generic Swedish identity.

This shift in attitude is apparent half a century later, in the revised edition of *Läsebok för folkskolan*. There, the entry for Bohuslän reflected a more positive attitude toward nature. The author remarked that on Marstrand

> lies the west coast's largest and finest beach. Do you see how beautiful and welcoming it lies in the sunlight on the northeast beach of that rocky island, from whose summit the fortress, redolent with memories, looks down on sea and rocks! . . . It is an old city, and its history goes all the way back to the early Middle Ages. (Lindwall 444)

References to history and memory were common strategies for national Romantics in the efforts to foster an emotional attachment to Sweden's history and geography. They recognized the need to replace the social identity lost by the depopulation of rural communities. With the move from village to city, tens of thousands of Swedes lost the network of social relations that gave their lives structure and meaning. In 1880, 20 per cent of Swedes lived in towns, but by 1930, that had changed to 50 per cent (Sörlin/Sandell 13).

In order to maintain social stability, a replacement to village social relations had to be found. The demographic crisis resulting from the population shift from country-side to city was exacerbated by emigration. Between 1880 and 1910, Sweden lost almost a fifth of its population to emigration, motivated primarily by famines, land reforms and religious intolerance. Most Swedes had friends or family members who left the country never to return. This loss was experienced as a failure and contributed to an identity crisis that generated negative feelings about conditions in Sweden. National Romantics diligently combated these by offering a vision of the nation as nurturing, enduring and essential to the Swedish individual's sense of place in the world.

The seismic demographic shift occurring in late nineteenth-century Sweden affected not only the cultural identity of individuals but also their health. Urban mortality in nineteenth-century Sweden, as elsewhere, was high, particularly among infants and adult men. Conditions were most chronic in Stockholm and the region around lake Mälar, Sweden's most densely populated area, and therefore the one most prone to problems of sanitation and contagion. This situation was antagonized by a mistrust of doctors on the part of peasants and the working class, which persisted until the end of century. A general change in attitude occurred during the final two decades, largely the result of labour and other social movements, when leaders were able to allay the fear of their members so that they would listen to the advice of doctors and undergo medical examinations. Attitudes toward doctors had a direct effect on bathing resorts, since visitors were generally sent there at the recommendation of their physician. Initially, medical visits were an upper-class activity, not only because the best educated members of society trusted doctors while the populace at large did not, but also for financial reasons.[2] Medical check-ups were, until the 1890s, paid privately, and few Swedes had either the money to pay for a doctor's services or the leisure time to devote to a cure. Spending several weeks at a bathing resort entailed expenditure far beyond the means of most Swedes at the time. It is not surprising then that a perusal of resort guest lists prior to 1890 reveals an exclusive company of aristocratic and wealthy guests.

In Sweden the years around 1900 witnessed a formative development of outdoor life in connection with the growth of organized activities. Concern for public health was, significantly, bipartisan: both political liberals and conservatives sought to ameliorate living conditions among the population in general. Unions arranged weekend outings for their members and families, and the Swedish Tourist Association and *Friluftsfrämjandet* encouraged public interest in Swedish nature and provided information on affordable ways of enjoying it. *Friluftsfrämjandet* in particular was associated with liberal/socialist politics, and outdoor life and contact with nature were considered one strategy for realizing its social vision (Sandell/ Sörlin 44). Another aspect of Sweden's 'sound mind in a sound body' policy on both an individual and societal level was the emphasis on gymnastics, which reflected the pietistic Lutheran belief that each member of society had a responsibility to be a healthy and productive member (see Ambjörnsson).

Although the Swedish parliament did not legislate two weeks of paid vacation for all workers until 1938, the working classes had been taking vacations, particularly beach vacations, since the turn of the century. Their presence radically changed the character of sea bathing and resorts. Until the end of the nineteenth century Sweden's rugged west coast was considered ugly, and the numerous bathing resorts along its shores purposefully omitted in their advertising images or descriptions of the locales. Because the housing and socializing requirements of the aristocratic and affluent demanded ample space and a degree of luxury, those locales able to provide them developed first. It was only later that the quaint fishing villages with crowded congregations of tiny cottages emerged as bathing resorts. It was above all the middle classes who pioneered the touristic colonization of these places. Not only were they generally uncomfortable mingling with the high society of established resorts, but their pocketbooks were frequently insufficient to fund extended vacations in places like Gustavsberg or Marstrand. Instead of living at hotels or building villas, a strong trend among the affluent middle class, beginning around 1900, was to hire rooms in the homes of local inhabitants and later in rustic fishing cottages, which often lacked the comforts of lighting, electricity and indoor plumbing. This activity provided important income for local peasants and fostered a closer relationship between guests and natives.

After 1900 resort guests began to appreciate the picturesque charm of the fishing villages, and the natives became participants in the summer spectacle. Then guests began buying cottages in well-preserved villages such as Fiskebäckskil, the West coast home of the national romantic painter Carl Wilhelmson, who recorded the religious, diligent natives with a coarse dignity fostered by the rugged landscape they inhabited. In his handbook J. Wallin made the peculiar observation that the fisher folk of Bohuslän were, along with the native Sami, lowest on the ladder of human development in Sweden. This condition he attributed to their eternal struggle with wind and sea, their subsistence level of existence and their 'exile' on a rocky shore, 'unsoftened by even one of nature's beautiful and moderating influences' (Krantz 280). The popularization of seaside bathing and resorts was also facilitated by the development of steamboat traffic, especially in the Stockholm archipelago, which made remote islands rarely visited by outsiders accessible to the public on a regular basis. Anders Zorn and August Strindberg were among those travelling by steamboat to the outer archipelago in the mid-1880s to resorts such as Dalarö and Sandhamn. As the resorts and islands closest to the cities became crowded, those seeking a solitary nature experience explored less populated areas.

Also joining those seeking distance from Stockholm and an unfettered relationship with nature was the painter J.A.G. Acke. His 1906 painting *Östrasalt* (Fig. 8.2, the name of the rock on which the men stand, literally 'East Salt'), celebrated the vitalist imperative for direct bodily contact with nature and the sea. Critics admired it for its 'ideal clarification of strength and beauty' (Romdahl). Vitalist impulses infused art and literature in turn-of-the-century Sweden as evidenced in an excerpt from a poem by Karl-Erik Forsslund:

> I wake, glide down to the lake
> move out into the clear, pure
> blessed, cooling water.
> I stand up and stand worried
> with closed eyes and head held high

Figure 8.2   J.A.G. Acke, Östrasalt, *1906. Oil on canvas, 113 × 175 cm. (Göteborgs Konstmuseum, Sweden)*

in the sun's burning light, in the summer's
brilliant, high, warm air.
Strong, delightful, purifying bath,
in earth, in water, in air and fire
divine bath of rebirth.

(quoted in Lagerlöf 197)

Acke was part of a colony of artists and writers, which formed on the island of Östra Lagnö in 1894 and included Bruno Liljefors, Albert Engström, Edvard Alkman and Gustaf Ankarcrona. Among its visitors were Anders Zorn and the prominent national romantic writers Gustav Fröding and Verner von Heidenstam. These men were united in the belief in the beneficial and strengthening qualities of direct bodily contact with sun and sea. As previously mentioned, until the end of the nineteenth century, excessive bodily exposure to the elements was considered unhealthy, and it was not until the 1890s that bathers ventured in significant numbers onto open beaches. It was also at this time that vitalism attracted the attention of Swedish artists and intellectuals, who ventured to locations where they could bask in sun and sea naked and undisturbed. In depicting three unselfconscious women on the verge of bathing in bracing Baltic waters, Zorn anticipated by more than a decade in *Out of Doors in Dalarö* what emerged as a growing trend.

In Acke's painting three lanky young men pose on a rock in shallow water off the coast of Ornö, an island in the Stockholm archipelago. They savour the rays of the midnight sun and the salty air, their bodies splashed by the chilly sea. Historically, women have been constructed as more 'natural' and associated with the physical landscape (Mother Earth). And consistent with this image, Zorn's women seem at ease in their setting, whereas the poses of Acke's men are awkward, as if they are not completely comfortable in their environment. Zorn's women are seated on the rocks—they are in greater physical contact with the earth, the forest and fast land, where Acke's men seem stranded on a rocky outcropping in the sea and, by standing, maintain a greater distance from the earth. Furthermore, Zorn's women comport themselves in a casual and natural manner, whereas Acke's men pose for the artist and are isolated from one another both psychologically and physically; they seem involved in a private communion with the sea, whose choppiness contrasts with their stasis.

Patricia Berman has shown in a painting by Edvard Munch from 1907–8, one similar to Acke's, that the men represent the modern, strong Norwegian nation-state, emancipated from Sweden in 1905. She demonstrates that as nature became a crucial signifier of national identity, of Norwegianness, it was redefined as a masculine space rather than a feminine one (Berman). The same process of a masculine appropriation of nature occurred in Sweden as an integral part of the construction of national identity. Instead of nurturing and provident, nature was remapped as a physically challenging site where male individuals honed their physical prowess in order to build a strong and wholesome nation state. Indeed, Klas Sandell has asserted that 'The national romantic feeling at the turn of the century seems to have had a decisive significance for attitudes toward the accessibility of Swedish outdoor life'.[3] The differences in the paintings by Zorn and Acke visualize this transition in attitude. Acke's close friendship with prominent national romantic ideologues suggests that he shared their ideas concerning the importance of forging a healthy, egalitarian, Swedish society in harmony with nature.

Thus, the association of health and naturalness with nude sea bathing evoked in Zorn's image was transformed two decades later by Acke into a muscular declaration of national identity. Just as cold-water bathing itself democratized around the turn of the century, so did nude bathing. While continuing to be a largely private practice, it became a commonplace by the mid-twentieth century, losing its political edge as it was assimilated into a natural aspect of a generic Swedish identity.

Notes

NB All translations are the author's.

1. Speculation as to the reasons for the strong collective spirit of Dalarna's inhabitants, as well as for their reluctance to conform to mandates issued by a central Swedish authority have occupied scholars and been a subject of general interest. An introduction to this problematic and fascinating question is found in Bortas.

2. Doctors were mistrusted by workers and peasants because they represented civil authority; see Edvinsson.

3. Sandel 56; George Mosse has demonstrated how an escalating interest in nudism accompanied the search for symbols of national identity.

9

The Ideological, Aesthetic and Ecological Significance of Water in Twentieth-century German Garden Design

Joachim Wolschke-Bulmahn

Water has been, over the millennia, not only an absolute necessity for gardens and gardeners, but also one of the most fascinating phenomena in the world of gardens. A quotation from Frank A. Waugh (1869–1943), an American landscape architect and important garden writer of the early twentieth century, reflects this fascination. Waugh described in his 1928 *Book of Landscape Gardening* the significance of water for garden design in the following:

> Water in any form furnishes an ever pleasing addition to a garden, whether as a bubbling fountain, a sparkling brook, or a cool and quiet expanse of a mirror-like surface. In brooks and ponds it furnishes one of the most delightful resources of the landscape gardener . . . The possibilities which are open to the landscape gardener in the treatment of water surfaces are so magnificent and manifold that neither description nor enumeration is practicable here. We can only declare with all emphasis that when water surfaces are brought into a landscape composition an immeasurable field of pleasing variety is opened for cultivation by the resourceful gardener. (Waugh 27–8)

'An immeasurable field of pleasing variety', Waugh's characterization, also points out a problem this author confronted when deciding how to focus this essay. Even its title, 'Ideological, Aesthetic and Ecological Significance of Water in Twentieth-Century German Garden Design', left elbowroom for, to use Waugh's wording, an almost immeasurable variety of different essays. The study has finally been focused on issues of water as discussed in one specific German landscape architecture journal, *Die Gartenkunst* (Garden Art), which appeared from 1899 to 1944. Other journals and publications, for example, books like *Die künstlerische Verwendung des Wassers im Städtebau* (The Artificial Use of Water in Urban

119

Architecture, Volkmann), will be considered only marginally. Since 1949 its successor, *Garten und Landschaft* (Garden and Landscape), has been published by the Association of German Landscape Architects. In its character and significance *Die Gartenkunst* is considered an equivalent to the prestigious American journal *Landscape Architecture*, the journal of the American Society for Landscape Architects, or the Danish journal *Landskab*. This essay analyses changing garden design theories as presented in *Die Gartenkunst* and *Garten und Landschaft* and shows how they have been realized in practice over the past century in close connection to politics, culture and ideology.

Water Issues as Discussed in the Journal *Die Gartenkunst*

Die Gartenkunst and *Garten und Landschaft* cover more than a century, a time span that includes such different political systems in Germany as the Imperial period, the Weimar Republic, National Socialism, the German Democratic Republic and the Federal Republic. Although already focused mainly on one journal, the following discussion has to remain fragmentary and mainly addresses issues of water in public parks and private gardens.

The period around 1900, when *Die Gartenkunst* first appeared, was a period of fundamental political change in Germany. During the nineteenth century, as part of the process of industrialization, the political power of the nobility and landed gentry decreased, and rapidly growing cities and their administrations gained influence. Beginning around 1870, parks departments were established in German cities to improve living conditions for the urban population. These fundamental changes also affected discussions of garden and park design in *Die Gartenkunst* and other professional journals. Of course, one can still find articles from around the turn of the century that introduced the parks of the nobility to *Die Gartenkunst*'s readers. Nevertheless, these princely parks and their lakes and ponds were no longer exclusively presented as retreats for the nobility. They were now often discussed as part of a system of public open spaces intended to serve the recreational purposes of urbanites.

Die Gartenkunst began to dedicate increasing attention to the growing number of public parks newly created by the parks departments of such cities as Berlin, Leipzig and Hamburg. Until 1900 these parks, often characterized by large lakes, were still designed in the landscape style of their princely models and predecessors of the nineteenth century. Their lakes and ponds had irregularly shaped shorelines, and, in those days, the citizens of even the smallest German cities wanted to have their own swannery like the nobles of earlier centuries.

The designers of these new public parks were particularly fascinated by artificial waterfalls, often realized under great financial strain. Such waterfalls were often found in parks of cities, such as Hamburg and Cologne, situated in Germany's flat regions lacking natural waterfalls. Constructing them involved taking advantage of the slightest difference in elevation. The modest waterfall in the so-called Elbberg Gardens, a public park on the Elbe river in Altona near Hamburg, was enthusiastically described in *Die Gartenkunst* in 1903 as 'one of the newest creations in the field of landscape gardening' and as a magnificent waterfall, 'which falls roaring and murmuring down 16 metres like a mountain creek' (Jung 205). The sketch of this waterfall (Fig. 9.1) might indicate the author's enthusiasm as well as the exaggeration of his statements. Another such artificial waterfall was

Figure 9.1   Sketch of the waterfall in the Elbberg Garden, Altona (Gartenkunst 1903: 206)

designed for the Klettenberg Park in Cologne. The terrain of the Klettenberg Park was praised by park director Fritz Encke[1] (1861–1931) for the following reason: 'Ten metres of difference in elevation can rarely be found here on flat ground, so that making use of this difference in conjunction with artistic design will result in park motifs lacking in Cologne's other parks' (Encke 91).

Such ideas about waterfalls and garden design were explicitly discussed by garden architect Willy Lange (1864–1941), who published, beginning in 1900, his concept of a nature garden. It had a strong racist component.[2] Lange saw the nature garden as the highest stage of evolution in the field of garden design, therefore appropriate for the Nordic race. For Lange, garden art was a constituent of national culture, and culture could only be national. He vehemently rejected the idea that 'art could be international', declaring: 'Let us find the national style for our gardens; then we will have art, German garden art. As long as different nations exist, different national styles must exist' (Lange, 'Garten' 364). In 1901 Lange presented his ideas about the use of water in natural gardens in a series of articles entitled 'Water in the Landscape'. He claimed that natural gardens and each garden feature, including water, had to be designed according to the laws of nature. Therefore, he carefully studied waterfalls, lakes and other natural bodies of water. He rejected adding artificial water features because they would not be true to nature. Lange conceded that in the small nature garden a spring could be created by using a water pipe. 'But then', he said, 'in the small garden one has to be content with a spring of natural size and should not want to have little waterfalls, little bridges and ponds in a garden of only a few square metres' (Lange, 'Wasser' 439). Architectonic water basins, water terraces and cascades were for Lange the business of the architect, not of the garden designer; they had no place in his natural garden.

Ideas about naturally designed water features, particularly artificial waterfalls, were fashionable around 1900. A spectacular example of an artificial waterfall as the main attraction in a public park was the one designed for the Viktoriapark in Berlin. It was first planned in the 1880s by Hermann Mächtig (1837–1909), park director of Berlin, not as a natural waterfall but as a formal water axis leading from the monument on the Kreuzberg, which commemorated the wars of liberation against Napoleon (1813–15), down to the city. The Kreuzberg waterfall is of special interest because it elucidates most clearly how politics and ideology influence the use of water in garden design. When plans were developed to design the Viktoriapark, named after crown princess Viktoria, Mächtig considered a baroque water cascade appropriate for a public park honouring a member of the royal family. One goal of open-space politics in those days was to educate the people through park design to be good citizens. Therefore, Mächtig developed a formal design that would heighten the effect of the monument: a cascade lined with rows of pyramidally growing trees, broad steps and sculptures. The whole design was to follow 'a patriotically oriented program' (Nungesser 86). These plans were not

Figure 9.2   Waterfall in the Viktoriapark in Berlin (c. 1910)

realized, because of the immense costs and because a formal water cascade was apparently considered by some representatives of Berlin as being 'too good' for Kreuzberg, a proletarian neighbourhood (Nungesser 86). A natural-looking water-fall was created instead and it is still an attraction today (Fig. 9.2).

During National Socialism Adolf Hitler and his architect Albert Speer developed gigantic plans for redesigning Berlin as the capital of the German Reich. These plans would have had a considerable impact on the Kreuzberg waterfall. A model of the intended redesign of this area was published in *Die Gartenkunst* in 1938 (Fig. 9.3). It is emblematic of the ideas held by the National Socialists concerning the appropriate design for urban spaces and the role of water in them. Instead of a people's park with a romantic-looking waterfall, Hitler's architects planned a monumental, formal axis from the Schinkel memorial to the Tempelhof airport. Four cascades were to flow down from the monument to the airport building. This shows that architecture was one of the means by which the Nazis strove to convey power over the population.

The Time of the *Kaiserreich* and the Weimar Republic (1918–33) – Water in People's Parks

However, the beginning of the people's parks movement at the start of the twentieth century needs further discussion. The public parks created in Germany

*Figure 9.3   Redesign of the Viktoriapark and its waterfall by National Socialist planners
(Gartenkunst 1938: 58)*

around this time were, in terms of their use, of a more formal character. Their use
was determined by bourgeois paternalistic ideas about good behaviour. The public
was not allowed, for example, to go onto the lawn and use it as a playground. Rather,
people were expected to walk on paths, to look at nature and to admire the patriotic
monuments. A report by Berlin's city council covering the years 1861 to 1876
noted that the newly established parks in Berlin should serve the people foremost
as 'a source of a true perception and an ethical enjoyment of nature' (quoted in
Hennebo 384). Particularly with regard to members of the working class, the report
expressed the following goal: 'It is indisputable that such well maintained parks
are a suitable means to raise the mind above the worry of material existence and
to temper the raw mind, wherever it exists' (quoted in Hennebo 384).

However, as part of the political transformations and the industrialization process
at the beginning of the twentieth century, the workers' movement was flourishing,
and socialist parties and trade unions were gaining increasing power. Along with
these socio-political changes ideas about the purposes and the appropriate use of
public parks also changed – and all this impacted ideas about water. In the course
of democratization new parks were designed, and existing ones opened to the
population for a variety of leisure activities. Children in particular became an
important clientele for the landscape architect. It was revolutionary in Germany
when people were first allowed to go onto the lawn and use it for games, dancing

Figure 9.4   Wading pool with sand beach in the Eppendorf Park (Gartenkunst *1929: 13)*

and – during the Weimar Republic – for political gatherings. In 1909 *Die Garten-flora*, another garden design magazine, reported on the newly designed Schillerpark in Berlin: 'For the first time here in Berlin opening large parts of the lawns to the public on a grander scale, according to the English model, will be tested' (Fischer 210). And in 1929 the Communist Party had a gathering with tens of thousands of participants in the very same Schillerpark.

Some progressive landscape architects played an important role in the demo-cratization of park use in Germany. Among them was Ludwig Lesser (1869–1957), the leading figure in the German people's park movement. In 1913 Lesser founded the German People's Park Association and in 1927 published his modern ideas about the design and use of public parks in *People's Parks Today and Tomorrow*. He criticized the fact that traditional parks were not accessible to all parts of the population and could be used only in very restricted and limited ways. People's parks should offer, he said, sunny lawns for play, shady alleys, music pavilions and athletic fields. Water, for Lesser, was an imperative feature of a people's park. He advocated not only drinking fountains and ornamental water basins but also 'areas of water, parts of which could be used as bathing pools' (Lesser 6) (Fig. 9.4).

As previously mentioned, these changes regarding the use of water in public parks were revolutionary for Germany, which is clearly reflected in *Die Garten-kunst*. This becomes evident, for example, in a series of articles in 1909 entitled

'How Can the City´s Gardens and Grounds Be Made Usable for the Population in a Practical Way?' One of the topics discussed in the series was 'sport and bathing places on urban grounds'. The author, Wolfgang Singer (1865–1942), head of the parks department in the city of Bad Kissingen, welcomed the new trends of nudism, fresh air and sunbathing, which arose in the years after 1900, but also stated regretfully that 'the general view of life in our country is still not advanced enough for open-air swimming pools . . . in public parks to be admissible without further ado. Densely fenced-in enclosures, protected against viewers, have to be created particularly for the adults' (Singer 42).

In the years between 1900 and the beginning of the First World War, water played a special role in German society in many different senses. The various life-reform movements, such as the youth movement, nudism, sports, etc., gave special attention to public health issues. Within this context, swimming gained importance for an increasing number of people. During their sports lesson many school children now learned how to swim. Many so-called public river baths had already come into being before 1900. With the beginning of the twentieth century the first official public open-air swimming pools were established. Water also attained outstanding importance in a totally different sphere, the military world. In the struggle for world power Germany spent billions of Reichsmarks to expand its navy. Fascination with water, the sea and with German strength and technological development as reflected in battleships may explain why the sailor suit became the typical Sunday garb for many children (Fig. 9.5).

The First World War briefly interrupted the discussion of the social significance of water for public parks in Germany. Not unexpectedly, the discussion of water in *Die Gartenkunst* also changed. No longer were there many articles about people's parks; instead garden fountains, for example, were now promoted as memorials for fallen soldiers. In his article 'The Memorial in Park and Garden', landscape architect Wilhelm Heilig promoted the idea of erecting memorials in one's own garden for fallen relatives, particularly for members of the navy, whose corpses could not be transported back home to Germany. 'Would it not be possible', Heilig asked the readers of *Die Gartenkunst*, 'to erect a memorial at an appropriate place in the garden, perhaps at the favorite spot of the deceased, thereby creating a place that is dedicated to him?' (Heilig 4). Sketches illustrating his vision showed grove-like garden settings with memorial fountains.

After the end of the First World War and with the breakdown of the Imperial Reich, the Weimar Republic brought new rights to an increasing number of people – women, for example, gained the right to vote for the first time in German history. This period of democratization furthered the creation of people's parks, and this caused an explosion of articles in *Die Gartenkunst* about people's parks and issues related to a socially oriented park policy. In contrast to park director Singer's regret in 1909 that German social norms discouraged adults from swimming in public

Figure 9.5   Children in sailor suits (c. 1910)

parks, it now became the rule to include wading pools and often swimming facilities in people's parks (Fig. 9.6).

From the beginning private gardens had been a topic in *Die Gartenkunst*. And, of course, water fountains and ornamental water basins, adding a picturesque and romantic touch, were often an important feature of the middle and upper-middle class gardens that the journal introduced to its readers. One can find pools and ponds of similar design in *Die Gartenkunst* over the following thirty years. It is interesting to note that during the Weimar period, a small group of German landscape architects strove to have avant-garde ideas incorporated into garden design.[3] They were inspired by avant-garde artists and often collaborated with

127

Figure 9.6   Wading pool in a park in Hannover (c. 1930)

architects of the *Neue Sachlichkeit* (New Functionalism). One of their objectives was to strip garden design of Romanticism. Hans Friedrich Pohlenz (1901-?) was a representative of this group and one of the most innovative German landscape architects of his time. In 1927 he published a brief article in which he presented a very unusual water fountain, which he titled 'Water Disc Fountain' (Fig. 9.7). His work was inspired by an antique source, whose forms he tried to translate into a modern, avant-garde language. To quote from his article: 'In Meersburg on the Bodensee you can find an old fountain: a female figure holding both arms at head-height at her side, and a water disc plays between her hands. Jets of water emerge out of the palms of her hands. I used this motif, stripped of its romanticism, for a fountain construction in the Bergische Land' (Pohlenz 159).

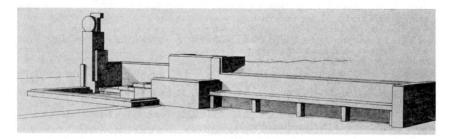

Figure 9.7   Design for the water disc fountain by landscape architect Pohlenz
(Gartenschönheit 1927: 159)

128

A fascinating water-related project of the Weimar period, which addressed in a unique way issues of sports, leisure-time activities, hygiene, recreation, health and social welfare, was published in 1928 by J. Goldmerstein and Karl Stodieck under the title *Thermenpalast*.[4] This 'Thermal Palace' was planned to accomodate about 30,000 visitors a day in a huge hall of more than 150 metres in diameter with a ring-shaped water basin and a spacious artificial beach in the center. Artificial landscapes painted on a circular screen twelve metres tall were to cover the interior walls. Laundries, tub baths and other facilities for hygiene, health and entertainment would complete the programme. The authors intended to provide the population of Berlin with a year-round equivalent to vacation and Mediterranean summer weather. The project was calculated in such a way that the poorer parts of the population could also have afforded to enjoy its artificial and artistic nature. This project was never realized, in all probability due to National Socialism, and was totally forgotten in the second half of the twentieth century (see following essay for details).

National Socialism (1933–45)

With the beginning of National Socialism avant-garde trends and socially oriented projects in the arts and garden design ended abruptly, and the work of the garden designers involved was defamed as 'degenerate'. *Die Gartenkunst* and other landscape architecture journals could no longer introduce to their readers such water features as Pohlenz's 'water disc fountain' or Goldmerstein's and Stodieck's 'Thermal Palace'. This indicates how National Socialism destroyed a complex set of progressive and innovative ideas about water, hygiene, recreational activities, garden design, landscape and nature.[5]

All facets of life in Germany were totally altered with the takeover of National Socialism. In the field of landscape architecture, for example, the Nazis forced out important exponents of a progressive park policy from their positions. The National Socialist state had no interest in a democratic park policy or in an unrestricted and self-determined use of public parks. Rather, the Nazis wanted total control over the population and, in particular, the youth. This included monitoring all aspects of life from work to leisure time. Understandably, in view of National Socialism's totalitarian character, articles about public parks and their unrestricted use more or less disappeared from *Die Gartenkunst* after 1933. However, several articles addressed the redesign of some people's parks for National Socialist purposes. Parade grounds were emphasized instead of extensive water areas, which were apparently no longer of interest.

Water did not disappear from parks but – compared with the Weimar Republic era – only a few articles dealing with public parks during National Socialism appeared in *Die Gartenkunst*. The shift in topics discussed in German landscape architecture journals included a focus on new areas for professional activities. This becomes evident in a 1933 article entitled 'The Tasks of the German Society for Garden Art', which dealt with the reorganization and future activities of the Deutsche Gesellschaft für Gartenkunst (German Society for Garden Art) under its newly appointed National Socialist presidency. The author, Georg Gunder (1894–1950), vice-president of the society, listed private gardens and the National Socialist office of *Schönheit der Arbeit* (Beauty of Labour) among the areas requiring special attention. Public parks were no longer a relevant issue (Gunder 101).

The National Socialists had various propaganda campaigns designed to promote their idea of the so-called *Volksgemeinschaft*, the people's community, and to prove to the German people that the National Socialist state would look after their interests better than the Weimar Republic had done. One campaign, *Schönheit der Arbeit*, is of interest for this discussion of water and garden design. The National Socialist state used this slogan to announce a major undertaking for the benefit of the working population, i.e. the beautification of factories and other industrial and commercial buildings. A special office, the *Amt Schönheit der Arbeit* (Office of Beauty of Labour), was established in the *Reichsarbeitsfront* (Reich Labour Front) to coordinate this effort. Its activities did not have much to do with the reality of working conditions in German factories but served above all as a propaganda tool.

Landscape architecture magazines also promoted this 'Beauty-of-Labour' campaign. In the spring of 1935 a special issue of *Die Gartenkunst* dealt with the initiative for the first time. From then until the beginning of the Second World War numerous articles in *Die Gartenkunst* focused on the gardens and grounds of factories and other commercial buildings, for example, 'Schönheit der Arbeit' (Landmann 1938), 'Schönheit am Arbeitsplatz: Ein Weg in die Zukunft der Gartengestaltung' (Beauty at the Workplace: One Way into the Future of Garden Design, Kolbrand), etc. The articles emphasized the significance of such gardens for workers and employees, and water was of special importance. One should remember that ornamental water basins were probably still characteristic of only the elite's gardens. Nevertheless, several of the articles about 'Beauty-of-Labour' gardens included photographs of water basins. These were intended to depict the luxurious design and care that the National Socialist state provided its working population. In 1938 landscape architect Hermann Aldinger (1895–1972) published an article titled 'The First Factory Garden in Stuttgart'. The garden (Fig. 9.8), designed by Aldinger himself, was introduced in the following way:

> Stuttgart has its first factory garden! It is situated in the middle of an austere quarter of the city, for the recreation and pleasure of 40 to 50 people, and has replaced a very ugly and poorly arranged factory yard . . . At the special request of the work-force a water basin with water lilies and irises was built . . . This first factory garden in town is an exemplary social achievement. (Aldinger 217)

*Figure 9.8   Water basin in the garden of a Stuttgart factory (*Gartenkunst *1938: 217)*

Such articles were supposed to help reinforce the social approach of National Socialism despite real-life conditions.

Private Gardens and National Socialism

Another shift in topics in *Die Gartenkunst* after 1933 was from public parks to private gardens. Of course, essays on private gardens had comprised a substantial part of the overall number of articles since *Die Gartenkunst*'s initial issue in 1899. Nevertheless, articles about public parks and other urban open spaces had been considered of equal importance, particularly during the Weimar Republic. One reason for the shift was the National Socialists' disinterest in an unrestricted use of parks, particularly by young people. Another was that people's parks were often identified with the political program of the workers' movement and the socialist parties of the Weimar Republic. A third important reason can be found in the National Socialist *Blut-und-Boden* (blood-and-soil) ideology, which glorified the healthy family as the nucleus of a future strong Germanic race. The private house garden of the middle-class family played a substantial role in promoting this ideal in many a garden design and landscape architecture journal.

In 1933, immediately after the takeover of the National Socialists, the editor of *Die Gartenkunst*, Herbert Jensen (1900–68), explicitly announced the change in focus. In his programmatic article 'Zeitgemäße Aufgaben der Zeitschrift *Garten-kunst*' (Current Tasks of the Journal *Gartenkunst*) he refers to recently repeated reproaches that *Die Gartenkunst* had dedicated too much space in the past to 'the great tasks of garden design, especially the design of public green spaces' (H. Jensen 140–1). Thus, according to Jensen, discussions of such public spaces would recede in the future in favour of those of the private garden. 'The private green space, one's own garden, will increase in coverage . . . We will have to make sure to use our influence so that the small house garden for the inexpensive one-family house is designed in the right way' (H. Jensen 141). Consequently, after 1933 numerous articles presented house gardens, often with illustrations that showed children playing happily (Fig. 9.9).

House gardens were supposed to correspond to the National Socialists' family ideal and be unpretentious and free of so-called foreign influences. As mentioned above, the Nazis vilified modernism and avant-garde trends in the arts, including garden design, as an outgrowth of what they called international and particularly Jewish influence. The majority of landscape architects no longer dared to experiment with garden design. Instead, intellectual boredom overtook the field. The resulting programmatic decline is reflected most clearly in the first important garden exhibition after the Nazi takeover. The 'Annual Exhibition of German Garden Culture' took place in Hannover in the summer of 1933. Heinrich Wiepking (1891–1973), a leading National Socialist landscape architect, praised it as

Figure 9.9   Children playing in a pool in a private garden (Maasz 61)

follows: 'Of all great German garden exhibitions I liked the one in Hannover the most. Nothing happened there' (Wiepking-Jürgensmann 162). Wiepking commented on the exhibition gardens as 'being genuine and not posed. They are all aimed at the ideal of simplicity, of practicability, of the house garden as well as the usable garden' (Wiepking-Jürgensmann 163).

During this time the genuinely German garden, suitable for the German people as the elite of the so-called Aryan race was the rule, and this recalled Lange's ideas from the early 1900s. Since *Blut-und-Boden* ideology closely connected Germans to their home landscape and soil, natural garden design became dominant. Informal design was favoured over the use of geometric forms; native plants were preferred over foreign ones. The exclusive desire for them became an important ideological vehicle that defined the National Socialist garden ideal.[6] Interestingly enough, this ideology hardly affected the discussion of water in garden design. One reason might have been that it was expensive in the 1930s to make natural-looking, that is irregularly shaped water basins, usually fashioned from stone or concrete, for middle-class house gardens.

One of the few articles in *Die Gartenkunst* that included a picture of a naturally designed pond was published by the American landscape architect Jens Jensen (1860–1951). He had strong ties during National Socialism to German colleagues, among them Michael Mappes (1898–?), who served as editor of *Die Gartenkunst* from 1936 to 1944. In July 1936 Mappes wrote a letter to Jensen in which he thanked him for articles about his (Jensen's) own work and stated:

> From the issues of 'Die Gartenkunst' I edited myself you will see that not only I but a number of German garden designers strive for similar ideals. That is a result of the spiritual change since the coming to power of Adolf Hitler. I urgently ask you to send me as soon as possible all of the pictures you published in the newspaper as well as photographs and, if possible, much more material, because I intend to publish your work in our journal in an effective way. (Mappes)

And indeed, in 1937 a longer article by Jensen, 'Die Lichtung' (The Clearing), appeared in *Die Gartenkunst*. The following quotation from the article indicates the proximity of Jensen's ideas about natural garden and landscape design to those of the National Socialists. Jensen described his own design motives to the readership of *Die Gartenkunst* in the following way:

> The gardens I created myself shall, like any landscape design, it does not matter where, be in harmony with their landscape environment and the racial characteristics of its inhabitants. They shall express the spirit of America and therefore shall be free of foreign character as far as possible . . . The Latin and the Oriental crept and creeps more and more

Figure 9.10   Natural pond, designed by the American landscape architect Jens Jensen
(Gartenkunst 1937: 180)

over our land, coming from the South, which is settled by Latin people, and also from other centers of mixed masses of immigrants. The Germanic character of our race, cities and settlements was overgrown by foreign [character]. Latin spirit has spoiled much and still spoils things every day. (J. Jensen 177)

Large, natural ponds similar to the one in Jensen's article (Fig. 9.10) also existed, of course, in National Socialist Germany. But during National Socialism it was apparently considered inappropriate to present such upper-class gardens in *Die Gartenkunst*. The garden of the 'ideal' member of the so-called *Volksgemeinschaft* (people's community), the modest middle-class garden in its various gradations, was the favourite object of garden writers in the 1930s.

During National Socialism the discussion of water in natural garden design was thus not really expanded. Yet, surely many people did not want to do without formal basins, fountains or other artificial water features. Ponds designed in a natural style would become fashionable forty years later, in the 1970s and 1980s.

The Period of the Federal Republic (1949–)

The period of the Federal Republic was marked by new trends in the use of water in garden design. Examples of public parks and of the evolution of swimming pools and water basins in the house garden illustrate such trends. The era of people's parks – that special concept of public parks with explicitly democratic goals – had passed with the Weimar Republic, and they never experienced a revival as originally conceived. However, public parks were created in numerous German cities in the 1950s and 1960s, but without the wading pools and paddling ponds of the Weimar parks because of hygienic concerns. In the public baths of these boom years luxurious swimming pools with circulation pumps and chlorine facilities became the rule. Absolute cleanliness, the shining white of 'Persil' and other laundry detergents became the ideal. There was also a thriving market for washing machines. Numerous advertisements in newspapers and on television reflected these growing concerns about dirt and the danger of illness. In many cities the parks departments were no longer allowed to install children's pools without pumps or chlorination. The head of the parks department in Berlin-Tempelhof, for example, introduced his 1956 article on water play gardens in the journal now named *Garten und Landschaft* as follows: 'According to a decree of the main public health office in Berlin, paddle ponds without concrete bottoms, circulation pumps and chlorine installations can no longer be opened to the public' (Kynast 8).

In the 1950s Ulrich Wolf (1902–67), parks director of Düsseldorf, developed special water playgrounds that would meet such hygienic concerns. His 1956 article on Düsseldorf's water playgrounds addressed the question of hygiene regarding public paddle ponds as follows:

> The water cannot attain a sufficient level of cleanliness unless an expensive circulation pump is installed like in big swimming pools, or unless we have to drain the water everyday, clean the basin and fill it again, as is done, for example, in the city of Basel. Over the past years the public health administration of Düsseldorf has stopped the operation of all paddle ponds for safety reasons, because of the occurrences of spinal polio. (Wolf 326)

Wolf instead developed his concept of water playgrounds, which employed traditional climbing frames equipped with water jets and nozzles. These apparently met the hygienic concerns of his time. It is uncertain whether in the following decades wading pools and similar water features totally disappeared from public parks in Germany, for Wolf's article is one of the last in *Garten und Landschaft* to address this issue. As already indicated, hygienic reasons – or perhaps an 'over-hygienic' reaction – and the high costs involved in building hygienically correct pools that could meet the new standards were a main reason for the disappearance of such pools from Germany's public parks.

*Figure 9.11   Swimming pool in a 1950s garden (*Garten und Landschaft *1959: 194)*

From Swimming Pool to Eco-Pond – Water in the Private Garden

The 1950s and 1960s were a period of economic prosperity in the Federal Republic. More and more people were able to hire landscape architects, and the gardens presented in *Garten und Landschaft* thus became more luxurious. Outdoor swimming pools became a status symbol for many middle-class families. *Garten und Landschaft* provided numerous examples of beautiful pools in private house gardens (Fig. 9.11). In 1958 the *Deutsche Gesellschaft für Gartenkunst und Land-schaftspflege* (German Society for Garden Art and Landscape Care) announced in the journal its newly published book *Wasserbecken im Garten* (Water Basins in the Garden), written by Paulhans Peter and Ludwig Roemer. It included numerous examples of extravagantly designed swimming pools. But, apart from being an important status symbol, these pools were expensive to construct and maintain, space-consuming and of no use at all during most of the year because of Germany's climate. This situation was soon reflected in *Garten und Landschaft*, and over time the presentation of swimming pools disappeared almost completely from it.

In the 1970s many members of the middle class, stimulated by the political and social impulses of the student movement of the late 1960s, exhibited an increasing ecological and environmental awareness. There is no space here to elaborate on these developments in an adequate way. Landscape architects also jumped onto the bandwagon, and this seemed to offer new perspectives for professional activities. Starting in the late 1970s, articles with titles such as 'A Garden Pond Habitat' (A. Wolf) appeared in *Garten und Landschaft*. This and other articles criticized traditional garden design – sometimes in arrogant and ignorant ways – as non-functional and cliché-ridden. For example, Eike Schmidt (1941–1990), the then editor of *Garten und Landschaft*, wrote: 'Joe Sixpack, who has his own garden, unfortunately wants to have an artificial lawn, wants a swimming pool, a Hollywood swing, over-bred roses, a Christmas tree, colourful flowers, some kind of barbecue grill in addition and even colour on the artificial stone path' (Schmidt 884).

Another article, 'Natural Gardens in an Urban Milieu', stated in a similarly patronizing manner that most of the private gardens 'have degenerated to the sterile conformity of made-up decoration. In often touching, but still helpless, endeavours to fashion them, only highly commercial models are reproduced. The stereotype wins again . . . The systems produced are biologically foreign and require endless care' (Spitzer 457). Instead, the author announced: 'Environmental problems are being discussed a great deal, and this leads to the consideration of how gardens may be fashioned according to ecological viewpoints . . . The centuries-old European conception of man as lord and exploiter of nature, which probably has Judeo-Christian roots (Genesis 1:28), is here supplanted by the knowledge that man himself is only part of the whole' (Spitzer 458–9). Man as 'part of the whole' – as a result of this kind of promotion of so-called ecological garden design many a garden owner naturally wanted to create the 'whole' in order to be able to become a part of it in his or her own garden. And a garden in the 1980s without an eco-pond lacked the character of 'wholeness'.

Eco-ponds were considered a necessary feature of natural gardens; they became emblematic of ecological balance in the garden and of their owners' environmental awareness. Gardens no longer primarily served owners' needs, but preserving nature became the objective. In the 1979 article on garden pond habitats the goal is described as follows: 'As a rule the objective should be the construction of a balanced, self-regulating natural system with a variety of flora and fauna. [Floral and faunal variety] does not imply a botanical or zoological garden, but a stable community of plants and animals . . . Properly planned, such ponds can become valuable semi-natural areas within a very short time, with an important role for the preservation of wildlife' (A. Wolf 443).

The change from formal ornamental water basins and swimming pools to inform-ally laid out eco-ponds was made possible by the often condemned chemical industry. Specially developed plastic sheets enabled many garden owners to create affordable ponds on a large or small scale, in almost any desired shape or form, but most easily in one that looked informal and organic. Gardens in the 1980s were literally flooded with such eco-ponds. It would be interesting to know how many animals died in the name of ecology and nature preservation in order to create these new ecological paradises in highly urban settings. Lizards, frogs and other animals considered an imperative component of such ecological paradises were either bought in pet shops or caught in the surrounding landscapes and then brought into the garden.

But many garden owners started to realize that to keep such pseudo-ecological systems alive was a difficult and somewhat anti-natural enterprise, requiring permanent and careful maintenance. Many of these ponds thus disappeared over the years. By the end of the 1980s some skeptical voices were also raised in *Garten und Landschaft*, for example, in the articles 'Urban Green between Ecology and Garden Art' (Schmid) and 'Water between Design and Ecology' (Luz). These later contributions clearly reflect the search for a balance between two different concepts – garden design as an artistic and social issue, and garden design as primarily a contribution to the preservation of nature.

The search for a balance between different concepts of water seems to be the latest step in the changing role of pools and ponds in the garden. With the rejection of the open-air swimming pool as a luxurious and anti-ecological garden feature and with the departure of the mere eco-pond, the most recent fashion in the use of water in the garden seems to be a combination of the two. This new trend reached *Garten und Landschaft* in the early 1990s, when the first articles on this topic were published. 'What to Do with Ruined Open-Air Pools? The Return to a Natural Pond' (Konold/Rolli 41) was the question and answer given in the title of one such article, but the authors suggested a solution that included both natural pond and swimming pool. In the same year Eduard Neuenschwander's book *Beautiful Swimming Ponds* appeared. The author juxtaposed, rather manipulatively, a photograph called 'Glamorous Life at the Swimming Pool' with one titled 'The Other Kind of Bathing Pleasure', the latter showing a happy father with his daughter. In the text one reads the following comment: 'This kind of luxury and its artificiality have reached their limit. Our longing for the natural comes through once again; our understanding of nature and our attitude towards it are in a process of radical change' (Neuenschwander 8).

Conclusion

A goal of this discussion of the ideological, aesthetic and ecological significance of water in twentieth-century German garden design was to illustrate how ideas about water in gardens and parks in the journal are connected to ideology, politics, technology, philosophy and other spheres of human life. My analysis, although already focused mainly on one landscape architecture journal, could not be comprehensive within the limits of this essay. Nevertheless, it described the change from a more representative use of water in public parks during the Imperial period to the wading pools of the people's parks of the Weimar Republic. This new emphasis on usefulness and accessibility contrasted with the ostentatious nature of the earlier parks, where water was only to be admired passively. The essay also connected the disappearance of wading and swimming pools in public parks to the National Socialist destruction of progressive concepts of park design. Water, when included at all, was again used to impress and control, in part by suggesting the state's concern for its German workers. There was, however, more of a focus on private, 'natural' gardens. The study then elucidated how changing values in postwar Germany have been connected with innovative ideas about pools and ponds in both private gardens and public parks. These latest uses of water have reflected a general sense of prosperity as well as new hygienic and environmental concerns. One can assume that subsequent trends in the use of water in garden design will continue not only to depend, for example, on new socio-political and economic conditions and perceptions about nature and culture but also to further or challenge them. Perhaps this paper will stimulate analyses of *Die Gartenkunst* against other landscape architecture journals in order to compare developments in Germany with those in other countries. But independent of such studies, water in all probability will remain one of the most fascinating elements in the garden.

Notes

1. See Gröning/Wolschke-Bulmahn, *Grüne,* regarding the biography of Encke and other German landscape architects of the early twentieth century.
2. See Wolschke-Bulmahn/Gröning, 'Ideology', for more detail about Lange's racist ideas about natural garden design.
3. See Wolschke-Bulmahn 'Avantgarde', for more detail about avant-garde ideas in early twentieth-century German landscape architecture.
4. See for more detail about the *Thermenpalast* the contribution of Gert Gröning and Joachim Wolschke-Bulmahn in this same volume.
5. See Gröning/Wolschke-Bulmahn, 'Entwicklung'; Wolschke-Bulmahn, 'Peculiar', for more detail about the impact of National Socialism on German landscape architecture.
6. See Wolschke-Bulmahn, 'Search', for more detail about the significance of racism for ideas about natural garden design in Germany and the United States.

10

The *Thermenpalast* (Thermal Palace): An Outstanding German Water-leisure Project from the 1920s

Gert Gröning and *Joachim Wolschke-Bulmahn*

In the course of the 1980s many municipal indoor swimming facilities in Germany experienced a severe loss of visitors. Some Germans questioned the objective need for such facilities, concluding that further construction was no longer necessary. Since the end of the 1970s, private companies had increasingly assumed the construction of so-called 'fun-and-leisure' swimming facilities. These 'new' sites provided space for participation in a number of related indoor activities besides just swimming. In contrast to the seemingly purely functional architecture of buildings housing municipal swimming facilities, these fun-and-leisure swimming sites offered a variety of architectural spaces designed to communicate a sense of relaxation. Designers even introduced plants to counteract the sterile atmosphere of most municipal facilities. These sites thus alluded to the summer holidays many Germans experienced on the Mediterranean.

The case of Hamburg, for example, demonstrates this change in emphasis from municipal to private swimming facility. In the fiscal year 1980, Hamburg's deficit from managing municipal swimming facilities reached 50 million Deutschmarks, equivalent to $US 25 million. Leisure experts, employing empirical research methods, sought to analyse the reasons for such a loss. One reason for the decline in visitors to the municipal facilities was a change in leisure habits. Visitors missed *Gemütlichkeit* and wished to do more than merely take a swim. Instead of 'cold tiles', they would have preferred an artificial lawn. Other preferences included a cafeteria and restaurant, special areas for fitness training, tanning studios, music, flowerbeds, underwater illumination, water-current generating devices, chairs and benches, and small, secluded areas where guests could retreat from the otherwise lively atmosphere (Opaschowski). Advocates of the new, enhanced swimming facilities thus claimed that visitors from all social strata would be willing to pay a much higher entrance fee. However, considering the growing unemployment and sinking wages of the late 1970s and early 1980s, such an assertion reads like pure

Figure 10.1   Exterior view of the Thermenpalast, *sketch by Professor Poelzig, Berlin*

propaganda (Krieger). The same claim, however, provided support for those who had viewed the reduced availability of swimming facilities as a loss of social orientation (Caspar). Yet there was a perception that private companies, not municipal governments, were more capable of offering these desirable expanded amenities. On the other hand, a conflicting view portrayed those visiting indoor swimming centres as members of a new hydro-thermo-subculture with the brains of tadpoles (Herbel).

Over the last two decades of the twentieth century, the notion that the public is responsible for all members of a community deteriorated even further. There are at present no models for public fun-and-leisure swimming establishments under discussion. Yet Berlin's *Thermenpalast* (thermal palace) from the late 1920s deserves serious reconsideration. Karl Stodieck and J.Goldmerstein developed the concept and design for this outstanding water-related project. It was never realized, in all probability due to the worldwide economic crisis of 1929 and the political crisis of the National-Socialist takeover of Germany in 1933, and was later forgotten. To our knowledge, no one since has developed a more comprehensive or more socially convincing idea for a public indoor swimming facility. This is why we refer to it again here.

In 1928 Goldmerstein and Stodieck published their concept of a thermal palace for Berlin in *Thermenpalast: Kur-, Erholungs-, Sport-, Schwimm- und Badeanlage*,[1] as the project apparently was close to realization. Acknowledged institutions and experts had already approved the overall feasibility of the *Thermenpalast*, including its technical, medicinal and hygienic as well as social and economic soundness.

Goldmerstein's and Stodieck's introductory remarks indicate the modernity of their ideas. By presenting entertainment, beautiful nature and lovely landscapes the *Thermenpalast* was to offer the population of the city of Berlin a year-round equivalent to a summer vacation. Goldmerstein and Stodieck anticipated today's advertising experts when they wrote:

In the summer we enjoy pleasant hours at the beach. We look for relaxation and recuperation at seaside resorts. The beautiful countryside and nice summer weather refresh the heart and senses. But, unfortunately, these recreational areas are usually far away and can be reached only during the short summertime under great financial effort. In comparison, the recreational facilities with beach, artificial sun etc., which are to be created based on the project presented here, will be accessible all year round . . . So many people go to the water, to the sea or the river in order to romp around after work, lightly dressed, in the open air and in the water. The short summertime vacation offers only scant opportunities for this. A small income often does not permit a summer journey at all. Here, our health, sports and recreational centre will step in. In the spacious, airy and bright hall the visitor will feel as if in open air. The hall's periphery will be equipped artistically, helped by modern stage technology, with all kinds of graphic and three-dimensional objects to give the visitor the impression of being in a borderless room with a vast panorama. Painted landscapes, twelve meters high, circling the hall's interior like a panorama, will present a friendly, sunny environment. Coldness, rain and all the unpleasant natural phenomena will not bother our guests. Here, there will always be sunshine, always a blue and laughing sky. Visitors will find everything a natural beach has to offer. (Goldmerstein/Stodieck 6–7)

In order to perfect the enjoyment of nature, the lighting experts consulted for the project suggested sun lamps and additional lighting from coloured bulbs and colour filters, 'so that, e.g., aside from a beautiful and delightful sky, a sunset or the glow from the Alps (*Alpenglühen*) can also be simulated. A centrally fixed machine (*Wolkenapparat*) would project slowly moving clouds'. Another expert consultant suggested planting flowers, shrubs and small trees on the balustrades and in the galleries to further the impression of a natural environment.

The overall concept of the *Thermenpalast* with its manifold program was described as follows:

The main hall is dominated by a huge, circular water basin with a spacious beach on both sides. The inner circular beach rises toward the centre, where there is a two-story restaurant. The inner beach is connected to the outer one by four bridges, each of them three metres wide. Daylight enters the hall through 72 skylights, each 110 square metres in size, and through a huge dome of 600 square metres in the centre of the hall. Thus the hall is turned into a friendly and sunny place. 17,800 adults and 15,000 children per day

Figure 10.2   Interior view of the Thermenpalast *hall with hill, circular pool and outer bathing beach*

will be able to participate in the amenities that the hall offers. They will be able to relax for about four hours after a day's strenuous work. They will enjoy themselves by bathing, swimming, doing gymnastics, running, jumping, walking, eating, drinking, lying on the warm sand and listening to the music. If they are looking for company and entertainment, they will find it there. The hall will provide recuperation, pleasure, social life, entertainment, care for the body through gymnastics and all kinds of sports, health care through medicinal baths, physiotherapy, and drinking and lying treatments, all under artificial sunlight. (Goldmerstein/Stodieck 6)

The water basin and the beaches were described as follows:

The circular water basin is 19 metres in width and from 280 to 400 metres in length. The area covered by water is 6,700 square metres. Of this space, 4,300 square metres can be used for swimming. The basin holds 9,800 cubic metres of water. The greatest depth is four and a half metres, sufficient for dives from a height of ten metres. Two high-diving platforms, ten metres high, are planned . . . The circular design of the water basin creates a one-directional, endless swimming lane. In addition, the radius is so large that swimmers will hardly notice that they are swimming in a circle. The beach on either side of the water-circle will have surfaces on which up to 2,650 visitors can lie; each surface is 1.2 x 2.2 metres large. The outer ring offers 345 plated and 640 sandy places on which to lie. On the inner side of the circular water basin 1,665 sandy places are planned. All of the places are to be heated. Visitors are supposed to feel as if they are actually at a natural, sun-warmed beach on a beautiful, sunny summer day. (Goldmerstein/Stodieck 7)

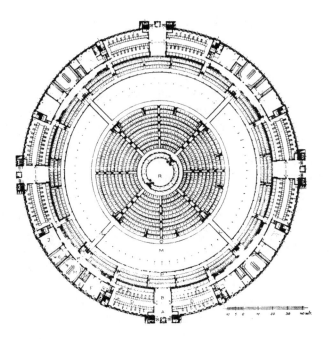

Figure 10.3   Ground plan of the Thermenpalast

In addition, plans included facilities for a broad range of sporting activities, e.g., several gymnasiums for running, jumping, boxing, apparatus gymnastics, rhythmical gymnastics and other sports.

With regard to the arts, entertainment and culture in general the *Thermenpalast* could easily match the programs of today's indoor swimming halls. Goldmerstein and Stodieck announced additional artistic programs in their publication as follows: 'There will also be no lack of entertainment in the palace. The visitor can listen to music. There will be all kinds of artistic performances as well as slide lectures, gymnastic performances, water shows, light shows and similar events. These events can also serve educational purposes' (Goldmerstein/Stodieck 8).

Considering the living conditions of hundreds of thousands of Berliners in those days, the designers offered another intriguing facet of this unique facility. Visitors could have their clothes cleaned free of charge and their shoes repaired while they were there. Obviously, the *Thermenpalast* would have provided all the major amenities of today's swimming halls, and even more. In the entrance halls and waiting rooms, huge glass walls were to allow guests 'to witness as spectators the life and activities within the huge hall' (Goldmerstein/Stodieck 10). The purpose for the walls was to have incoming visitors see others enjoying themselves. Descriptions of late twentieth-century swimming palaces emphasize time and again this particular objective, i.e. putting guests in the proper mood as soon as they enter the building.

A key aspect, especially nowadays, of this fascinating historic concept of a fun-and-leisure-time swimming centre is its social dimension. One of the project's major objectives was to improve the quality of medical care in the city. Goldmerstein and Stodieck stated: 'A very important task of the thermal palace is in the field of health care, be it the care of the healthy through personal hygiene, or the healing of the ill through bathing and drinking treatments, physiotherapy, inhalation, electric baths, etc.' (Goldmerstein/Stodieck 8). They thus planned facilities for medicinal baths, physiotherapy, artificial sunlight, etc. as well as special recovery areas for the ill.

But above all, Goldmerstein and Stodieck's social conscience was reflected in plans 'to ensure that fees were kept within limits so that all parts of the population could visit the thermal palace' (Goldmerstein/Stodieck 11). In order to achieve this goal inexpensive architectonic solutions for the construction of the *Thermenpalast* were required, thus keeping the entrance fees low. Experts from different disciplines, e.g., architects and engineers, the director of a public bath and the director of the Hygienic Institute of the University of Berlin, had also been asked to evaluate the project from an economic point of view. Their expertise confirmed that it would have been possible to build and operate the *Thermenpalast* by raising entrance fees only slightly above those of regular contemporary public baths. The various firms that had calculated the costs for the different construction aspects, such as building, electricity, installation, etc., were ready and willing to do the work for the quoted price.

Even at that time of economic recession the city of Berlin could have brought the project to completion. However, the *Thermenpalast* was never built. Today, we can only speculate about the reasons why. Perhaps the political takeover by National Socialists led to the failure of the project, since its social dimension clearly reflected the tradition of peoples' parks during the Weimar Republic, which were discontinued after 1933 (see Chapter 9). Or perhaps during National Socialism some of the experts involved in the project were no longer allowed to work, e.g., as architects, engineers or other professionals in related fields. This could have been the case with Goldmerstein. We could not find any information about him after 1933. His name could indicate a Jewish origin, and he may have been persecuted by the National Socialists. His co-author, Stodieck, however, worked from 1928 until the end of the Second World War as an honorary professor for industrial architecture at the Technical University of Berlin.

Seven decades ago the *Thermenpalast* would have been a completely new form of public swimming hall. It would have superseded by far all other comparable facilities in Germany and many other European countries. The fun-and-pleasure baths (*Spaß-* and *Vergnügungsbäder*) of the 1980s and 1990s can be considered only poor and incomplete copies of the *Thermenpalast* of the 1920s. Even today its concept can offer new perspectives for public swimming halls, both in its design and, particularly, in the continuing relevance of its social objectives.

Notes

1. Goldmerstein/Stodieck; all quotations were translated by the authors.

II

Hungarian Spas

Terri Switzer

Not far from the banks of the Danube lies a spring that first attracted the Romans, who built there a spa town they called Aquincum, referring to the abundant waters of the area. This spring is only one small, warm-water spring of more than 120 that lie underneath modern-day Budapest and more than 1,000 that gurgle up through cracks in Hungary's ground. Aquincum's hot spring beckoned the Huns and later the Magyars, who both settled near the ruins and graves of those who had first recognized the healing properties of warm water, for waters here seemed to cure sicknesses from leprosy to back ailments, and other springs with similar powers were soon discovered on the banks of the Danube. A settlement emerged in response to their popularity and later became the site of Budapest. Although the use of bathhouses in Budapest fluctuated in popularity over the centuries according to the morals and social habits of the time, this spa culture revolved primarily around structures built during the Turkish occupation and the later addition of modern facilities that catered to the nineteenth-century obsession with the waters. The following discussion details the changes in Budapest's spa culture through the ages from one of hot springs serving a purely medicinal purpose to one of luxury spas intended to attract tourists to the region. These shifts in emphasis on function are connected to the varied architectural styles of Budapest's baths.

Thermal waters have been used around Budapest for more than 2,000 years, with bath origins dating to the establishment of Aquincum on the hills west of the present-day Óbuda district. An early bathing history is evident in excavations of this Roman resort town. On the edge of the Roman Empire, Aquincum emerged as a military town; the settlement was elevated to the rank of *colonia* in AD 194, ushering in organized development. With the advent of urban planning stone houses replaced adobe brick and wood. A temple, an extensive aqueduct system and – owing to the beneficial mineral waters flowing from limestone rocks – thermal baths were added. As civilians began to increase the initially military population, additional bathhouses – perhaps as many as ten – were constructed (Lôvei 5). The baths satisfied Roman priorities for hygiene, but their medicinal properties became famous throughout the Empire. The high number of deformed skeletons found in excavations of the military hospital-bath complex suggests that soldiers were sent from across the Empire for treatments of rheumatism and other ailments (Jacobs 25). The baths were also recognized for their entertainment value, with the Roman practice of mixed bathing persisting until the rule of Emperor Hadrian. Although Aquincum died out with the loss of Roman authority at the beginning of the fifth century, the thermal springs continued to attract settlers during the Migration period; for example, popular belief holds that Attila based his mid-fifth century winter camps here to take advantage of the warm waters (Lázár 70).

In the mid-twelfth century, religious organizations – namely, the St. István and St. John nursing orders – were drawn to the healing properties of the Gellért thermal springs and established hospitals not far from the Aquincum ruins in the northern half of present-day Buda at the foot of Gellért Hill. Locations selected for wells to supply these institutions would remain significant for the Hungarian bathing culture in future centuries. For example, the well created in 1178 to provide waters for the St. John hospital now serves the twenty-first-century Gellért Spa-Hotel; medieval resorts were also constructed north of Buda at locations that later became the Lukács and Császar Baths. Throughout the thirteenth century, patients with a variety of ailments – even leprosy – visited springs at the foot of Gellért Hill. However, despite strong belief in the miraculous power of the waters, the dual nature of the early baths – medicinal versus hedonistic – persisted, prompting condemnation from medieval church leaders for rumours of immorality and lewd behaviour among bathers; it is perhaps for this reason that in 1233 Buda leaders sought to regulate the use of thermal water (Grove 64). Certainly, changes in bathhouse personnel coincided with ecclesiastical protests of immorality. For example, a barber-surgeon oversaw facility finances and maintenance – as well as 'blood-letting and other minor operations' – in thirteenth-century Hungarian bathhouses (Rubovszky 15; Jacobs 26). Fourteenth-century bathhouse rosters included the position of 'bath-girl', whose addition did little to convince church leaders of the purely medicinal purposes of such establishments. A fourteenth-century manuscript from the collection of Renaissance King Mátyás Corvinus portrays this new attraction wearing only a transparent apron as she performs her duties of 'washing her client, drying him . . . massaging and shaving him, and cutting his hair' (Jacobs 26).

Aristocratic use of bathhouses multiplied from the fourteenth to fifteenth centuries, particularly during the reigns of Sigismund of Luxemburg and Mátyás. Conflicts with Turkish invaders occurred repeatedly throughout this period. In addition, European Crusaders passed steadily through the region en route to and from the Holy Land. Western travellers journeying through Buda – like the French knight Bertrandon de la Broquière, who praised the 'very beautiful warm waters' enjoyed at the bathhouse at the foot of Gellért Hill in 1433 – helped foster recognition among non-Hungarians of the waters, which contributed greatly to an increase in tourist bathers (Rubovszky 15).

During the sixteenth century dramatic political changes in Hungary profoundly affected the Hungarian bathing culture. Supported by his Black Army, King Mátyás had been able to check Turkish invaders during his lifetime. Upon his death in 1490, however, his standing army was dismissed, leaving the nation vulnerable to attack. In the early 1500s there was a new crusade against the Turks, which coincided with a failed peasant revolt in 1514. The Hungarian nobility responded to the uprising by denying peasants the right to bear arms even as the Ottomans threatened the nation, and class tensions escalated during the first decades of the century. Roughly simultaneously, humanist Míklós Oláh elaborated on the considerable powers of the Gellért thermal springs for healing rheumatism and fevers. In his text *Hungaria et Attila*, Oláh also distinguished between baths worthy of the king – where facilities boasted menials and barber-surgeons to attend to the needs and ailments of upper-class patrons – and the few attended merely by 'peasants and vine-dressers', for whom cleanliness was traditionally not a priority, and who typically purchased what medical relief they could afford either from wise-women or at fairs (Jacobs 26; Rubovszky 15).

Despite persistent belief in the medicinal power of the baths, public interest in taking the waters declined as Hungarian patrons yielded to Church censure for the reported licentiousness of bathers and staff. As in other parts of Europe, the use of perfumes to mask body odours overwhelmingly reduced the need to visit thermal waters for hygienic purposes. However, within Hungary, decreasing interest in bathing among Hungarians was a reaction to the undeniable emphasis placed on bathing by the religion and culture of Muslim invaders. In Budapest, because the Ottomans regularly used the baths, Hungarians avoided the waters, for they were reluctant to frequent sites popular among their oppressors, particularly bathhouses dramatically renovated or completely rebuilt in the Turkish architectural style. Bathhouses in Budapest thrived during Ottoman occupation – albeit not among the native inhabitants – for Islam required followers to observe strictly daily ritual bathing before prayer. Hungary fell under Turkish rule in 1526 when Suleiman the Magnificent crushed Hungarian knights at Mohács and then turned his troops northward to sack and burn Buda. In 1541 the city became the centre of Ottoman Hungary and remained under Turkish control until 1686. During this time, Turkish administrators fully utilized pre-existing springs and constructed bathhouses to replace any structures destroyed in the sack of the city, and this dramatically expanded the number of functional baths (Farbaky 69).

Turkish architects constructed two types of bathhouses, both *ilidje*, or hot-water thermal baths, and *hamman*, or steam baths. Of the nine thermal baths constructed in Buda during the sixteenth century, four are still functional (Farbaky 69). The facilities have been structurally altered in varying degrees – and most have experienced name changes – but these stand as excellent examples of Ottoman-Hungarian architecture. These include the *Veli bey* Baths, known as the *Császár*

Figure 11.1 The Veli bey *baths (present-day* Császár Fürdő*) during the Turkish period. (Courtesy the Bibliotheca Nationalis Hungariae/Országos Széchényi Könyvtár, Budapest, Hungary)*

(Emperor) Baths after the Turkish occupation; the *Kaplu ilidsha*, presently called the *Király* (King) Baths; and the *Rudas* (Pole) and *Rácz* (Serb) Baths. Borrowing from the traditional Roman bathhouse plan, each shared a common layout of vestibule, antechamber and bathing room or *harara* (Farbaky 69). Structural differences occurred in the treatment of interior space: thermal baths generally consisted of a cupola or dome covering a round or octagonal inner pool, whereas with steam baths interior space was partitioned into nine separate segments (Farbaky 69).

Three of the remaining structures are associated with Sokoli Mustapha, Pasha of Buda during the 1560s and 1570s. The first of these is the *Veli bey* Baths, currently contained within the *Lukács* Bath complex. These were built on the site of springs used by Romans and were later purportedly visited by Attila and Árpád. The village that arose here was known as *Felhévíz*, or 'upper warm waters', and boasted a hospital built in 1330 by the *Szentlélek Lovagrend*, or Knights of the Holy Spirit. Many residents of Felhévíz were thus employees of the hospital-bath complex and worked as either barber-surgeons or bath-servants. In his text differentiating between baths frequented by aristocrats and peasants, Oláh specifically referred to Felhévíz waters as a court favourite during the reign of King Mátyás, probably due to an extensive complex catering to aristocratic demands. These baths were also included in the first scientific treatise on Hungarian waters, *Hypomnemation de admirandis Hungariae aquis*, written by a German doctor, George Wernher, in 1511 (Jacobs 27).

Completion dates for the Turkish facility there are indicated on a wall plaque that lay forgotten until a doctor rediscovered it in the 1830s: the plaque indicates that the bathhouse – begun by Veli, *sanjakbey* of Hatvan – was completed between 1571 and 1572 by Bosnian-born Mustapha (Iván 72). The plaque declares, 'He built a bath, the likes of which the heavens have never seen' (*Osztrák-Magyar* 508). Additional plaques praise the waters' restorative powers, as well as the beauty of the structure. For instance, a bather of 1584 described the 'unforgettable' marbled interior of the 'enormous, magnificent bath', with its central pool large enough for a bather to actually swim in and the nine smaller baths situated around it (Iván 72). The *Veli bey* construction was therefore unique, combining the nine-part floor plan traditionally used for steam baths with the dome framework typically of thermal baths; four smaller corner domes surrounded the central dome. Another pleased patron from the early 1600s, English doctor Edward Browne, pronounced *Veli bey* the 'world's most beautiful bath' (Iván 72).

Mustapha's name also appears on the walls of the present-day Rudas Baths, located in the region formerly known as *Alhéviz*, or 'lower thermal spring', later called the Tabán. The springs for this facility were used for baths during the late fourteenth- and early fifteenth-century reign of King Sigismund, and when he assumed power in 1556, Sokoli completed construction begun by his Turkish predecessor. *Direkli ilidszaszi*, its former Turkish name, referred to green marble columns supporting a dome with stained-glass openings above the central octagonal pool. Damaged during World War II, the Rudas Baths have been restored, and the interior maintains Ottoman features. Mustapha was also responsible for the construction of a smaller facility similar to the Rudas. This miniature structure was known during the Ottoman period as *Kaplu ilidsha*, loosely translated as 'Rooster Tower Baths'. The Király Baths – so called today – were constructed within the old town walls of *Vízváros*, Buda's 'water town' district. This facility was initiated by Arslan, Pasha of Buda between 1565 and 1566, and completed in 1570 by Mustapha. The smaller facility provided Muslim soldiers with a means of bathing even when under attack. Although the structure served only a secondary role in the sixteenth century – and even today admits only eighty bathers – the interior is remarkably well preserved. Except for the Baroque-period vestibule, visitors today can bathe in the original octagonal bathing room under a dome with stained-glass openings (Farbaky 69).

The fourth still-functioning example of Ottoman bath architecture in Hungary is the Rácz Bathhouse, a facility – like the Rudas – located in the Alhéviz, or Tabán region, and whose reputation has historically ranged from one extreme to the other. As with other Turkish-built facilities, a bath existed here prior to Turkish occupation. In 1864, the Hungarian paper *Vasárnapi Ujság* detailed the pre-Turkish history of the bath; by the nineteenth century, the Rácz had become notorious for its seedy neighbourhood clientele, to the extent that Buda residents had apparently forgotten its glory days ('Ráczfürdô' 242). Thermal springs on this site originally served the royal palace of King Mátyás, and Oláh noted the beauty of the facility in his 1536 text. Turkish occupiers constructed an Ottoman-style octagonal vaulted structure, alternately referred to by the Hungarian word for 'king', *Király* – alluding to fifteenth-century royal patrons – and by the Turkish for 'little bath', *Kücsük ilidzsaszi* – reflecting the new facility's simpler architectural approach ('Ráczfürdô' 242). Despite a less ornate interior, *Kücsük ilidzsaszi* was noteworthy when the seventeenth-century Turkish traveller Evlija Cselebi praised its waters in healing chronic arthritis, muscle and nerve pain (Rubovszky 15). However, the demographics of the surrounding neighbourhood changed, and the facility fell into disrepair and acquired a wretched reputation primarily due to its environs ('Ráczfürdô' 242). Hungarian aristocrats avoided the region, and the facility gradually became known as the *Rácz* (Serb) Baths, reflecting the heritage of poor non-Hungarian residents who settled near it.

Buda first acquired its reputation as one large bathhouse during Turkish occupation, and Hungarian bathing culture absorbed the bathing habits of Ottoman invaders and has retained features of it to the present day. Under Turkish rule the sexes were strictly separated in the bathhouses, preventing the interaction that had led to accusations of licentiousness by the medieval Church. During the Turkish period, men frequented bathhouses in the mornings; Hungarian women were admitted in the afternoons or evenings.[1] A seventeenth-century German visitor to the Buda bathhouses remarked on the particular attraction that bathhouses held for upper-class Hungarian women, for these venues afforded them a freedom denied elsewhere in daily life, such as an opportunity to abandon servants and gossip freely with friends (Jacobs 28). However, the Rudas Bath – ostensibly the finest of the Turkish bathhouses – denied women access and, even today, maintains its long-standing tradition as a male-only venue.[2] Although the Turks are often remembered in Hungary for their destructive acts, the bath architecture they created during their century-and-a-half occupation of Buda drew praise from a diverse body of fifteenth- and sixteenth-century visitors, several of whom have been mentioned. In his Budapest cultural guide, art historian Michael Jacobs describes a varied group of Western European bathhouse admirers. A sixteenth-century German pastor en route to Constantinople expressed amazement at the lavish marble interiors; a Belgian diplomat visiting a decade later remarked on the cleanliness of the facilities and the efficiency of bathhouse staff (Jacobs 28). Jacobs also recounts the tale of an injured German prisoner of war held in Buda in 1610, who was so impressed with the remarkable healing waters that 'had he been a free man, he would have liked nothing better than to have spent the rest of his life there'.[3] In 1638, Browne – the Englishman whose admiration for *Veli bey* was previously quoted – reportedly described Buda baths as the 'noblest' in Europe, both for the quality of their springs and for the 'magnificence' of their architecture (Jacobs 28).

Turkish occupation ended during the final decades of the seventeenth century, when the Habsburgs replaced Ottoman rule following a failed Turkish attempt on Vienna. The ensuing six-week siege of Buda in 1686 destroyed much of the city, including its Turkish bath architecture. The subsequent chaos encompassed every aspect of daily life for city residents and resulted in a long period of decline in Hungarian bathing culture. These factors were further compounded by an outbreak of the plague in 1693, which caused the long-term closure of several bathhouses. Maintenance of the baths was neglected, and structures deteriorated to the extent that when Italian tourist Domenic Sestini visited Buda in 1717, he expressed his disappointment at their loss of 'oriental luxury' (Jacobs 29). Several facilities fell into private ownership during the early Habsburg years; for example, the Császár Baths, as they came to be known, passed into private ownership in the eighteenth century, after having been purchased by János Ecker in the late 1600s and sold again within only a few years. Others – like the *Veli bey* Baths – continued to show scars acquired during the siege. Although fewer tourists praised the sites, the *Veli bey* Baths were still noted in a German study of architecture – *Entwurff einer historischen Architektur* (*Design of a Historical Architecture*)– published by Fischer von Erlach in 1721 (Farbaky 69). Although *Kaplu ilidsha*, or the Rooster Tower Baths, survived the 1686 siege, they also passed into private hands and acquired Baroque structural additions between 1717 and 1727 (Török 98). The facility was eventually purchased in 1796 by the König family, from whom the baths took the new name of *Király*, the Hungarian form of *König*. The Rácz Baths, located in the dilapidated Tabán neighbourhood, deteriorated during the eighteenth century and attracted a disreputable lower-class population represented by Serbs, Greeks, gypsies and Hungarians reportedly involved in the shady riverboat trade. As Jacobs writes, the area was infamous for its abundance of 'taverns, gambling dens and whores', and respectable Buda citizens went to great lengths to avoid the area (Lukács 35). Thus, bathhouses like the Rácz, their hygienic function much reduced, were more often frequented by disreputable patrons seeking the variety of non bath-related sexual services offered by scantily-clad peasant women.

The use and condition of the baths declined during the struggles at the end of the seventeenth century and beginning of the eighteenth as revealed by the physical deterioration of facilities and by the negative reputations acquired by certain sites. Standards of acceptable bathhouse behaviour – namely, modestly garbed, segregated sexes seeking either medicinal relief or bathing strictly for religious purposes or cleanliness – dramatically lowered as rule of Buda transferred from Turkish to Habsburg hands. Whereas Turkish rulers monitored bathhouses for religious reasons due to ritualistic Islamic bathing requirements, the Habsburgs – who had no such religious motivation for bathing – did not consider the activities of bathhouse patrons of great concern to the Empire. Although church leaders might protest declining morals, government administrators were faced with seemingly greater priorities in the wake of Turkish rule. Without strict monitoring of the separation of sexes implemented by Ottoman rulers, mixed bathing again became the norm. The misbehaviour that resulted from these changes prompted from the Buda City Council in 1713 and again in 1785 decrees indicating that bathhouses were again dens of 'revelry and moral misdeameanour [sic]' (Jacobs 30). As reputations sank and reports of shocking incidents within their walls multiplied, the facilities were shunned by upper-class visitors. The aprons or shifts used during the reigns of Mátyás and the Ottomans were abandoned, and with mixed nude bathing, Buda bathhouses hence became synonymous with 'brothel'. In 1708, for example, a young woman fell under public censure when witnesses reported she had bathed nude with a group of soldiers at one of the Buda baths (Tóth 197–8). Robert Townson, a British visitor in 1797, described the 'young men and maidens, old men and children, some in a state of nature' that he witnessed at a Buda bath, where bathers were seen 'flouncing about like fish in spawning-time' (Jacobs 30). Efforts at combating these problems and attracting a higher-class clientele by promoting Buda tourism – like a 1733 German-language guide to the city baths – were generally futile (Jacobs 30).

Thermal bathing thus fell out of fashion, and many shunned the baths during this time of looser standards; in response, perfume usage again increased as interest in the hygienic attractions of bathing declined. However, a number of Hungarian aristocrats continued to seek medicinal benefits for rheumatism and gout from warm thermal waters, although upper-class visits were generally limited to remote spas rather than Buda facilities; only the very sick or very rich continued to seek its healing powers. For example, although he lambasted the spas of 'that sort' that his kinsman visited, seventeenth-century Palatine György Thurzó prayed for God's blessings on the bathing cure sought by his wife in 1616 (Tóth 197–8). Ailing rich aristocrats frequented rural sites so much that Thurzó himself remarked that he almost feared getting 'gout from the excess of bathing' (Tóth 197–8). Bathing attendants – often duplicating the former barber-surgeon's services – offered bloodletting, massages and various healing treatments. For upper-class residents of draughty stone castles, these skills were so valued that peasants on the Batthyány estate complained of their expense, for the Batthyány barber-surgeon 'would not touch a poor man for as much as two groschen' (Tóth 197–8). Thus, the medical relief offered at bathhouses was prohibitive enough to discourage peasant patrons, who generally turned to other avenues – primarily, the so-called village 'wise-woman' – for cures.

The benefits of thermal waters prompted eighteenth-century scientific inquiry, and Laurence Stocker published the first study of Buda's thermal waters –

Thermographia Budensis – in 1721. Works like Stocker's contributed to the beginning of the balnaeological obsession that would emerge across nineteenth-century Europe and England. With the dawn of nineteenth-century bath culture, upper-class patrons returned to spas to partake of the waters. Facilitating visits to thermal baths outside one's own country, railway construction across Europe between the 1830s and 1840s made the world a smaller place. Therefore, the highest echelons of Hungarian society rarely restricted their bath visits to Buda or even to rural Hungary and, as a sign of status, travelled outside the nation for holidays. They often frequented Carlsbad or Marienbad, where higher quality spa hotels better suited their taste (Lukács 103). The offerings of well-known non-Hungarian spas and the benefits found there were detailed by the press: for example, a *Vasárnapi Ujság* article described the history of bathing habits and the benefits Western Europeans found in their thermal waters ('Fürdôk' 590). These priorities revealed themselves early in the century when the development of rural spas also became essential, for these provided the nobility and the gentry lacking sufficient funds to travel to more costly sites with suitable vacation resorts. Popular Hungarian spas outside of Buda included Pöstyén in northwestern Hungary and sites in the Tátra mountain region; between 1800 and 1848, spas like Balatonfüred also sprang up around Lake Batalon and became favoured resorts for the gentry and Jewish middle classes.[4]

Across Europe attendance at spas and bath resorts flourished, and spa organizers began offering various options for entertainment, including cotillions, casinos, theatres and drinking halls. Hungarian facilities likewise sought to satisfy the social needs of visitors, and proprietors constructed restaurants, performance halls, parks, gardens and gaming rooms to increase attendance. Although patrons continued to frequent the numerous Hungarian baths purely in pursuit of their medicinal value, nineteenth-century bathing resorts also became important social venues. In Hungary as elsewhere, vacationers were entertained by concerts, balls and excursions, and these facilities became stylish places to see and be seen for political figures, actors and actresses, aristocrats, and financial and cultural leaders of the nation. Contemporary accounts in the daily press of these social venues and their entertainment programs reveal the public fascination with the bathing culture in general, as well as with specific sites and the famous and infamous who frequented them.[5]

An 1815 report by Viennese scientists indicates that the Buda baths still some-what retained an image as venues for lower-class amusement; however, city priorities on the modernization of Turkish baths allowed Francis Schams in his 1822 book to note 'immeasurable' improvements in Buda facilities (Jacobs 30). An 1847 German guidebook espoused medicinal benefits – including cures for rheumatism and spinal conditions – offered at fourteen admirable Hungarian spas (Grove 64). Furthermore, efforts at attracting tourists to Buda conveniently coincided with Orientalism and the Western European obsession with the Near

East, and the unique Ottoman legacy within Hungary proved advantageous. The sexually titillating imagery of Turkish baths and harem life produced by Western artists like Jean-Auguste-Dominique Ingres or Jean-Léon Gérôme arguably facilitated tourism in Hungary, for the Ottoman-constructed Buda bathhouses unquestionably reflected architectural priorities of the so-called Orient. Western images like Gérôme's *Harem Bath* and *Moorish Bath* or Ingres' series of Turkish bath images depicted locales similar to those in Budapest, which were certainly of a more exotic nature than could be found in Western European spa towns.

The relationship between the bathing craze and tourism encouraged not only architectural expansions, but also the need for technical improvements. Efforts at modernization included improved digging techniques in the 1850s and engineering advances to expand the number of accessible thermal springs in the city. Between 1865 and 1866, engineer Vilmos Zsigmondy tapped new springs on Margaret Island, situated in the middle of the Danube between Buda and Pest (*Osztrák-Magyar* 506). Within a decade, Zsigmondy also drilled for thermal springs on the Pest side of the river, in *Városliget*, or the City Park, and both of these boreholes allowed construction of new facilities. These priorities were facilitated by the Compromise of 1867, which granted Hungary an equal role within the Habsburg Empire. The Compromise allowed local government to monitor the use and expansion of thermal springs, and when Buda and Pest were unified in 1873, efforts towards implementing an official bath policy intensified (Buzinkay 113; Jacobs 33).

St. Margaret Island – known in the Middle Ages as *Nyulak szigete*, or Island of the Hares – was home in the thirteenth-century to the daughter of King Béla IV, who reportedly gifted the island nunnery with his four-year-old daughter Margaret in gratitude for divine deliverance from Mongol invaders in 1242. After Turks destroyed the nunnery, the island remained largely uninhabited for several centuries. In the middle of the Danube River, the island was difficult to access until the nineteenth century. Early in the century, the Palatine of Hungary – also a Habsburg archduke – used the island for recreational purposes by building a hunting lodge there. The introduction of steamboats facilitated river transportation, permitting island excursions after about 1860. Zsigmondy's discovery of thermal springs on the island in the mid-1860s allowed construction to begin on the Margaret Baths in 1868. Consisting of three wings topped with a Renaissance-influenced octagonal dome, the neo-classical structure designed by architect Miklós Ybl – 'the greatest and most influential Hungarian architect of the second half of the nineteenth century' – was destroyed during the Second World War (Sisa, 'Hungarian' 174, 182). Excursions to *Margit-sziget* increased with the building of a hotel on the island, and in the 1890s visitors could also tour excavations of the medieval nunnery. In 1901, the island became even more accessible, for the new Margaret Bridge linked Buda and Pest with the landmass.

The Császár Baths were renovated under the direction of architect József Hild, who between 1841 and 1844 rebuilt the facilities in the neo-classical style, adding a *gyógyudvar*, or 'healing courtyard' (Csapó 73). After renovation the Császár was reputed to be the most elegant Buda bathhouse and served as a venue for evening balls and concerts during the second half of the century. According to an 1863 article, bathers could also enjoy musical entertainment during their daytime visits; this article detailed medicinal treatments offered and described structural changes made by Hild, including 'delightful' walkways and expanded bath and pool facilities for both men and women ('Császárfürdô' 184). The Császár is also noteworthy for wall tablets left by visitors who found relief from ailments there. It is among these that one finds the plaque naming Sokoli Mustapha as responsible for the construction of the bathhouse. Although current guidebooks to Budapest often appear to use the names *Császár* and *Lukács* interchangeably for this complex, during the nineteenth century, the Lukács Baths were a separate, neighbouring facility, attracting a lower class of bathers than the upper-crust circle who frequented the elaborate social functions at the Császár (Kósa 58).

The dregs of nineteenth-century society could still be found at the Rácz Baths, which remained problematic due to the unrestrained nature of the Tabán riverfront neighbourhood. In his travelogue on Buda and Pest between 1843 and 1907, Adolf Ágai recounted childhood memories of the Rácz: the noisy, unrestrained nature of the bathers as well as the ugliness and filth of the facility (Porzó 70–1). In 1864 *Vasárnapi Ujság* underscored its seedy nature, stating that the bathhouse structure 'was so neglected before 1860 that only the poorest classes visited here' ('Ráczfürdô' 242). János Heinrich Nepomuk purchased the facility in 1860 and engaged Ybl to renovate it. Ybl was a favourite of Hungarian aristocrats and the 'most prolific and popular architect of public buildings' in Budapest during the 1870s and 1880s (Sisa, 'Hungarian' 174). His involvement with the renovation of such an unpropitious project was certainly ambitious, and – to a certain degree – successful. Although the poor reputation persisted throughout the century, *Vasárnapi Ujság* praised the renovations, writing that 'those who've seen . . . [the Rácz] . . . in the last year gaze with amazement at the magical transformation' ('Ráczfürdô' 242). Despite these efforts – and although the seediest elements of the neighbourhood had been dislodged by the turn of the century – the district of Tabán 'was still there, catering to men with a liking for good cheap dishes, good cheap wine and . . . good cheap women' (Lukács 35).

In addition to renovations the turn-of-the-century construction of completely new baths in Budapest heightened the popularity of Hungarian spas. The most significant of these were the Széchenyi Baths – an immense complex in the middle of the City Park – and the art nouveau Gellért Baths within the spa hotel of the same name. Although the Széchenyi Bath's architectural structures were built only between 1909 and 1913, the facility rested on thermal springs discovered by engineer Zsigmondy during the 1870s; Zsigmondy is memorialized with a statue that stands outside the Baths. The City Park was a massive undertaking completed in 1896 to house the Millennium celebrations of 1,000 years of Hungarian statehood, and the neo-baroque spa designed by architects Gyôzô Czigler and Ede Dvorszák augmented the park's already considerable attractions. When constructed, the Széchenyi facility was reportedly the largest health spa complex in Europe and remains even today one of the largest of its kind. The Széchenyi featured not only outdoor and indoor thermal baths and swimming pools but also an impressive menu of medical treatments and steam rooms. All of this is housed within a neo-baroque structure boasting a dome – the interior of which is decorated with art nouveau mosaics – gigantic chandeliers, sculptures of Neptune and Venus, open courtyards, gardens and the added attraction of water chess played on floating chessboards. A northern wing designed by Imre Francsek was added in 1927, and the expansion provided for the large number of patrons who visit the spa throughout the week, and on weekends when other spas are closed. Current attendance at the Széchenyi is estimated at two million annually, and a notice at the Baths boasts their success at treating 'degenerative articular diseases, arthritis, gout, orthopaedic and traumatic deformations, spinal complaints and barrenness' (Pearce 23).

Construction work on the other major turn-of-the-century spa began in 1908. The Gellért Baths are considered by many to be the best in Budapest; they are also the most expensive. Housed within the Gellért Spa Hotel, the facility rests at the foot of hill where the orders of St. John and St. Elizabeth maintained a twelfth-century hospital (Éber 143). Springs here were considered powerful enough to warrant their use in the treatment of leprosy, and today are noted for their benefits in treating back problems, arthritis, gout and heart disease. Designed by Ármin Hegedûs, Artúr Sebestyén and Izidor Stark, the light-grey stone structure with orientalized domes and art nouveau interior is a unique and almost magical landmark on the Danube banks, for 'unlike other buildings, which go black with time, it grows whiter and whiter' (Török 113). Built during the inter-war period and opened in 1918, the Gellért was considered noteworthy enough to warrant an article that same year in *Magyar Iparmûvészet*, a decorative arts journal that regularly featured discussions on the Hungarian-ness of ornamentation and on linkages between folk and modern art. The Gellért certainly fits these priorities. The interior of the entrance hall includes stained-glass windows illustrating the 'Death of Buda', a nineteenth-century epic poem by János Arany, which glorified a Hungarian legend. The distinctive blue and green majolica tiles from the Hungarian Zsolnay factory are covered with folk-inspired floral details and decorate the thermal bath for men (Éber 142). Mosaic waves cover the floor of the large swimming pool; mosaic swans and fountains featuring blue porcelain lions, dolphins and cherubs add to the art nouveau treatment.

At the time of the Gellért construction, Budapest had embarked on a conscious campaign to turn the capital into a city of baths, and for this reason, no holds were barred: the Gellért aimed at being not only the pride of the capital, but the 'best of its kind world-wide' (Éber 143). Together with the Széchenyi, the Gellért can be credited with helping the city realize its goal, for even as Budapest became known as the largest spa in the world, tourism to the nation doubled between 1895 and 1912, with an estimated 250,000 visitors annually (Grove 64; Lukács 57). Added to the recently renovated Turkish baths of Rudas and Rácz, the city had also expanded bath offerings with the new facility on Margaret Island. The recently renovated Császár complex was gradually united with the neighbouring Lukács swimming pools, and this expanded institution included restaurants and garden areas to make it more attractive. The Császár-Lukács facility eventually became known simply as the *Szent* (Saint) *Lukács* Baths and became from the 1950s on the favoured spa for political dissidents and intellectuals, who used the facility as a seemingly harmless gathering site for politically motivated discussions (Török 175; Móra 175).

In 1929 when the Hungarian Parliament established the National Commission on Spas to safeguard and monitor these Hungarian treasures, thermal baths throughout the nation were unquestionably the basis of tourism. Recognition of the nation's importance in this field can be seen in the location selected for the first International Spa Congress: Budapest (Buzinkay 113). Despite political and social tensions during the inter-war years, baths continued to open in Hungary throughout the next decades. Hungarian advertisement of these facilities emphasized their long-standing tradition. For example, when a new bath opened in the 1940s in *Római-part*, or the 'Roman shore' district of Budapest, a poster announced 'Aquincum Spa – Reopened After 2000 Years' (Móra 177).

The legacy of the Second World War was particularly harsh for Budapest's spa culture, with virtually all of the bathhouses sustaining some damage. Although restoration work continued even into the last two decades, most of the baths have now been restored to their former glory; an exception to this are the *Margit Sziget* Baths, which were completely destroyed during the war. Other problems now threaten these national treasures, however, the most serious being a decline in Hungarian water tables. During the 1950s the Soviets heavily mined the region for bauxite and coal, a process that removed large quantities of water in order to access the deposits. Writing in *New Scientist* in 1994, Fred Pearce revealed the severity of the situation: water supply to the largest thermal lake in Europe, the Hungarian *Héviz*, is 50 per cent lower than before the introduction of mining (Pearce 25). Although the mines have been closed for the past decade, as of the mid-1990s water continued to be pumped out, which lowered the levels available for thermal baths. The situation is further compounded by the regional decline in rainfall over the past twenty years.

Water pressure continues to decrease even as new spas are created, which increases the demand for the water. Between 1956 and 1977 alone, at least 115 new thermal baths were opened across Hungary (Grove 64). Hungary still encourages thermal bath expansion despite the potential hazards to the industry and pre-existing bathhouses. For example, the springs supplying the Császár-Lukács complex have declined so severely that now water must be pumped from the Széchenyi boreholes on the Pest side to supplement demands at Lukács.[6] Despite this, throughout the 1990s, the Danubius-owned *Thermal Hotel* line opened luxury spa-hotels in Aquincum and on Margit Island as well as the Helia Hotel on the Pest bank; meanwhile, the Gellért reportedly added two hundred rooms to its facility (Kenneally 49). The rationale for continued expansion when water levels are unquestionably declining is reportedly to 'provide income for investment in the basic system: repairing pipes, preventing pollution, and maintaining the buildings' (Pearce 24). However, the overuse of thermal water is a very serious problem for Budapest: as water levels decline, water pressure also decreases, and with water spending less time at former depths, temperatures of the waters are also dropping, and the chemical balance of the hot springs is thus altered. The very minerals that allegedly provided bathers with cures since Roman times are therefore also at risk. Thus, the Hungarian tourism industry that the Budapest thermal springs support now threatens the availability of those same springs for future bathers.

Notes

1. There is no evidence of a special bathing time for the few Turkish women living in Budapest at this time.
2. Women are not admitted to the Rudas thermal baths, although they are now allowed to use the swimming pool at the facility.
3. Josef Wilden, mayor of Nuremberg (1610), in Jacobs 28.
4. *Pöstyen* (present-day Piešt'any) and the Tátra resorts are now in Slovakia.
5. For more information on famous patrons – primarily of rural baths – see Kósa.
6. The chemical composition of the Széchenyi borehole springs is a different chemical composition (Pearce 24).

Part III

Ecology and Economics

12

Water Recreation Resources and Environmental Pressures along Bulgaria's Black Sea Coast

Vassil Marinov and *Boian Koulov*

Introduction

This essay discusses an area of prime concentration of natural resources – the Bulgarian Black Sea coast – as a politically contested arena. It considers the value that the coastal waters hold for different users, especially for the tourist industry. The authors examine the changes in ownership, rights to use and authority over the coastal water resources. The identification of the actors and geographic scales affecting these resources informs their sustainable management.

Utilization of Bulgaria's Coastal Water Resources

On a number of geographic scales the Bulgarian Black Sea Coast represents a prime concentration of natural resources of vital importance to recreation, biodiversity and economic development. The combination of seawater, coastal wetlands and mineral waters sustains the most developed international tourism region in Bulgaria, which accommodates about 5 million foreign tourists annually (*Tourism* 2001). Both the relative proximity to the largest consumer of tourist services in the world, the European Union, as well as the traditions in servicing Western tourists further enhance the recreational and economic value of the coastal water system.

At the same time, the Black Sea coast is geographically a part of Via Pontica – the second most important bird migration route in Europe. The ten to thirty kilometres-wide land strip along the coast contains most of the natural wetlands in Bulgaria. One of their most important functions is to provide habitats for different animal species, especially birds, many of which are significant to European biodiversity. Thus, Bulgaria has the responsibility to protect some of the richest areas in bird species on the continent. These areas are essential also to the development of its tourist industry.[1]

Last, but not least, the coast functions as a gateway to Bulgaria: its ports provide access to the world ocean and enable low cost transportation of exports and imports. At the same time, the coastal area houses Bulgaria's largest chemical plants, numerous food processing and construction materials industries, all of which compete for scanty water resources. Bulgaria's third and fourth most populous urban areas, Varna and Burgas, as well as extensive agriculture and aqua-culture production also figure among the largest water consumers along the coast. The different priorities given to these concepts of the coast's significance underlie the competing strategies for developing and protecting it.

Recreational Value of the Sea Water

Over a third of Bulgaria's territory – about 40,000 km^2 – is suitable for leisure and recreation. Seaside recreation, however, is the most preferred and developed branch of the Bulgarian tourist industry. The specific seawater characteristics, in combination with the local climate and relief (sand beaches, dunes, cliffs, bays and caves), explain the highest concentration of recreation establishments, mostly hotels and restaurants, in the country.

Seawater temperature is over 18 °C between 130 and 140 days a year (Iordanova 54–72). The absence of dangerous sea fauna, the considerably lower salinity of the water (16–18 parts per thousand), as well as the very small tides, are additional features that attract foreign and domestic tourists, especially during the summer months. Water sports are the third most popular visitors' activity (31 per cent), after shopping and sightseeing.

While the concept of eco-tourism has been discussed among academics and planners since the 1980s, this relatively new branch of recreation became popular in Bulgaria at the beginning of the 1990s. Tour operators realized the increasing attractiveness of eco-tourism, especially for West European visitors, and decided to capitalize on the relatively unspoiled natural resources in Bulgaria. Local environmental non-governmental organizations (NGOs) and branches of political parties with ecological emphasis (e.g., Ecoglasnost, the Green Party) were also extremely active and, at the same time, quite powerful in that period (Koulov 146–9). The opening of the country at the very beginning of the 1990s enabled and facilitated cooperation between Bulgarian and Western NGOs (e.g., Blue Flag Movement, Ecoglasnost-Burgas, Bulgarian Society for Bird Protection), which positively influenced eco-tourism development along the coast. Coastal seawaters up to a depth of six metres are most important to eco-tourism and biodiversity preservation. About 126 fish species periodically or constantly inhabit this depth

(Prodanov/Dencheva/Ivanov 547–66). The dolphin sub-species *Phoceana rupicapra* and *Tursiops truncatus* are among the endangered endemits (Georgiev 9).

The climate characteristics compare favourably to both the hotter Mediterranean and colder North Sea and Baltic resorts. Water temperature, sunshine hours per day[2], average air temperature during the day, minimum air temperature during the night, all fare better than those at the vast majority of European and North African resorts. The average daytime air temperature does not exceed 25°C, and the minimum night temperature during the summer months is 15°C. The length of the period with air temperature over 18°C is 100 to 120 days (Mishev/Popov/Tishkov). The active season for sea recreation continues for four to five months, while favourable conditions for climate therapy and prophylactics last for a much longer period.

The sand beaches, which occupy about 28 per cent of the 378 km long Bulgarian Black Sea coast, are the most attractive tourist resource. Over 70 large and small beach strips cover an area of over 16 km². The beaches can accommodate up to about one million people at the same time, and only 42 per cent of their capacity is currently utilized (Marinov 557). There are some overused areas. However, the longest and widest sand beach strip along the Bulgarian sea coast, south of the Kamchia River, still remains largely untouched by the tourist industry.

Most of the beaches are situated south of the Stara Planina (Balkan) Range, where the climate is a sea variety of the transitional continental and transitional Mediterranean type. They are protected from northern winds and receive ample sun radiation from early in the morning, due to their eastern exposure. The sand in the western part of Burgas Bay has high magnetite content and, presumably, curative properties.

The most attractive relief form along the Bulgarian coast, appreciated since the ancient Greeks, is Cape Kaliakra (Greek for 'the Beautiful Cape'). In the south, along the most indented part of the coast, Medni Rid, tourists visit the few tiny Bulgarian Black Sea islands: St. Peter, St. Ivan, St. Kirik near Sozopol, St. Anastasiya near Burgas, and Zmiiski Island. The two large bays, Varna and Burgas, boast extensive sand beaches. However, both are used as ports, and their coasts are heavily industrialized and urbanized. Most pristine are the beaches and waters of the southernmost section, due to their proximity to the border zone with Turkey. These geographic conditions have made the coast an important tourist resource, and it is therefore not surprising that Black Sea beach tourism has existed for over a century.

The recreational value of sea bathing received official recognition in Bulgaria at the end of the nineteenth century. In 1889, the first facilities were built along the Varna beach and, in 1921, this city officially acquired resort status. Five years later, the newly built Central Baths accommodated the first foreign tourists, mainly from Eastern Europe. Before the Second World War, Czech, Romanian and Polish vacationers regularly visited the towns of Varna, Nesebar and Sozopol.

Politics, ideology and economics determined the post-war valuation of the coastal resources. A specialized state tour operating company, Balkantourist, was set up in 1948, and in 1955 the government decreed the construction of large-scale 'resort complexes' along the coast.[3] The dominant reasons for this were, on the one hand, the typical obsession of command economies with centralization and scale and, on the other hand, the availability of sparsely settled and less used land along the coast. This explains the three largest resorts with over 12,000 beds each – Sunny Beach, Golden Sands and Albena – which still dominate the recreation industry. In the early 1960s Bulgaria emerged on the international tourist market as a typical 'sun, sea and sand' destination (Bachvarov, 'End' 48). This opening to the world aimed mainly at bringing in much-needed hard currency while displaying the benefits of socialism to the rest of the world.

The tendency towards construction of large-scale 'complexes' reversed about 20 years later, and smaller (1,000 to 2,000 beds each) resorts – Duni, Elenite, Riviera and Sunny Day – came into operation. This reversal corresponded to attempts to decentralize the economy at large as well as to the state planners' gradual realization of how limited tourist resources were. Significantly, different forms of informal tourism in small villages and towns have been increasing since the 1970s. In the 1990s the highest level of tourist construction along the coast took place in these types of settlements.

At the end of the twentieth century, the international and domestic tourist industries in Bulgaria still relied overwhelmingly on the coastal resources.[4] In the words of the 1998 Tourism Investment Guide of the Ministry of the Economy and Tourism, 'The principal product at present is sun and beach'. Indeed, over 83 per cent of the overnight stays in hotels and about two-thirds of the hotel beds are concentrated along the Black Sea. The seaside hotels accommodate most of the foreign visitors (68 per cent) and have the highest occupancy rate (48 per cent) in the country, including the capital of Sofia (*Tourism* 1999). The continued success of this industry also depends on protecting the coastal wetlands and mineral waters.

Wetlands

While the man-made lakes along the Bulgarian coast are of limited recreational importance, the tourist industry, particularly medical tourism, values the natural wetlands along the coast, mostly for their high quality peloid (curative mud) deposits.[5] Their effectiveness for prophylactics and therapy for certain diseases has proved to be considerably higher than most other methods of treatment.[6] Additionally, the wetlands' proximity to the sea enables a combination of the use of peloids with that of mineral water, lye[7], herbs, seaweed, sand and the sun. The simultaneous application of different methods of healing coupled with diverse cosmetic, anti-stress programs and diets accounts for the successful blending of both medical tourism and seaside recreation. The employment of medical procedures extends the tourist season in the autumn and spring months and increases the industry's profitability. For the purposes of eco-tourism, however, the unique potential of the coastal lakes, swamps and river mouths is still largely unrealized.[8]

Natural Lakes and Swamps

Due to the attraction of nearby seawater, coastal lakes in Bulgaria are seldom used for recreational activities, either. However, they possess important resources, especially curative mud and unique wildlife, which have long been attractive for tourists from Bulgaria and abroad.

Archaeological findings date the balneological utilization of peloid resources along the Black Sea Coast back to the ancient Greek colonization between the thirteen and sixth centuries BC. Balneotherapy has always been a part of traditional medicine, and many spas were functional during the rule of the Ottoman Empire. After Bulgaria regained its independence in 1878, Russian doctors introduced mud therapy to Bulgarian medical practice. In 1906, a sanatorium in Varna used for the first time peloids from the Balchik Tuzla for treatment of bone and joint tuber-culosis, and five years later a mud therapy station opened near the lake. Mud therapy thrived in Varna until the Second World War and gradually spread to other settlements along the coast. In the period of the 1950s to the 1970s, the towns of Varna, Burgas, Nesebar and Pomorie acquired specialized balneological facilities, which increased significantly the medical and recreational use of the peloid resources (Kazachka 185). These facilities are still in use, although most of them are in dire need of modernization.

Currently, there are eighteen lagoons, firths and landslide lakes along the Bulgarian Black Sea coast with a total area of 8,600 hectares (ha) (Georgiev 43). The medical tourism industry assesses the quantity and quality of their peloid reserves as follows: Varna and Mandra lakes – about 3 million tonnes each; Pomorie Lake – 1.3 million tonnes; Atanasovo Lake – from 0.5 to 2 million tonnes; Shabla and Balchik Tuzla – 200,000 and 38,000 tonnes respectively (Kazachka 188). Other coastal lakes (Beloslav, Taukliman, Karaagach, Stomoplo and Alepu) also have significant peloid reserves, but most are insufficiently studied, since they are of lower quality and largely unused. About half of the total of the 6 to 8 million tonnes of peloids are of good quality and can be used without further processing (Kostadinov/Karakolev 11; Iordanova 58). Less than 3 per cent of the seaside vacationers take advantage of the peloid resources, mostly due to a severe shortage of modern facilities.

Water overconsumption, agricultural run-off and industrial pollution decrease the quality of the peloid reserves. Oxygen content is within the norms (8 mg equv/dm^3) only in the northernmost lakes. Due to pollution, the rest have a yearly average of 6.5–7.0 mg equv/dm^3 (Georgiev 47). Inadequate projects, aimed at maintaining the lakes' water balance, have caused additional damage. Artificial canals, which were built to regulate seawater flow in some of the lakes, polluted the peloid deposits with solid particles and upset their salinity balance (e.g., Shabla and Pomorie lakes, as well as Balchik Tuzla). Despite these problems, Kazachka argues that, if properly managed, Bulgaria's peloid reserves are practically inexhaustible (Kazachka 201).

The state institutionalized the protection of peloid deposits in 1975. Nevertheless, most of the eight coastal resorts that offer peloid treatment simply discard, rather than regenerate, the mud after use. Only three resorts, Pomorie, Burgas Mineral Baths and Balchik Tuzla, utilize local resources. The vast majority, including the largest centre for medical tourism in the Balkans – Albena – transport curative mud from Varna Lake. The geographic discrepancy between deposits and resorts further increases transportation and recycling costs.[9]

Medical tourism and public health have vested interests in the sustainable use of the mud resources along the Black Sea coast. However, the exceptional variety of rare and endangered species, mostly birds, makes the lakes and swamps attractive also for eco- and specialized tourism. Three, out of a total of five, Bulgarian wetlands, protected by the international Ramsar Convention (1971), Atanasovo, Durankulak and Arkutino, are situated along the coast. Since most lakes and swamps there do not freeze in winter, they constitute convenient resting, nesting and breeding grounds along the Via Pontica, the migration route from northern Europe to the Mediterranean.

Most important for bird biodiversity are the Varna-Beloslav, Shabla and Pomorie-Burgas lake complexes. Georgiev identifies in their waters between 185 and 291 different bird species respectively (Georgiev 99–132). This account includes between 95 and 170 species from the Endangered Birds of Europe List, as well as between 56 and 83 bird species from Bulgaria's Red Data Book of Endangered Species (Georgiev/Dereliev/Yankov/Profirov 139–47; Yankov/Dimitrov/Kostadinova 118–19).

The richest ornithological site in Bulgaria, Atanasovo Lake, is included in the list of Ornithologically Important Sites in Europe. At the time of migration, it supports the highest concentration in Europe of the Curly-headed (*Pelecanus crispus*) and Pink Pelicans (*Pelecanus onocratulus*), and ranks second, after the Bosphorus, in concentration of the Small Crying Eagle (*Aquila pomarina*) and White Stork (*Ciconia ciconia*) (Georgiev 119–20; Profirov/Michev/Dimitrov/Nikolov/Yankov/Stoinov 115–17). Almost all of the world's 60,000 representatives of the Red-breasted Goose (*Branta ruficollis*) winter in the protected areas of Shabla Lake, also on the List of the Ornithologically Important Sites in Europe (Georgiev 99). Shabla and Ezerets lakes provide habitat for seven fish species from the Red Data Book of Bulgaria, as well as for the otter (*Lutra lutra*), a rare and endangered mammal in Europe. Several fish species from Atanasovo Lake are also listed in the Red Book. Shabla Lake also hosts one of the largest areas of the rare and endangered species of White Water Lily (*Nymphaea alba*) and Yellow Water Rose (*Nuphar lutea*).

An elaborate and increasingly stringent system for the conservation of the coastal lakes and swamps as unique bird habitats of Europe-wide significance is in place. Part of Atanasovo Lake, for example, was first declared a protected area in 1974. In 1980, it became a 1050 ha reserve with a buffer zone of 900 ha that includes the surrounding freshwater swamps and wetlands.

River Mouths

On the international scale, the lower reaches of the largest Bulgarian Black Sea rivers – Kamchia, Ropotamo, Veleka-Rezovska and Batova – are most important for biodiversity protection and ecotourism, due to their position on the Via Pontica. These areas have the highest nest density in the country for a number of bird species (Yankov 47). Eight, out of the total of 257 bird species identified in the Ropotamo Valley, are rare and endangered on the global scale; 144 species are under European protection; and 71 are listed in the Red Data Book of Bulgaria (Georgiev 145). The Kamchia River mouth is registered as a European Important Bird Area, due to the presence of 118 species of European nature protection significance. Bulgaria's Red Data Book includes at least 58, out of a total of 234 bird species in the region (Georgiev/Dereliev/Yankov/Profirov 136–8).

The rich fauna coupled with vegetation diversity prompted the establishment of the 'Kamchia' Biosphere Reserve (842 ha) and the 'Kamchia Sands' Protected Area (373 ha). The reserve allows for protection of several snake, lizard, frog and turtle species. Land turtles have experienced very heavy anthropogenic stress in the last decade. People harvest them for food, export and alleged medical purposes. The river mouths also display significant fish diversity and are the most interesting areas for observing rare and endangered reptiles and amphibians. Particularly interesting for eco-tourists are opportunities for observing larger mammals, including the otter (*Lutra lutra*). Kaliakra Cape in the northern section of the Bulgarian coast and Maslen Cape near Ropotamo River are considered the last habitats of the globally endangered monk seal (*Monachus monachus*). However, there is no proof that it exists there now.

Another exotic attraction at some river mouths is the endemic forest biotope, called 'longoz'. Once widespread in southern Europe, the longoz forest is presently very rare on the European continent. Outside Bulgaria, longoz forests are still preserved only in Spain and northern Turkey (Georgiev 47). These are very dense and difficult to penetrate forest formations, which are flooded during the autumn and spring high waters. The unusual coexistence of ash, oak, elm, alder and maple trees, with many kinds of lianas climbing among their branches, creates the impression of a tropical forest. Characteristic for the Ropotamo and Veleka valleys are also the relic forests of Durmast oak (*Quercus polycarpa*) (Georgiev 141). The nearby resorts, e.g., Dyuni and Primorsko, have not presented significant environmental threats to the seasonally flooded forests. Most harmful since the 1990s is the unregulated and illegal construction of private 'summer houses'.

Parallel to conservation, the exceptional floral diversity at coastal river mouths presents valuable opportunities for the development of eco-tourism. In 1999 about 59 plant species in the Ropotamo lower valley, including the exquisite Sand Lily, were registered as rare and endangered (Georgiev 143). Their habitats are protected by the 'Ropotamo' Reserve (1,001 ha), which has a buffer zone of 771 ha and includes the old riverbed, the protected areas 'Water Lilies' (14 ha), 'Stomoplo' (40 ha) and 'Alepu' (17 ha). The mouth of the Veleka River is also protected (1,128 ha), due in part to the rare and endangered Yellow Water Rose (*Nuphar lutea*). Typical for Kamchia's mouth is a rare and endangered medical plant, the Swamp Snowflake (*Leucoyum aestivum*), as well as several buttercup species. The populations of White Water Lily (*Nymphaea alba*) make the scenery particularly attractive for tourists.

On the domestic scale, the specific combinations of brackish to fresh waters, sandy beaches and dunes, specific wetland vegetation and wildlife in a particular area induce different types of tourist activities. Beach recreation, swimming, bathing, fishing, boating, hiking, hunting and eco-tourism are most typical for the coastal river mouths in Bulgaria.

Mineral Waters

The Bulgarian Black Sea coast is uniquely endowed with mineral waters of all major types.[10] Their high qualities have been recognized since ancient times. The Burgas Spa, for example, was the best known and most visited spa in the Eastern Roman Empire (Kostadinov/Karakolev). Modern, science-based use of coastal mineral waters dates back to the beginning of the twentieth century.

At present all major coastal hotels use local, most often thermal, mineral water in open-air and covered swimming pools. In addition, the best-known resorts, e.g., Albena, St. Constantine and Helena, Golden Sands and Sunny Beach, offer mineral-water treatment in modern, specialized medical centres. The wide variety of waters enables year-round application of over 120 different therapeutic and prophylactic procedures, including bathing, drinking, inhalations, irrigation, cleansing, underwater massage and gymnastics. Indications for their use include diseases of the lungs, upper respiratory system, heart, blood system, nervous system, skeletal and muscular system. Most beneficial for the international tourist business and public health are the opportunities to combine balneological resources (mineral water and curative mud) with climate and phytotherapy.

Due to the relatively high cost of peloid and related therapies, foreign tourists have dominated the medical establishments at larger resorts since the 1990s. The largest medical centre in Albena can serve up to 400 customers daily, and interest is high. Smaller, traditional spas, e.g., Balchik Tuzla, Nesebar and Varna, also employ mineral waters in combination with curative mud treatment. The most severe problem here is the decrepit state of the facilities. Additional impediments include transportation of mud from Varna Lake, lack of mud regeneration, almost complete absence of marketing and the high maintenance costs of the Western equipment. These reasons account for the lack of foreign visitors and the decreasing number of Bulgarians. Mostly elderly people visit the sanatoriums to receive subsidized treatment. The modern 250-bed sanatorium, which serves exclusively the petrochemical complex near Burgas, is a rare exception. Its occupancy rate is 60 to 70 per cent on average, and during the winter the rate is close to 100 per cent.

Proponents of eco-tourism and environmentalism thus have complementary views about preserving the region's waters. In contrast, other groups compete to manage them for very different purposes.

Privatization of the Tourist Industry: The Struggle for Control over the Coastal Recreation Resources

In the early 1990s international financial institutions and experts advocated rapid privatization as the only remedy for the problems of the former centrally planned economies. In Bulgaria, the structural adjustment of the tourist industry proceeded under conditions of economic crisis and political and legal instability. There was neither clarity nor social agreement on the goals of ownership transfer. Acute, partisan struggle resulted over the spoils of privatization and control of resources.

A specific feature of Bulgaria's tourist business is the concentration of a considerable number of the hotels and restaurants (about one-third of the bed capacity) in so-called 'tourist or resort complexes', some with over 12,000 beds.[11] Privatization started in 1990 without a clear concept for the post-privatization management of these complexes. The absence of experience or of any dependable state or civic control delayed and greatly obscured the process. Oversimplified notions of capitalism and free-market economics spurred a 'get-rich-quick' mentality and extremely individualistic behaviour.[12] Media reports widely accused company managers and public officials of corruption and 'crypto-privatization', i.e. manipulating the restructuring process to eliminate competition.

The illegal practices employed in the tourist industry were very similar to those in the rest of the economy. Directors intentionally led their companies to bankruptcy to dissuade other buyers and acquire the assets at lower cost. Tourism managers leased property to private entrepreneurs under questionable financial conditions (Kostova). The lessees were entitled to buy off the property later on preferential terms. Tourist offices abroad refused reservations and falsely claimed that hotels were fully booked. Frequent replacement of managers on partisan grounds contributed further to the overall economic insecurity.

One of the most important dilemmas became whether to privatize entire resort complexes or individual units (e.g., hotels, restaurants etc.). Managers and employees adamantly opposed the administrative breakup and piecemeal sale of the resorts.[13] Competition among and within the different coastal resorts on the international tourist markets proved unprofitable. International experience also corroborates the advantages of larger hotel groups in terms of brand image, marketing and bulk purchases (Williams/Shaw). Finally, the state Committee of Tourism reorganized the coastal resort complexes as state joint stock companies, preserving their trademarks and common policy-making capabilities.

In the first half of the 1990s the private sector grew after the establishment of new, predominantly small companies. In 1996 privatization of the resort complexes accelerated and, by the end of 2000, the industry was largely in private hands. Some resorts (Albena, Riviera, Slanchev Den) were privatized through the sale of larger packets of shares (30 to 60 per cent of the respective company), which enabled them to preserve a more centralized management structure. Insufficient domestic capital and absence of strategic foreign investors, however, necessitated the piecemeal sale of the largest resorts (Golden Sands, Sunny Beach, St. Constantine and Helena), mainly to management-employee companies. Incidentally, this type of privatization placed most former managers in charge of the property transfer, and many were elected presidents of the newly formed joint stock companies. Company employees were entitled to buy up to 20 per cent of the shares of their respective firms on preferential terms. Nationalistic arguments also favoured the management-employee privatization. Balkan Holidays' president, for example, advocated the management-employee option, rather than allowing Western tour operators to obtain a majority stake in his company (Troev).

Additional groups of stakeholders with interests in recreational resources emerged as a result of the land restitution process of the 1990s. Private individuals and municipalities claimed pre-1944 ownership of land parcels, which had later been appropriated by the state and included in the territorial limits of certain resorts (in the case of Albena – about 80 per cent of its territory). The Shabla Tuzla mud deposit, according to a 1905 decision of the People's Assembly, the Bulgarian

Parliament, is the property of the Municipality of Balchik. The state Forestry Committee also demanded compensation for the State Forestry Fund lands included in some resorts (Kostov). At privatization, tourist companies had to set aside some of their shares to satisfy such restitution claims.

Conflicts over control of the coastal resources took place between and within every geographic scale. Central and local authorities, as well as private citizens and groups, clashed over access to resources. In some cases, private companies unlawfully restricted public use of beaches, which are state property. In other instances, resort administrators and municipal governments argued over the authority to issue vendor permits on resort grounds. Company managers and private 'entrepreneurs' sought to benefit from the withdrawal of the state from most areas of public life and pursue short-term self-enrichment goals often in total disregard of resource preservation and conservation. Unregulated private construction became probably the most flagrant example of natural resource abuse along the coast. The very resources on which leisure and recreation depend experienced the heaviest shock from the post-socialist change.

The effects of the transition to capitalism on tourism have been quite dramatic. In the 1988–99 period, officially registered tourist overnight stays decreased by more than five times (from 62.3 to 11.6 million) (*Tourism* 2000). The sharp drop was particularly pronounced for domestic tourists (by 5.9 times versus 4.5 times for foreign tourists) (*Tourism* 2000).[14] Notably, while a slow and fluctuating increase is characteristic for the overnight stays of foreigners, the decline for Bulgarians has been steady. Nevertheless, in comparison to the rest of the Bulgarian economy, the tourist industry appeared less affected by the host of unfavourable internal and external conditions and, in fact, performed quite well. In 1999, for example, tourism accounted for 15 per cent of Bulgarian exports and covered 41 per cent of the balance-of-payments deficit (Balance).

Environmental Problems and Resource Management Actors in the Post-Socialist Period

Despite the substantial advancement of Bulgaria's environmental legislation and policy-making in the last decade of the twentieth century, the main actors that affect the environmental state and recreational value of water resources remain largely the same. Urbanized areas, industrial and transport centres, agriculture and tourist development itself continue to exert serious pressure on the coastal ecosystems, mainly by depleting, polluting and disrupting the natural water cycle. The important difference at the beginning of the twenty-first century is that most users and offenders are no longer state companies but recently privatized enterprises.

On the international scale, the 1982 United Nations Convention on the Law of the Sea made river mouths which coincide with international borders politically important for the delimitation of maritime boundaries. Unfortunately, such river mouths became quite vulnerable to manipulation regarding their direction. Attempts to relocate the Rezovska River mouth, which separates Bulgaria and Turkey, inflicted significant environmental damage in the 1980s, especially on the rare longoz forest.

On the state level, the 'gateway' function of the Bulgarian coastline has attracted concentrations of heavy industry and urbanized areas. While beaches and mineral waters are much less affected, the largest and environmentally most valuable lake complexes – Varna-Beloslav and Pomorie-Burgas – are situated in the immediate vicinity of some of the most heavily industrialized and urbanized areas in the country. Thus, the sedimentation lakes of the largest petroleum refinery in the Balkans are located very close to Mandra Lake, part of which also served for a number of years as the household waste dump for the city of Burgas (population 192,000). Even neighbouring Burgas Lake is severely contaminated with oil products, which have filtered through and damaged Atanasovsko Lake (Georgiev 116). Industrial and household waste depots are found in the immediate vicinity of Beloslav and Burgas lakes. The state legally assumed responsibility for the pre-privatization environmental damages.

Coastal water resources suffer also from overexploitation of surface and ground water for irrigation, drinking and land acquisition. The Devnya Industrial Complex and the city of Varna (population 308,000) use substantial amounts of water from Devnya Springs at the expense of the freshwater inflow into Beloslav and Varna lakes. In fact, most coastal lakes are artificially connected to the sea to restore some of their water volume. The large variations in their water levels and salinity, however, destroy the spawning grounds of aquatic species.

Bulgaria's transportation needs led to the construction of a navigable canal, in 1909, that connected Varna Lake to the Black Sea. As a result, the freshwater species disappeared from the lake. The canal has been subsequently enlarged, and its regular dredging continues to inflict significant damage on the breeding grounds of different species, including rare and endangered fish listed in the Red Data Book of Bulgaria.

Extensive flood prevention structures, typical for most Bulgarian Black Sea rivers, also severely damage their water balance and regimes. The dams, dikes and drainage canals in the Kamchia, Ropotamo, and especially Batova river basins dry up the surrounding swamps and the seasonally flooded longoz forests. The ensuing microclimatic changes also threaten wildlife habitats and biodiversity. The damming of Mandra Lake in 1963, for example, eliminated spacious swamp vegetation areas in its shallowest part and liquidated the nesting and breeding grounds of the last colony of Curly-headed Pelicans (*Pelecanus crispus*) (Yankov 33–44).

The lack of checks and balances under the totalitarian regime, before 1989, also took a significant toll on the environment in the river mouths. In 1978, for example, a government decree excluded about 367 ha from the national park 'Ropotamo' to build yet another official residence. Six years later, the government redesignated 149 ha of this territory for construction, paradoxically, of an International Children's Ecological Centre.

Democratization and the transition to a market economy benefited the coastal environment in some respects. The dramatic decrease of industrial and agricultural production in the 1990s relieved the seawater's oxygen zone from the habitual overuse of artificial fertilizers and pesticides, which had often led to increased eutrophication and massive death of fish. The return of private control over agricultural land and the ensuing sharp rise in fertilizer prices also improved the situation. Another positive trend has been the prioritization of environmental protection investments along the Black Sea coast in the last fifteen years: state policies emphasize the construction of waste-water treatment stations for all sea resorts.

The geopolitical reorientation of Bulgaria towards the European Union has also benefited the environmental protection of the coastal wetlands. For example, in 1994, the country joined the European Union program on Coordination of Information on the Environment (CORINE), which collects, coordinates and distributes information for the state on the environment and natural resources in Europe.[15] The lower reaches of Kamchia and other rivers to its south are designated CORINE sites. A number of Bulgarian and international non-governmental organizations, including the Blue Flag Movement and the Bird Protection Society, collaborate with the state environmental protection programs along the coast. The joint Program for Biodiversity Preservation between Bird Life, Switzerland and the National Nature Protection Service of Bulgaria, for example, includes ten projects in the coastal wetlands.

The economic crisis of the 1990s and the pauperization of the majority of the population since the introduction of a market economy, however, intensified some environmental problems and facilitated the emergence of new threats. Fishing and bird hunting in the wetlands increased, including international hunting tourism. Such activities take place outside permitted time periods, with illegal methods and in prohibited areas (Georgiev 93). Non-existent or inefficient control also allows egg poaching, which threatens rare and endangered species. Illegal gardening and grazing of livestock in the vicinity of the lakes can result in trampled nests and/or burnt swamp vegetation (Georgiev 111–15). The larger number of land carnivores – foxes, jackals, stray dogs and cats – also threatens the populations of many, particularly ground-nesting, birds. A study of Shabla Lake, for example, reveals that 14 bird species, previously reported to nest there, were not detected between 1992 and 1994 (Ivanov 130).

The rapid affluence of a certain social stratum, on the other hand, has translated into a drastic intensification in the use of recreational resources in more remote and previously less accessible areas, especially in the Veleka-Rezovska region. Illegal construction of private summer homes boomed in the 1990s, bringing most extensive damage to the Veleka River mouth, the village of Sinemorets and the protected area 'Silistar'. The construction of the International Ecological Centre continued, under a different designation, only 500 metres from the Arkutino Swamp, which is of European-wide ornithological significance (Georgiev 146–7).

Policy implementation and enforcement of environmental regulations, however, may have become the most challenging problem of the post-socialist period. First, a discrepancy persists between the boundaries of the natural ecosystem and the territorial structure of leisure and recreation administration. For example, the Council of Ministers directly administers two of the three lakes within the Shabla wetland system, which are part of a state residence. The Ministry of Health manages the third lake, due to its specialization in medical tourism (Georgiev 98–9).[16]

Second, state institutions still have missions whose objectives are hard to reconcile. The Ministry of Health, for example, emphasizes curative mud and water protection, while the state of the flora and fauna in the wet zones remains on the back burner (Milchev 277–90). The National Agency of Forests, on the other hand, is directly responsible for regulating the logging industry, the longoz reserves and the hunting tourism.

Last but not least, multiple state institutions and companies outside the tourist industry own summer homes along the coast and, thus, use and manage its water resources. The large number of managers, for whom leisure and recreation is a secondary, often part-time activity, hinders common policy implementation and enforcement of the environmental laws. The fragmentation of ownership, which resulted from the post-1990 privatization, brought about a further, much more dramatic increase in the number of resource owners and managers. However, there was no parallel increase in the resources of the environmental protection agencies or the respective non-governmental organizations. Under these conditions, the enforcement of environmental protection obligations, undertaken by the new owners according to privatization contracts, becomes quite dubious.[17] It is not coincidental that local interests have succeeded in delaying for several years the parliament's passing of the proposed Black Sea Coast Act, due to its presumed restrictive character. Such developments, however, are certainly going to influence negatively highly environmentally sensitive Western tourists.

Conclusion

The geographic characteristics of Bulgaria's coastal water resources determine their unique significance for European biodiversity, seaside recreation and infrastructure development. Yet, the abrupt politico-economic change in Bulgaria and, particularly, the rapid pace of the privatization of the tourist industry intensified some environmental problems and led to the emergence of new threats to water resources, the access to them and, ultimately, to seaside recreation.

The state retained, however, its ownership over the most important natural resources as well as its main environmental management responsibilities. Thus, the Ministry of Environment and Waters controls all water bodies. Additionally, the ministry directly administers the coastal waters as well as the one kilometre-wide strip of coastal forests, all of which are protected territories and exclusive state property. The Regional Development Ministry, on the other hand, handles beach and mineral-water concessions, which can extend for periods up to 20 years. Local administrations also have substantial water-use authority. In view of the multi-scale functions and threats to Bulgaria's coastal ecosystems, their sustainable management structure has to be adjusted to reflect their geographic, rather than administrative boundaries, in order to advance coast-specific standards and regulations.

Notes

1. On one per cent of Europe's territory, Bulgaria harbours 74 per cent of its species plus twelve additional species which are not yet included in the European List (Georgiev 9). Bulgaria was one of the first European countries to publish in the mid-1980s a 'Red Data Book' for its rare and endangered plant and animal species.

2. Pomorie, in the middle section of the Bulgarian seacoast, receives between 2,173 and 2,360 hours of sunshine annually (Kazachka 78).

3. The term 'resort complex' roughly corresponds to 'artificial' or 'planned' resort, built on 'empty space'.

4. In 2000 Bulgaria's income from international tourism was about $US1 billion. In terms of contribution to the Bulgarian economy, the ratio between international and domestic tourism is 70:30 (Interview with the Deputy Minister of Economics and Tourism, December 2000).

5. The term 'peloid' is of Greek origin and unites different kinds of mud, formed in natural conditions. The lagoon-firth types originate as products of evaporation and sedimentation over thousands of years in salty water basins near the sea. They consist of organic and inorganic components and are applied for therapeutic and prophylactic purposes.

6. In Bulgaria, such are locomotory system malfunctions, central and peripheral nervous system, urinary and reproduction system, skin, stomach and intestinal tract, liver and gall bladder, and blood system diseases.

7. Lye is a product of the salt production, obtained after the crystallization of the salt.

8. A number of protected territories of different status are situated along the Black Sea: reserves (Kaliakra Cape, Baltata, Kamchia, Sand Lily, the Snake Island, Arkutino, Morski Pelin, Water Lilies); protected areas (Taukliman, Kamchia-South, the northwestern part of the Atanasovsko Lake, the western part of the Burgas Lake, Korenyata, the fjords and the Seal Cave around Maslen Cape); state parks (Golden Sands and Ropotamo); and local forest parks (Borovets, Kozluka, Otmanli).

9. The supply region of the Varna Lake peloid deposit also includes the Golden Sands, St. Constantine and Helena, Nesebar and the Burgas Spa.

10. There are over 190 different mineral water occurrences in Bulgaria, which surface in 520 springs with a total discharge of 3,200 litres per second (Kostadinov/Karakolev 7).

11. For example, the largest Bulgarian tourist complex, Sunny Beach, was reorganized without any prior announcement, publicity, pre-set rules or regulations, auctions or trade union participation.

12. For further analysis of environmental policy-making in Bulgaria, see Koulov 142–5.

13. Authors' interviews, 1993–99.

14. A part of the decline should be attributed to the sharp increase in unregistered tourists, particularly in the private establishments.

15. Bulgaria has 141 CORINE sites and 24 sub-sites in this program, which also includes 25 other European states (Kostadinova 14–17).

16. According to the Public Health Law and its Regulations, the Ministry of Health legally identifies and establishes the maximum capacity of the 'resort resources and areas', which include mineral waters, curative mud deposits, coastal beaches and the respective seawater.

17. The privatization contracts with the Privatization Agency include obligations of the new owners regarding the management of the respective resort complexes. Some of the most important are participation in the maintenance and development of the infrastructure, activities of common benefit and preservation of the environmental conditions, according to the Bulgarian legislation.

13

Water and Leisure in Moldova: A Social Perspective

Maria Vodenska

Until 1990 Moldova was a small part of the powerful Union of Soviet Socialist Republics (USSR). Because of its geographic situation and abundance of resorts by springs, lakes and rivers, Moldova was a designated resort destination for Soviet workers. This made leisure one of the many social activities that connected Moldovans to the other Soviet peoples. Yet, local Moldovans could seldom enjoy the comfort of their own recreational establishments due to the vacation policies of the Communist Party. Today Moldova is a country in transition and has a young, modern society still under the influence of its Russian 'big brother'. Its destination as a tourist spot available only to some has not changed significantly since Moldova's separation and subsequent declaration of independence. Once again, only a very small portion of the local population has access to the luxury resorts remaining from Soviet rule. Successful businessmen and the nouveaux riches comprise the social group of current vacationers who can afford the much higher prices of today's Moldovan leisure industry.

Any contemporary tendencies in leisure and tourism must be analysed by examining the republic's history, on the one hand, and its present economic situation, on the other. This essay explores the changes in Moldovan water-based tourism and leisure from a social perspective. Tourism refers to travelling great distances in order to reach a specific destination where the goal is to experience the non-ordinary. Tourists, for this reason, are demanding in terms of expected facilities, services and activities. Leisure, however, comprises a much broader range of local activities in which individuals routinely engage in their free time. The first part of the essay presents a historical and geographic overview of Moldova and the potential uses of its lakes, rivers and springs for health and recreation. The second part focuses on the development of Moldova's water-based resources into tourist and leisure sites. The final part of the essay is devoted to the social and economic changes affecting Moldovan water resorts since the collapse of the USSR. It concludes by analysing concomitant problems and suggests solutions.

Maria Vodenska

Historical Overview

Moldova has a long and rich history as a crossroads for migrating populations. Historians consider Geto-Dacians the most ancient population known to have inhabited what is present-day Moldova (Bruchis 7–8). Roman historians called this territory 'The Iron Gates of Europe' in the beginning of the second century AD. After the Romans' retreat in the mid-third century, Moldova became a passage for many migrating peoples: Goths, Huns, Avars, Slavs, Bulgars, Pechenegs and Cumans. In the tenth century it was called 'The Land of Interpreters' because its inhabitants were fluent in many languages. The Principality of Moldavia, the first independent state, was founded in 1359 (King 13). To maintain its independence, it fought the Turks, Poles, Tartars, Hungarians, etc. In the fifteenth century, these lands were known as 'The Shield of Europe' since they served as the entry for invading tribes from Asia and held a strategic position on the trade route from the Black Sea to northern Europe (*Republic* 4). After a period of glory under the leadership of the national hero Stefan cel Mare (Stefan the Great, 1457–1504), the principality finally bowed to outside pressure and became an Ottoman protectorate in the middle of the sixteenth century. The Ottoman Empire ceded a part of Moldavia, i.e. Bukovina, to Austria in 1774 and another part, Bessarabia, to Russia in 1812. In contrast to the Ottomans, the Russians pursued a stringent, century-long policy of complete denationalization of Moldavian culture and language. In 1918 Bessarabia joined Romania, and in 1924 half of this territory formed the Moldavian Autonomous Soviet Socialist Republic (ASSR). The rest of the territory joined the Moldavian ASSR and, respectively, the USSR, in 1940 (*Republic* 5), whereupon 'Autonomous' was dropped from its name, thus the Moldavian SSR. Upon independence in 1991 Moldavia changed its name to Moldova and readopted the Roman alphabet.[1]

Although the curative and health qualities of mineral springs, lakes and waters were known even to Geto-Dacians, the Romans, famous for constructing baths and *thermae* wherever they established their power and administration, were the first to introduce them as places for recreation and leisure in these lands. The long centuries of wars, battles and migrations later caused the decline of these Roman baths until they eventually fell into disuse (*Moldova* 38). With the beginning of the Soviet period, when most of Moldova's resorts were constructed and it became a vacation site for the USSR population, thermal baths once again came into use.

Moldova's present diversity and its central location in Eastern Europe, relatively close to the major tourist-market countries in Eastern, Central and Western Europe, are an advantage for attracting visitors from different parts of the world to its recreation resorts, most of which are water-based. The country's ethnic composition is still extremely diverse. Besides Moldovans, who comprise at present 64.6 per cent of the population, there are representatives of more than sixty nationalities or ethnicities, mostly from the former Soviet Union. The most numerous are Ukranians (14.2 per cent), Russians (11.6 per cent), Gagauz (3.5 per cent), Jews (2.7 per cent) and Bulgarians (2.1 per cent) (*Republic* 7), and tourists from these groups come to Moldova to visit their friends and relatives. Thus, Moldova could become one of the favourite destinations for vacationers from all parts of the former Soviet Union.

Recreational Value of Moldova's Geography

The Republic of Moldova is a small state (33,800 km^2) situated in southeastern Europe and lies mostly between the Nistru and Prut rivers. Easily accessible, it is on the main transit highways between Russia and the rest of Europe, in keeping with its history as a crossroads. Due to ethnic and historic ties, Moldova has special trade and economic relations with Romania. In addition, as a part of the former Soviet Union the country is integrated within the CIS (Commonwealth of Independent States). Romania and the Ukraine, its border countries, and Russia are competing among themselves for political and economic influence over Moldova and have therefore moved investments and people into the country. This in turn is contributing to a certain extent to the development of Moldovan tourist facilities and services (*Sustainable Development* 6).

Moldova has considerable natural resources for supporting tourism. They include lakes and rivers, mineral springs, protected forest areas, highly scenic agricultural landscapes and river valleys, wetlands, bird sanctuaries, limestone caves for caving and steep hills for rock climbing. Since health and water-based tourism and leisure have a certain tradition in the country, present tourist developers can use this reputation to attract foreign tourists. What are the geophysical conditions for achieving this?

The most important natural phenomenon fostering Moldova's economic and tourist potential is its temperate continental climate. The warm, moderately dry and mild weather, which does not vary much throughout the country, is amenable to outdoor leisure activities. The exposure of most slopes is western (28 per cent of all slopes), followed by southern and eastern slopes (26 per cent each). This condition extends the tourist season, which lasts from the end of May to early October (*Ukraine and Moldavia* 58). The predominance of sunshine has earned the country the nickname 'Sunny Moldova'. Most of Moldova's resorts are situated on riverbanks or lake shores. Health, river and lake resorts have played a significant role in Moldova's present tourism development while sightseeing, cultural, rural, eco- and urban tourism are identified as appropriate forms of future development (*Sustainable Tourism* 13).

The country has about 62 natural lakes, with a total territory of about 62.2 km^2. They are fairly small, none of them larger than 0.2 km^2, and most are situated in the Nistru and Prut river valleys. Additionally, Moldova boasts 1,600 man-made lakes, which cover a total of 160 km². About 60 per cent of these are also relatively small, most of them covering an area of less than 20 ha each. Altogether, these lakes make up more than 1 per cent of the republic's territory (*Water* 24). Because of the sunny summer climate, water temperatures in July range from 22.6 to 23.9 °C in the Nistru and 21.7 to 23.9 °C in the Prut (*Sustainable Tourism* 9). Many of Moldova's small, shallow lakes freeze over in winter, allowing the local population, especially young people and children, to enjoy their free time ice-skating. Ice fishing has also become popular. Since there are no facilities in the real sense of the word to support these winter activities, only local residents participate in them.

Rivers also have long been a popular destination for vacationers. The picturesque riverside marshes and ponds are rich in fish and birds. Such conditions could create opportunities for eco-tourism, photo-tourism, fishing, etc. Moldova's most important hunting grounds are also situated near rivers and marshes. These attract people from all over the country to fish, walk along the banks, bathe, row boats, etc. More than 500,000 people from Moldova and abroad spend their holidays each year along the Nistru (*Sustainable Tourism* 12). Since the Nistru serves as the border between Moldova and the Ukraine and the Prut separates it from Romania, Moldova can make use of only half of the rivers' waters and only one of their banks. The potential exists, however, to develop with neighbouring Romania and the Ukraine joint recreational zones along these river basins.

The country is rich in mineral springs as well. Moldova has about 2,200 springs, attracting mostly local visitors. Three-quarters of the springs are concentrated in the northern and central parts of the country, where the most popular Moldovan spas and health resorts have been constructed. They specialize in treating various heart, kidney, gynaecological and other illnesses. Nowadays, some former sanatoria have been turned into hotels. A significant amount of the mineral water from the springs is bottled and sold on the national market for its supposed curative powers (*Republic* 18).

Development of Tourism in Moldova – A Social Perspective

The Soviet Legacy

For ideological and economic reasons internal, social tourism became the most widely practised form of recreation in the former Soviet Union. Social tourism comprises all forms of tourism and leisure activities that in one way or another are sponsored by a governmental organization. Vacationers pay a symbolic portion of the vacation cost, the rest being covered by the state budget. In former socialist countries the main sponsor was the state with trade unions acting as intermediaries. The state or the trade unions covered up to 80 per cent of the real costs of workers' holidays. The regeneration of the labour force and the general well-being of the population were state-sponsored priorities (Bachvarov, *Geography* 15). The length of annual vacations was quite generous (up to four weeks), inexpensive, and anyone could afford to spend them away from home. Social tourism in the USSR was not luxurious but comfortable. There was little price difference between modern and outdated tourist facilities. The large demand, especially for the more prestigious destinations, created a shortage of rooms at quality resorts in all of the former USSR. Such was the case with seaside resorts in its southern republics. Even seasons were of little consequence – centralized Soviet Union-wide management of social tourism and recreation ensured full occupancy of the holiday homes[2] all year round. Moldova therefore never had to promote its leisure facilities nor focus on improving their quality. This situation was also true for most eastern European socialist countries (Bachvarov, *Geography* 9).

Room shortage was not the only obstacle preventing social tourists from vacationing at destinations of their choice. They had to rely on the distribution of holiday vouchers, called *putyovka*, issued by the party-state. The Soviet system divided Soviet society into more than forty groups and subgroups with diverse privileges ranging from discounts for transportation and household electricity to larger and better-located apartments. The different strata of the party-state *nomenklatura* received vacation vouchers for specific categories of destinations. The resorts within the ex-Soviet Union fell into different categories: top, middle and lower, according to their location, resource quality, comfort and service. The establishments in the top group offered single rooms, waitresses in the dining rooms (there were no menus, and everyone ate the same fare), more chambermaids, large halls for watching television, dancing or playing games. Among the most prestigious holiday destinations were the Crimean Peninsula in the south of the Ukraine and the famous spas near Kislovodsk in the south of Russia. The geographic situation of Moldova placed the majority of its resorts among the destinations in the middle category. Reasons for this ranking included less luxurious surroundings and lower service quality. There were, however, a small number of high-quality resorts.

It was unthinkable for common workers to spend their holiday at an elite resort and vice versa. Usually the more privileged groups, i.e. the best workers and high-ranking party members and state officials, spent their holidays in the most desirable season, that is the summer months, and the lower strata often had to spend their holidays outside this high season. In fact, it was not uncommon for some to have to holiday at a seaside or a lakeside resort in winter. A factor in the state's awarding of a *putyovka* was the availability of state or enterprise-owned holiday homes scattered throughout the USSR. Generally, those whom the regime regarded as worthy obtained vouchers for the more desirable vacation spots, which included some of the more luxurious Moldovan resorts situated in the Nistru and Prut valleys.

The voucher system worked as follows. Workers or officials applied to the trade unions for a voucher to a specific destination. Trade unions at the enterprise level, in conjunction with the local Communist Party organization or, respectively, the Komsomol (Communist Youth Union), acted as filters. The trade unions evaluated in writing each application, affirmed or rejected it, at times changing the destination, time of year, etc., and then passed it on to the Party or the Komsomol authorities (for the younger population), who made the final decision. The KGB (Committee for State Security), however, had the final say over applications to destinations outside the USSR and restricted them to a token few who had proved themselves faithful to the Party and were therefore considered less likely to defect to the West. If a voucher went unused, it passed on to the next person in line.

The centralized distribution of vacation vouchers served other Soviet policies as well. To support internationalism among the over one hundred different nationalities and cultures, many vacationers were directed to spend their holidays outside the republics they lived in, but still within the USSR. Rivers, lakes and spas were among the most sought-after destinations because the recreational opportunities they offer have always been and still are the most attractive worldwide.[3] A limited number of prestigious destinations outside Soviet borders, e.g., Bulgaria's Black Sea coast, were available only to a carefully selected elite. Ordinary Moldovans, however, hardly benefited from this policy, which restricted their access to the resorts and campsites in their own territory. In fact, many felt they were victims of discrimination since they were given vouchers for trips outside their republic to places more often than not of lower quality. Naturally, the Moldovan party elite could have their pick of vacation destinations within and outside the republic (Bachvarov, *Geography* 31).

Present Economic and Social Conditions for Developing Tourism

At the beginning of the twenty-first century, economic and social conditions present new challenges for tourism. Moldova's economic situation is deplorable. Its GDP has decreased appreciably since 1991. It is among the poorest countries in the world; its poverty is severe and social welfare meagre due to dwindling budgetary resources and lack of implementation capabilities. Even job status does not necessarily affect poverty. Those employed are only slightly less likely to be poor than those who are unemployed or on unpaid leave. Wages are very low, and payment is often significantly delayed (*Republic* 13). The annual per capita income is less than 500 US dollars, and over half of the population lives on less than one dollar per day. Erosion of the few education, health and public services has further hurt the poor (*Republic* 13). Per capita foreign investments are among the lowest in Eastern Europe (*Republic* 14). Therefore, Moldovans have the means neither to take vacations nor to develop on their own a tourist industry attractive to foreign tourists. This means that the demand for private recreational facilities within the country is quite low. Moldova's population distribution, dense but dispersed, also diffuses the local demand for large-scale tourist and leisure services and creates a need for small-scale local facilities for the native population.[4] Moldovans use the natural resources of their country in an unorganized way. In their spare time, they go fishing, swimming, rowing, bathing, etc. in and on the numerous public rivers and lakes. At present, however, the Moldovan government does not have the financial resources to develop public leisure areas. The facilities in place are currently in such disrepair that companies and organizations are not interested in privatizing them. Their use is thus available free of charge.

The present economic situation in Moldova does not allow the parallel development of both leisure and tourism. Yet it has the potential to develop a viable tourism sector that can generate considerable income, foreign exchange earnings, employment, government revenues and other economic, social and environmental benefits. So far, the state has shown little awareness of tourism's potential contribution to the country's economy and society, and the low priority given to the development of tourism has led to a continuing decline in tourist activities. However, theory and worldwide practice show that the tourist industry is one of the easiest and least expensive ways of stimulating economic activity, a sure means for decreasing unemployment and attracting foreign investments (Mathieson/Wall 10). This is the reason why many countries in periods of transition or in a difficult economic situation turn their attention to tourism development (*Republic* 15). Tourism also indirectly affects other areas of the economy and can be a catalyst for other economic sectors, especially agriculture, fisheries, manufacturing, crafts and construction. For example, tourists visiting Moldova consume its traditional export products – grapes, fruits, vegetables (both fresh and tinned), grape wine, grape brandy, sugar and tobacco – and the economy profits from this 'invisible export' by saving the expenses of export and transportation. While the state is not yet focusing on tourism, private industry is investing in the development of new facilities along lakes, rivers and springs for foreign tourists rather than for Moldovans (*Republic* 27).

Issues Affecting the Current State of Water Recreation

The Republic of Moldova has special historical, cultural and natural resources as well as a number of resorts and spas, all of which could be conducive to a tourist industry. Other assets include an existing stock of hotel accommodations (although most hotels require renovation) and a few functioning tour and travel agencies. Yet, as a recently independent and relatively small country, Moldova and its tourist attractions are not well known outside Eastern Europe. The limited availability of funds prevents their being marketed internationally to any great extent, and the country's image as a desirable tourist destination is therefore very weak. Another reason for this is the decrepit condition of facilities across the country. Most were built in the 1960s and 1970s, have become obsolete and generally do not meet current international standards. Proprietors are trying to sell them at any cost. Buyers are most often individuals or organizations, related to the 'grey' and 'black' economy, and, having no experience in the leisure and recreation business, purchase them merely to launder money ('Tourist' 1). However, the legitimate private sector is working to establish a thriving tourist industry. For instance, private investors have begun resort renovation, but it is proceeding slowly because of limited financial resources (*Sustainable Tourism* 17).

Very little of Moldova's former leisure and recreation industry still exists. The number of foreign visitors in 1999 was a third of that before the beginning of the democratic changes. Ministry officials consider this information less than accurate, however, due to the inefficiency of gathering border statistics ('Recreation' 1). Nevertheless, the largest and most attractive recreational zones continue to draw visitors from Moldova and abroad, mainly from the former Soviet republics. One example is the resort area of Vadu-lui-voda on the Nistru River. Accessibility (only 16 km from the capital, Chishinau) and a good transportation infrastructure have helped maintain its popularity. Most of its vacation homes, situated within a small forest, are promoted as being as comfortable as any four-star hotel. A nightclub, billiard room, café, movie theatres, a ballroom, sports facilities, sauna and a library complement outdoor activities (Agentia Nationala 3). Although open to all, currently only businessmen and foreigners can afford a visit there. Moldovans who cannot afford such luxury frequent less expensive sites, such as local cafés along the Nistru riverbank. They also visit their 'second homes', that is their modest, former village huts. All social strata participate in quite similar recreational activities. However, the wealthy have larger boats, better fishing rods and more expensive equipment and outfits.

Exercise, while not a specific goal, is a natural part of the whole process of water recreation. Studies show that water recreation improves general health and physical fitness and increases resistance to colds and other illnesses. Furthermore, it reduces instances of temporary sick leave by a third and increases labour productivity by about 10 per cent (*Water* 34). For those whose health has already deteriorated water therapy is beneficial, especially when both external and internal mineral-water treatments are properly administered. These types of water therapy for the infirm are available at specialized spas or medical centres. The medical centre at Vadu-lui-voda, for instance, has contributed significantly to the area's popularity. Working closely with the Health Ministry, tourist companies such as 'Moldsindtur' and 'Sindbalneoservice-Moldova' offer water and mineral springs-based services combined with balneological treatment and medical consultancy at a number of other resorts. They include Nufarul Alb in Kagul, Kamenka and Kodru in Kalarash. Guests, after having obtained a medical recommendation, receive balneological medical treatment, physical therapy or prophylactic therapy. Indeed, the potential for Moldova's medical tourism, based on its water resources, should not be underestimated.

Another large resort, the Soroca group, is situated at the northern part of the Nistru River, in the vicinity of the ancient town of Soroca, and boasts more than 300 beds. During Soviet days, anyone possessing a tourist voucher could visit either the Soroca group or Vadu-lui-voda. Currently, the different social classes all may use the same rivers and lakes for recreation, but only the wealthy can afford to make use of the resorts by the water. Moldova's nouveaux riches and high-level state officials, who manage the Soroca group, have built luxurious private villas there (Agentia Nationala 4).

A noteworthy impediment to water tourism is the continuing armed conflict. After Moldova's emergence as an independent state in August 1991, internal fighting engulfed it till mid-1992. Vacation homes and infrastructure along the Nistru were made unusable, and full sovereignty over the whole left bank of the river (with the exception of three villages), populated mainly by ethnic Russians and Ukrainians, has yet to be fully established. An example of the different nature of tourism in the disputed area is the recreational zone in the picturesque valley of the Dubossary River, currently a part of the Russian-dominated 'Trans-Dniestr Republic'.[5] Attempting to preserve Soviet ways, the zone's administration is running a voucher system in the same way as in the former Soviet Union, but concrete evidence of its effectiveness is difficult to obtain, and no sources can be cited. Moldovans may vacation in this area but they seldom do, the poor for lack of money, the rich for lack of luxury or comfort. Nothing has changed in these areas since Soviet times, and there have been no improvements (*Sustainable Development* 7).

No visible tension between Russians and Moldovans existed in the resorts of the republic before the political reforms under Gorbachev's *Perestroika* (Reconstruction) in the second half of the 1980s. The multinational character of the republic mentioned above – about 35 per cent of the population were not ethnic Moldovans – gave the appearance of ethnic tolerance. Yet, antagonism, whether stronger (as in the Baltic states) or milder (as in Moldova), was always under the surface in Moldova as it was in all non-Russian Soviet republics; the iron rule of the central power suppressed it. The Soviet state promoted demographic colonization, de-nationalization of native populations and destruction of cultural values. Most Moldovans, especially those who were not members of the Party, were accustomed to being treated as people of lower quality. They had access neither to high-quality goods nor to the picturesque resorts, both reserved for 'Party' people. Only in the time of *Perestroika* was it possible to voice some displeasure with the existing reality. The hostility of today's Moldovans towards anything Russian began around 1989–92. This antagonism was based on the perception that all negative aspects, especially the poverty and lack of security connected to the breakup of the USSR, came from Russia. Although ethnic tensions between and among various groups of Moldova's population have become more open, Moldovans are quite united in their antagonism towards Russia (*Moldova* 18).

Social and economic transformations in neighbouring countries and in Russia have also affected Moldova's tourist industry. Russian visitors today differ substantially from former Soviet tourists. In the past, Russian workers not among the Communist elite had little choice of accommodations and were easily satisfied with Moldova's tourist 'product'. The present-day Russian businessmen and politicians visiting water resorts pay substantial sums of money for their lodging and off-duty leisure activities and are therefore much more particular. In fact, wealthy Russian and Moldovan tourists prefer holidays in Turkey, Cyprus, Greece or Italy, middle-class tourists Bulgaria, and the poor stay at home or visit Ukrainian resorts (*Statistical Yearbook* 57). Therefore, Moldova must become internationally competitive to regain its prominence as a tourist destination.

In contrast to the previous year-round usage, most recreational facilities on the Nistru and Prut rivers are now used only sporadically – for private celebrations, on weekends, as summer camps for schoolchildren, etc. Businesses also use them for organized events, like seminars, meetings, conferences, or to accommodate their foreign guests. Individual users are mainly local consumers who cannot afford a holiday abroad. In the period 1995–98 booked accommodations in Moldova decreased by 25 per cent (*Statistical Yearbook* 57).

Water pollution is another factor for declining tourism. During the immediate post-war years Moldova endured the Soviet policies of forced collectivization and excessive industrialization. Due to this, some lakes and rivers became polluted, but very few measures if any were taken to diminish the harmful effects. Moreover, it was not the policy of the Soviet state to make public any pollution, even in areas where it had been found to be extremely high, nor to discourage people from using polluted resorts. The Moldovan BASA-press reported on 12 June 2000 that not a single lake or water basin around Chishinau met national or international sanitary requirements, and the government therefore forbade bathing in them. Medical professionals confirmed in this report that this had been the case for the last three years and warned that epidemic diseases could spread from recreational zones. Since no information on water quality could be published during the Soviet period, no one knows when the pollution actually began. Before Moldova became part of the USSR, government control over the purity of water had been quite strict, and measures had been enacted to ensure continued water quality. Nowadays there exists no financial possibility to invest in water purification or quality control. No one has yet investigated the effect this situation has had on the number of balneological vacations. At present, the price not the quality of the water resources is what matters most.

Conclusion

During the Soviet period, Moldova's mild climate and rich water resources made it such a desirable holiday destination that its resorts were full without having to promote them. Independent Moldova is saddled with many economic, political and social challenges. The state has had no resources to develop a general strategy for the utilization of the numerous leisure establishments on its territory, which were constructed to satisfy the needs of a much larger number of vacationers. The majority of the companies that use and manage the resorts have no resources or experience in recreation and leisure. The old centrally planned system has been demolished, but a new one has not been created yet.

A gap existed in Soviet times between the privileged elite, who could afford the best resorts in Moldova's territory, and the rest of the population. Little has changed; the gap remains and is most probably even greater than before. There are several differences, however. The current disparity results from economy, rather than from ideology. Instead of the Soviet party-state elite, now Moldovan nouveaux riches and powerful politicians use the few high-quality resorts in Moldova. The demand for recreation has also changed dramatically. While the elite groups engage in the same kind of water-based activities as the rest of the population, they have much higher requirements for the quality of service and thus find the majority of facilities inadequate. Most resorts are in need of renovation, and long stays are beyond the financial means of the average Moldovan. As a result, they are used only sporadically, and this has had negative financial consequences. However, the fact that the facilities lend themselves to short stays compensates for their low quality and service; most Moldovans live within easy travel distance to a resort. In addition, visits to resorts are no longer mainly for medical purposes. Instead, resorts serve as places not far from home where one can spend leisure time with friends. At present unorganized leisure use of Moldovan recreational resources dominates over tourist use. If resort conditions improve, visitors will use them more often and for longer periods of time.

Moldova has only recently begun to formulate a state policy for the development of recreation and tourism. Previous decisions concerning tourist development had to be made on an ad hoc basis because there was no legal or regulatory framework. However, in May 2000 the parliament adopted the Tourism Act. It establishes a national tourism agency and covers a variety of issues, such as planning and marketing tourism, creating a tourism fund and licensing tourism enterprises. The latter includes rights and obligations, requirements for professional training of tourism managers, classification of hotels, protection and security of tourists, and international relationships, all according to policies set by the World Tourism Organization. It is too soon to know how this act will affect Moldova's tourism and economic situation.

For the time being, the lack of funding, but also of vision, has resulted in a complete absence of international advertising and promotion of the country's recreational resources. Therefore, I would like to propose the following recommendations. Moldova's government should move quickly to create the necessary environment for the infusion of know-how and capital by realizing the policies set forth in the Tourism Act. Meanwhile, private companies linked to the tourist industry need to sponsor aggressive promotion campaigns. Individual resorts should create and cultivate their own separate images and tourist products, e.g., water sports, medical tourism, etc., in order to attract specific types of visitors. Moldova's recreation and leisure industry should capitalize on the country's natural resources and its now dormant 'vacation-land' image to restore its past glory.

Notes

1. For the sake of consistency, further references to Moldavia/Moldova will use the republic's present name, Moldova. Likewise, inhabitants will be referred to as Moldovans.

2. A holiday home means a combination of hotel and sanatorium, where people could stay after obtaining a *putyovka* from the trade unions and the Communist Party.

3. 70 per cent of the world's tourist arrivals are at seaside or other water-based resorts (*Sustainable Tourism* 4).

4. With a total population of 4.3 million Moldova is one of the most densely populated countries in Europe. At the same time, however, the population is quite dispersed throughout the country, and large settlements are few. The capital city of Chishinau, for example (675,500 inhabitants according to the latest census of 1989), is the largest of a total of 21 towns (*Republic* 33).

5. Dniestr is the Slavic name for the Nistru River.

14

Water, Culture and Leisure: From Spas to Beach Tourism in Greece during the Nineteenth and Twentieth Centuries

Margarita Dritsas

Introduction

Greece extends over 15,000 kilometres of coastline, has 3,000 kilometres of sandy beaches, 337 inhabited islands, several hundred other uninhabited islands, hundreds of mineral springs and large and small rivers and lakes. Water is, therefore, a dominant element, and it is hardly surprising that Greek culture has concentrated over the centuries on the essence of water as a constituent part of human existence. Ancient Greeks borrowed many elements from other peoples and made bathing as important as literacy. Water cleansed, cured, rejuvenated, ensured immortality and, last but not least, it beautified and gave pleasure. Pindar considered water the epitome of excellence ('Ἄριστον μεν ὕδωρ'; Pindar). Water as border also united and separated, and, as means of transportation, was the main avenue of communication. In contrast to the notion of constant movement, of liquidity, and of adventure, the island (*terra firma*) was postulated as the corollary: a symbol of stability and permanence, a refuge and a source of strength, where all human needs were satisfied. Rivers, and especially springs, combined the two elements as life givers, ensuring a mystical bond between humans and earth. This culture became universal through the condensation of age-old traditions encapsulated in Homer's epics *Iliad* and *Odyssey* and in countless myths. Homer's adventures were set in the then known universe, the Mediterranean Sea, centre of the western world until the sixteenth century. It allowed communication and osmosis of cultures, provided resources for its different peoples, hosted many religions, and ensured the prosperity of different economies. People living along its shores acquired familiarity with water: Seafarers, travellers, adventurers, explorers – i.e. those philosophers and communicators who were quick of spirit and temper, and adaptable to a constantly changing environment – forged a cultural amalgam inherited by subsequent generations, which formed the basis of modern European civilization. Eventually the centre of this world shifted westward beyond the Atlantic, and much of European culture concentrated on ideas and principles cut off from the environment that had given birth to them.

During and after the Renaissance ancient culture was rediscovered. The new euphoria urged educated Europeans to travel east and south, in search of their assumed Greco-Roman past. They eventually went to Greece and thought they could discern the Greek *Volksgeist* in the writings of Herodotus, Aristotle, Plato, Strabo, Pausanias, Plinius and many others (cf. Castellan 24; Wordsworth 11, 197, 264, 351–2) who described the many natural phenomena that gave rise especially to springs. The Greeks bequeathed the habit of bathing in warm and cold springs to the Romans who, just like their predecessors, erected beautiful palaces and baths for therapy and pleasure.[1] The Byzantines later retained, if not the custom, certainly the structures and transmitted them to the Ottomans. Unlike the Moors in Spain, the Ottomans destroyed most of the old Roman/Byzantine installations but eventually developed a new tradition of indoor steam bathing.

Throughout Christianity, old legends survived and found expression in, among other things, 'holy springs' and 'fertility fountains'. These referred to libations of holy water accompanying all important moments of a person's or an institution's life and being particularly invoked in cases of ill health (physical or mental).[2] The flow was assumed to be cyclical, and thus water was an element both of the living and of the dead. Water determined the perception people had about the life cycle, and a strong female presence dominated legends about springs and the sea. Springs were indeed equated with the life-giving earth and were often personified as mothers shedding tears, milk or blood (cited by Meraklis 21–4), symbolizing at one and the same time fertility and virginity. This powerful symbolism was grafted onto the Christian tradition whereby the Mother of God is considered, and depicted as, a Holy Spring of life (*Ζωοδόχος Πηγή*). In many rural parts of Greece, many old practices, half-pagan and half-Christian, survive today as folk traditions and rituals and are re-enacted on particular feast days, whereas others are more formally institutionalized. The fusion of Christian and pagan elements of water culture has come to life again, as ancient myths have been resuscitated over the last three centuries through foreign travellers' narratives and depictions and through paintings by European artists.[3] Non-scientific explanations for the flow and characteristics of mineral waters often appear intact through time.[4]

Early Use of Spring Waters

Greeks appear to have been the first to use warm baths for leisure and mineral spring waters as remedies for disease. Mineral baths were part of their perception of the balance of harmony between a healthy body and a sane mind (*Νούς υγιής εν σώματι υγιεί*). Ancient baths, located in the forum and near gymnasia (or *palaistrae*) were popular places, where men could watch others train, listen to music, discuss politics, gossip or listen to philosophers. The curative powers of mineral waters were undisputed, as worship and healing intermingled, until the fifth century AD.[5]

The popularity of warm bathing gradually faded away and, as elsewhere in Europe, seemed to disappear with the advent of Christianity. First Spain, because of the Moorish influence, and gradually other places, after the Crusades (after the eleventh century), became reacquainted with the customs of the East and rediscovered warm baths. In Eastern Christianity throughout the Byzantine period, however, warm bathing was common among the aristocracy – although not so common among the rest of the population – despite hostility to it by monks and religious hermits, who considered care of the body the door to indulgence and sin.[6] Warm and cold bathing, both for leisure and curative purposes, came to other parts of Europe after the Ottoman conquest via those members of the Byzantine elite seeking refuge in the West. The progress of science and chemistry from the sixteenth century on and the rediscovery of ancient Greece and Rome eventually resuscitated the culture.

Modern and Contemporary Period

In modern times the mode of using mineral waters did not change much despite the proliferation of scientific theories and medical suggestions about their use from the eighteenth century onwards (cf. Althaus 283–4). During the early nineteenth century, spas in Europe were used mainly by the aristocracy. The process of industrialization accelerated the development of spas as cure/leisure locations for a larger public, and this was a qualitatively different phenomenon from the past. Early government preoccupation with the state of public health and the need for improvement were important factors, even if they took a long time to gestate. Use of the spas slowly started to spread, with emphasis initially being placed on their therapeutic value (strength and health). Gradually, spa use integrated leisure as well, to the extent that physicians warned their patients that 'indulgence in the pleasures of the table, gambling and excesses of every description could counteract the beneficial effects of a mineral water cure' (Althaus 305).

Patients/visitors took the water or the air along with hundreds of other visitors and collectively became consumers of new kinds of services and of natural and aesthetic resources. Springs were usually located in beautiful, natural surroundings, and a visit to the mountain or the seashore was advised as much for its intrinsic value as for its contribution to a cure, relaxation or resting. Residents of spa resorts were also likely, if not obliged, to follow medical recommendations to take the waters at the appropriate time of year and day, which usually implied a special sort of daily discipline (Filippakopoulos 29). This routine was appropriate for those who wished to improve their health and general well-being, either because they believed in the power of nature or because they were inspired by the new credo that science would improve modern society. For the more affluent users, confidence and the riches they had accumulated allowed them to integrate health improvement and luxury. Sumptuous palaces and luxurious hotels, including casinos, were built. Architectural designs provided for special walkways leading to the springs, comfortable benches and pavilions where spectacular views of the landscape could be enjoyed; high culture – theatre, music, dancing – was also available for the pleasure of the spa enthusiasts. The cosy atmosphere of the spas enjoyed by the rich and powerful, combined with efficient organization, made many resorts exclusive centres of international politics, diplomacy and business.

Spa organization spread beyond Central Europe and affected the subsequent emergence of modern resorts in other countries, including those along the Mediterranean. Southern countries changed from being destinations of the aristocratic culture-motivated Grand Tourists to becoming the object of desire for the ascending bourgeois professionals and businessmen from the north.[7] During the same period, the relation with the sea was much less developed. Sea water was considered dangerous, and bathing in it remained an individual pursuit until well into the nineteenth century. The beach was still rather an empty space where one could walk, admire the openness of the ocean and enjoy the sea breeze. Large numbers of people enjoying the pleasure of swimming were a phenomenon observed much later, coinciding to no small degree with the emphasis placed on the cult of the body, on eugenics and on sport. On the other hand, beach culture, associated with mass tourism, the feeling of total freedom and the pleasure of being in the water, came much later and revolutionized the pattern of holidays. The phenomenon coincided with post-Second-World-War political and economic changes. In addition to the liberation of many old colonies and the discovery of a whole new world, there was unfettered economic growth in the west for at least two decades with a consequent rise in income levels and in the standard of living. With the use of aircraft for mass travel, transportation and communications were revolutionized, too, and new consumer patterns arose (cf. Urbain, *Sur la plage* 106–7; see also Dutton). But until this happened, spa culture occupied the front stage.

Greek Spas

Few spas famous in ancient times were known to modern Greeks during the early nineteenth century, when Greece emerged as an independent nation-state. Some springs were apparently used only by local people familiar with old indigenous traditions/superstitions and perceptions about well being and the healing power of mineral springs.[8] These early modern users of thermal baths were rather of plebeian origins, simple folk who lived nearby and had first-hand experience with the qualities of the waters. By 1870, however, theories concerning the value of hydrotherapy had gained prestige among foreign and Greek physicians, both of whom argued that, along with hygiene and dieting, taking the waters was an important preventive measure against a wide array of diseases. Despite these views, no systematic development of spa resorts had taken place until the last quarter of the century, and conditions at least in one spa were described as 'appropriate for convicts rather than citizens'.[9] The situation began to change as visitors multiplied. Among them, numerous more affluent patients, disappointed by the results of treatment after having tried the waters at European resorts, were advised by their physicians to visit the more potent Greek thermals (Polyzoidis).

The case of two of the best known Greek spa resorts – Aedipsos in northwestern Euboea and Loutraki on the northeastern Corinthian Gulf – will highlight the process of development of a flourishing spa culture and its eventual substitution by the beach.

Aedipsos

In classical and Roman times, Aedipsos was a leisure/pleasure resort visited by Roman emperors and other illustrious personalities, but accessible also to common people as was then customary. Located near the sea and surrounded by mountains and woods, it was ideal for rest and remained in use throughout the thousand years of the Byzantine Empire, when aristocrats visited it again either for curative purposes or for rest and meditation. The Ottomans destroyed it in the fifteenth century, and although it fell into oblivion to the wider world, local inhabitants in the early nineteenth century believed in the curative power of the waters. A regular steamboat service linking Aedipsos with Piraeus several times a week brought in more visitors from the outside, which thus supported the modern development of the town begun in the second half of the same century. There was an almost complete lack of accommodation facilities, however, and those early patients, after initially trying to spend the night under the stars, built very temporary, rudimentary shacks. As the reputation of the 'miraculous' spa spread, new visitors began to use the waters, building more huts, each time slightly better than those constructed in previous years.

By 1875, Aedipsos attracted patients from all over the country and from overseas, and many scientists were also recommending mineral bathing as a way of improving public health (Polyzoidis). In 1890, according to one estimate, visitors were in excess of 4,000.[10] Land disputes being prevalent, however, it was some time before the economic potential of this new resource aroused the interest of local landowners like the Church, which built the first complex of baths only after foreign physicians had been praising the waters in their writings for at least ten years (Althaus). Meanwhile, the first modern Olympic Games in 1896 signalled a turning point in Greek tourism, the state designated the springs as national property a decade later and their first classification took place in 1906. During this time, Greek physicians and geologists began to publish more and more books about the springs, and manuals for prospective users referred extensively to the ancient culture. Other scientific and academic works, citing similar studies by specialists in Germany, Austria, France and so on, concentrated on the principles of hydro-therapy, on theories about the establishment of spas and on their characteristics. They all confirmed the healing qualities of any spa, while, on the other hand, they deplored the low quality of Greek facilities and the level of their equipment and management.

Clearly, the idea of health tourism was beginning to gather momentum but investing in its development remained restricted until after social policy and state involvement had provided protection and a market for the new activity. Labour legislation in Greece was still in its initial stages, workers and employees having no statutory rights to any vacation. On the other hand, wealthy businessmen and professionals, who could afford to travel to the large, well-organized spas of Central and Western Europe and enjoy luxury and high culture, were unwilling to experience the misery of Greek spas (unless absolutely necessary). Not surprisingly, service conditions at the end of the nineteenth century, although undoubtedly somewhat improved, were still described as 'semi-barbarous' (Dalezios 14, 28). However, as entrepreneurs in Aedipsos started to develop strategies that tapped into the new market of the many low-income and the few more affluent consumers, visitors started coming from all over Greece and especially from the overseas Greek communities in Egypt, Asia Minor, etc.

Between 1890 and 1940 developers of Aedipsos, along with those of several other Greek spas, imitated the standard features of European spas but adjusted some elements, such as architectural patterns, to local conditions. Mainly local landowners built modern hotels. One of the better hotels was named '*Thermai-Sylla*' for the Roman Emperor whose bath-tub archaeologists had unearthed near the springs. Like other big hotels elsewhere, it had a limited number of baths that used water from the springs. It was still in use in the 1960s.

After the First World War, state officials began to realize the potential of spas both for improving public health and attracting revenue from tourism (Boissonnas 54). Profound socio-economic changes had taken place in Greece with numerous effects. The borders were definitively fixed, and under the pressure of the influx of 1.5 million refugees after the defeat of the Greek army in Asia Minor in 1922, Greece had to mobilize all of its resources in order to recover. Domestic and foreign capital allowed a faster pace of development so as to absorb the newcomers economically, socially and culturally. Just as industry had its first 'promotion law' in 1922, which promoted industrial activity through land expropriation, freight reductions, tax exemptions, duty-free import of machinery, etc., so too did spas receive for the first time a coherent institutional structure. On the basis of earlier studies and classifications, new legislation was introduced that regulated owner-ship of the springs, planning of spa towns, operation of hydrotherapy centres, appointment of physicians, safety procedures and hygiene, and a framework for a tourist policy began to emerge.[11]

Greek spa development reached its heyday in the interwar period, but hydro-therapy was practised empirically and less systematically than in other parts of Europe. State involvement in planning had just started, and private initiative had not yet developed any long-term strategy. The market, nevertheless, had expanded, and competition was now intense. Not only did several Greek spa towns compete with each other for tourists, they also competed with foreign resorts in neighbour-ing countries like Italy and Serbia, which were preferred by the big tour operators of the period. One of them, Cook Travel, included in organized group packages stays at Italian and/or Serbian spas and promoted them as new, exciting and moderately priced destinations. Italy, with assistance from the state, had started to promote tourism much earlier and more effectively than Greece. Aedipsos, distant from international maritime routes, remained throughout the period a resort for lower-income domestic tourists. This was reflected in the type of hotels built and in the general infrastructure of the town. In 1934, the Directorship of Guests and Exhibitions of the Department of National Economy reported the unsatisfactory condition of bath facilities, the lack of physiotherapy equipment and the need to improve sanitation by building proper sewers. It recommended enhancing the environment by improving the sea front, by building a road where people could stroll and by constructing a pier, a market and public service facilities. It was clear that health tourism development was now seen as an area of state activity rather than of private initiative alone and as a sector oriented towards average-income domestic tourists, who were usually elderly.

This orientation found full expression after the end of the Second World War and the ensuing Civil War. Aedipsos retained its pre-war status as a resort for average-income visitors, and, as late as 1956, the local guest industry was made up of a multitude of modest rooms in private homes and mostly low-priced hotels. Only eight hotels were listed as class A and B, while most were class D and E (basic accommodation). During the same time, the beach began to attract younger visitors, often members of the same families who visited the spa. The situation has changed today, and Aedipsos is being upgraded to a modern integrated spa.

Loutraki

In sharp contrast to Aedipsos is Loutraki, which became its major competitor in the twentieth century. During the same period, Loutraki had 48 hotels, most of which (29 establishments) were listed as category A and B. The town also exhibited most of the features usually associated with European spa culture.

Since its discovery in the late eighteenth century, Loutraki was a popular spa in the Corinthian gulf. During the 1820s, rumour had it that Independence fighters bathed in its mineral waters (cf. Koukoulas, *Loutraki* 54, 57; *St'achnaria* 180–2). In the 1830s King Otto was persuaded by his Bavarian physician to visit the spa, which he liked so much that he had a pavilion built near the spring (Filippako-poulos 20). In 1843, the maritime firm Austrian Lloyd established an office there. Its steamships from the Ionian Islands, Trieste, Ancona, Patras and Aegion began to dock in the harbour, which contributed, along with royal patronage, to faster development of the whole region. The Customs House cleared passengers and goods; they were then loaded onto carriages departing for Athens and Piraeus. The town was well positioned on the international route of visitors, thereby enabling the curative qualities of its mineral waters to become more widely known. In 1847, Austrian Lloyd declared its readiness to invest in the new tourist venture by building proper baths after receiving a concession agreement from the Greek government. Competition with neighbouring Corinth for port facilities and planning permission, on the one hand, and the turmoil of the 1848 revolutionary activity in Europe, on the other, cut short the prospects, and the Austrian plans were suspended. The Customs House was eventually transferred to Corinth, and Austrian Lloyd closed its Loutraki office. Local patients using the mineral springs (cf. Koukoulas, *St'achnaria* 208) had to wait until 1870 when the town replaced early, primitive installations (wooden shacks) with ten proper baths and rented them out to an entrepreneur. The rooms in ten to twelve modest local cottages also proved to be insufficient and uncomfortable accommodations since each room usually housed one whole family or several friends. The Austrian Lloyd building and the house of a local merchant and notable (K. Oikonomou) were eventually converted into two hotels, which suggested that new visitors were more numerous, affluent, cultured and possibly more demanding.

A few years later in 1896, the opening of the Corinth Canal and the Olympic Games created new momentum for the region and the country in general. Foreign capital had for some time flowed into the country, and investors looking for profit-able ventures included a group of British businessmen, who promised to transform Loutraki into a spa town of European standard within five years. The proposal, however, failed to mobilize the necessary local economic and political support. Governments of the period were more interested in attracting capital for basic infrastructure and industry projects or in collecting taxes and duties from trade (directly linked with agriculture) than in supporting mineral springs and baths.

Loutraki reached its apogee between 1900 and 1940. Infrastructure improved, and the town was embellished, modern luxury hotels were erected and many good restaurants opened in the town and suburbs. The main mineral spring, feeding the baths and a fountain for drinking water, became the chief source of revenue for the town authorities. Serving tourists became the principal occupation of the local population and of the many newcomers from neighbouring villages. The central state had remained indifferent, and local authorities and entrepreneurs in Loutraki became the victims of their prosperity. Faced with limited finances, they adopted the short-sighted and arrogant attitude that patients flocking to Loutraki – and to other spas – to use the thermal springs would continue to use them in the future regardless of the quality of service or the efficacy of treatment. For a while, business appeared secure, as a large number of people continued to visit the thermal springs and to spend holidays with their families at the spa. Around two thousand visitors stayed in Loutraki in 1900 and used the four mostly privately owned complexes of baths attached to several of the twenty-three hotels. In addition, there were over forty more modest hotels and rooms available to tourists for longer periods. Important changes, however, were around the corner, as Loutraki, being only eighty kilometres away from Athens, was fast becoming a zone of secondary homes for professionals, businessmen and high civil servants.

Private initiative, meanwhile, had developed other side businesses, such as transporting and selling spring water to the hotels, as well as bottling and exporting it abroad, mainly to Egypt and later to the whole of the Middle East. A soft-drink industry was another spin-off. Exporting mineral water functioned as a kind of advertisement. Increasingly large numbers of Greeks from Egypt and other offshore communities started visiting the spa and eventually constituted the majority of patients/tourists during the inter-war and post-war periods. Tourists from abroad benefited in the 1930s and again in the mid-1950s from monetary stabilization (devaluation of the drachma in 1932 and in 1954) making Greece a very cheap country for a holiday. The impact of offshore Greek visitors on the town was reflected, among other aspects, in the names of many hotels (e.g., Egypt, Palmyra, Semiramis, Constantinople, Atlantic, England, Britannia, Canada, etc.). Most of the businesses were family-owned and run. Many started modestly, like the Karantanis, and in time integrated several separate firms and business activities, such as exporting water, running several hotels and restaurants, and managing both an insurance firm and a travel agency. Bottling factories proliferated and have changed hands many times since then; they are owned today by a multinational corporation, in which Greek capital has controlling interest.

Today, Loutraki is a bustling modern town with high-rise buildings and crowded beaches, very different from the past. During the early period when Loutraki functioned only as a health-resort centre, village life between May and October was very quiet. Visitors/patients spent long hours resting in their hotel rooms. They usually came out only in the morning and early evening to drink the mineral water as doctors recommended. Socializing took place in the few cafés where guests drank refreshments, read newspapers, gossiped or discussed politics. Strolling along the sea front or down the main road offered younger people opportunities for courting. With time, leisure and entertainment patterns already in fashion in the rest of Europe were ushered in. As the quality of hotels and services improved, so, too, did the chances to make useful acquaintances in hotel lounges through activities such as playing cards or even just socializing. Visitors enjoyed music and dance soirées organized in the more elegant establishments. After 1930 Loutraki's casino, offering new excitement for those who liked gambling, became the hall-mark of the spa for some time. In addition to expensive restaurants and bars in the centre of town, there were also *tavernas* and coffee houses on the outskirts, where traditional food and Greek folk singing and dancing offered alternatives to the more continental style of big-hotel entertainment. For the less affluent there were two cinemas, and for the very young (and their nannies), performances of 'Fasoules' or 'Karagiozis'. Churchgoing on Sunday, and on other days, especially to worship the 'miraculous' icon of 'Mother of God the Healer' was very common, particularly after 1928 when a larger church was built immediately after an earthquake had destroyed the town. A litany took place every year on 8 September, during the height of the bathing/tourist season. Excursions were also organized to the convent of St. Patapios (a sixth-century Egyptian saint) on the Gerania mountain ridge.

Development of the town accelerated when the main dispute over ownership of the springs was settled. Private initiative was involved in every aspect of business with the exception of the bathing facilities run by the state. Many hotels had, themselves, installed baths that received water from the springs, and also had drinking water transported to them. After the 1928 earthquake, development was entrusted to a new body, the Organization for the Rehabilitation of Earthquake Victims (AOSK), which received a considerable grant in the form of national land. The organization's scope included not only rebuilding and repairing houses damaged during the earthquake, but planning and constructing new therapy centres and opening the casino, the revenue from which was expected to help rehabilitate earthquake victims in the region. Since AOSK was in no position to assume the burden of redevelopment on its own, a public bid was announced. The casino opened after its manager had negotiated an agreement with the Athens-Piraeus railway for regular rail communication between Athens and Loutraki. In addition, a limousine service and four regular steamboat lines were available.

The resort was changing fast, having attracted for some time wealthy bankers and businessmen from Athens who built elegant summer residences (the casino was housed in one of them for a while). The local and national press praised the spa as an equivalent to the Riviera resorts or Monte Carlo, the casino's manager declaring that he was determined to make Loutraki 'a Greek Deauville'. Such lofty aspirations, however, depended on the success of a redevelopment plan for the town, which proved to be much more difficult than anticipated and brought local interests into direct conflict with foreign prospective investors. Of the Swiss, French and English groups that showed interest, British capitalists presented the most realistic proposal, but after a protracted bargaining process, it failed to receive the guarantee of the Greek government for what was still considered a risky venture (cf. Dritsas, 'Foreign Capital'). Such a risk might also have deterred AOSK, which was hoping, with the help of a loan from the National Bank of Greece, to remain in charge of both the rehabilitation process and further development (cf. Koukoulas, *St'achnaria* 354–8). However, a loan amounting to 280 million drachmas was earmarked by the state and granted to AOSK by the National Bank of Greece. This enabled anyone who had a house, a hut or a room affected by the earthquake to borrow (on paper) to rebuild. No cash was given to the borrowers, but they were allowed to exchange a sort of promissory note with contractors, who, in turn, were free to build according to their own specifications, thereby making enormous profits. Speculation thus prevented any rational, integrative development of the resort along European lines, and business and community leaders in Loutraki, though it was more developed than Aedipsos, did not avoid the consequences of ad hoc decisions.

Despite everything, however, the community managed to market successfully its reputation and to combine fragments of its old rustic simplicity with the veneer of European style. It was perhaps this charm that continued to attract a diversified public, from the political and economic elite to the average-income Greeks and the many affluent middle-class foreigners. Political patronage was present throughout this period. In the late 1920s and 1930s, Eleftherios Venizelos, twice prime minister of Greece (1910–15 and 1928–32), was a regular visitor to the spa, taking an active interest in its development, as did his successor, Panagis Tsaldaris (1932–35). In the next few years preceding the Second World War, new hotels and baths were built and trees and gardens planted. The new buildings were sturdier than before the earthquake, more comfortable and more luxurious with pleasant architectural designs. A new bathing/therapy centre was erected with thirty baths made of expensive porcelain, and including large rooms equipped with daybeds and armchairs, marble staircases, a large waiting hall and deluxe suites with lounges for VIPs. The road from the hotels to the baths and springs, which ran parallel to the seashore, was widened and made more pleasant for visitors to stroll under the shade of palm trees and laurel bushes. It became common for locals and visitors to cycle or take walks in the evening. There were benches at regular intervals, and the spring itself, where drinking water could be bought, was enclosed in a circular colonnade with fountains reminiscent of Roman structures and was decorated with a splendid mosaic inspired by mythological water scenes and motifs. The design incorporated the rock from which the spring water ran down quietly

into a marble pool. The new atmosphere was compatible with the new clientele of
the spa. Visitors were no longer locals, nor even all of them Greek, 40 per cent
being residents of foreign countries (Koukoulas, *St'achnaria* 397). Other spas
lagging behind Loutraki envied it, and in 1934, a special meeting called by the
Ministry of National Economy to discuss ways to promote spa tourism in Greece
excluded Loutraki from any future plans (cf. National Bank of Greece, Series
XXXIV, folder 0–034). What other spa towns and the authorities could not foresee
was the tide of a new fashion focusing on the beach.

Although there is evidence that around the end of the nineteenth century people
travelling to Aedipsos also bathed in the sea, beaches did not start attracting ever
growing numbers of Greek enthusiasts (usually among the affluent clients) until
the twentieth century.[12] In the inter-war period Loutraki was one of the first places
where *bains mixtes*, or joint baths for both sexes, were organized, meeting below
the Casino, on the rocky coast, and on a small pocket of sand behind the expensive
hotels. Bathers were few; others still preferred walking along the shore, content to
breathe in the sea air or gaze at the half-naked bodies of the swimmers. This new
fashion, however, was gaining in popularity day by day. Soon a new fifty-metre
beach was designed behind the large hotels, sand was transported and a pier was
built. Trees and flowers were planted and fountains installed to enhance the new
walk. The reputation of the place spread, and in 1936 a German firm showed
interest in investment. Germany had already made economic headway in the
Balkans, and the prospect of collaboration with the semi-fascist regime of Ioannis
Metaxas, who had taken power in Greece in the same year, obviously opened new
possibilities. However, local resistance and Metaxas's own views about foreign
policy and tourism frustrated this initiative. During his rule, until the outbreak of
the war, centralization increased and authoritarianism went rampant. His government dissolved AOSK and transferred all its assets to the state; accordingly, the
baths and the casino were to be managed by the state National Tourist Organization
(founded in 1930), which depended on the Ministry of Press and Propaganda.

The war disrupted plans for future development. After the war, even though
Loutraki maintained its character as a health spa until 1960 (when it had over forty
hotels and over 3000 beds), the tide had turned. Several efforts were made to
revive the spa tradition, for instance, by organizing medical conferences between
1957 and 1960 related to diseases curable at Loutraki, but these attempts failed
(Koukoulas, *St'achnaria* 149–59).

The Beach

Before the war, Loutraki was considered wealthy and successful enough not to
need any state assistance. In the 1960s, it did not receive a high funding priority,

either, because of its focus on domestic health tourism. State policy now emphasized the massive attraction of foreign tourists – and the consequent import of foreign currency – in order to maintain a healthy balance of payments. Moreover, the virtual annihilation of Greek communities in Egypt, Turkey and elsewhere, as a result of indigenous nationalism, caused a severe decline in spa tourism that lasted almost a decade.

These causes, however, were not the only, perhaps not even the most important ones, leading to its decline. As with so many mentalities and perceptions, the idea of holiday changed after the war, as did consumer trends. The concept of freedom affected every aspect of life, and the sea and beach emerged as the epitome of exhilarating liberation. In contrast to dramatic, if not tragic, legends about spas and springs, those about the sea have stressed sensual delight, bliss, pleasure, love, joy and have also had an impact on culture. (e.g., Aphrodite rose from the waves on her seashell, and Leander swam for love). It has been argued that the beach has a hedonism of its own and symbolizes liberty and democracy (e.g., by the removal of clothes – signifiers of social rank, income level, aesthetic preferences – and the removal of the shame of lying idle in the sand); the visual perception of the beach imparts a feeling of openness (see Dutton 13–17). Since the beginning of the twentieth century, bathing, swimming and sunbathing have gradually almost replaced mineral bathing for improving health and have been strongly recommended by physicians.

Figure 14.1   Periclis Pantazis, On the Beach, *mid-19th century oil on canvas (Benaki Museum, 30663. Athens, Greece)*

It is, therefore, no simple coincidence that all Greek spas declined as beach tourism started to develop. Indeed, since the 1970s the very essence of holiday for millions of people, including the average Greek, was no longer the countryside, the mountain, or the mineral spa resort but the beach and the islands. Beaches in the Attica region, near the capital, and on some of the closest islands in the Saronic Gulf – Hydra or Spetse – were the first to arise. Rhodes in the Dodecanese and Corfu in Heptanesa also developed fairly early since there had been a long tradition of dealing with foreign travellers. At the same time, island tourism was promoted as part of a more general policy of regional development, aimed at raising incomes in areas poor in natural resources and/or deserted by emigration and at improving the living standard of their populations.

Beach tourism accelerated the diversification already underway in Loutraki. Foreign tour operators no longer marketed the town to the new tourists primarily as a thermal spa but as a leisure resort. Improvement of communications and a new motorway built in the 1980s shortened the journey from Athens, thereby stimulating growth. The town became mainly a zone of semi-permanent or secondary residences for Athenians, and the new style of rather drab high-rise buildings with repetitive architectural designs, typical not only of Athens, now dominates there, too. Health (thermal) tourism was restricted more and more to domestic and some 'diaspora Greek' visitors.

Since the mid-1990s a new situation has been emerging with as yet no definite characteristics. As a result of the devolution of power from central administration to local authorities, supported and encouraged by the European Union, regional and local development companies are enacting community-based plans to expand tourism. The policy, undoubtedly, has both positive and negative effects. In the case of Loutraki, the target of the new 'Thermae-Loutraki Town Enterprise for the Loutraki-Perachora Tourist Development' is the integration of thermal and general (beach) tourism. The enterprise has undertaken an ambitious project to modernize and extend thermal bathing facilities, favouring only one side of the targeted plan. Simple observation confirms the lack of integration of the two distinct forms of tourism. Differences between the two are flagrant as foreign and younger tourists visit the town mainly for the beach and the sunshine, and, to a lesser extent, also because Loutraki is close to some of the ancient archaeological sites that make up the standard itinerary of the average foreign tourist (Corinth, Mycenae, Tiryns, etc.; cf. Lozato-Giotart 65). Conversations with local entrepreneurs indicate that hardly any of the foreign visitors know about, or show interest in, the mineral water springs or the history and tradition of the spa.

This sharp divide determines the whole spectrum of services offered – the level of comfort, price range of accommodation and composition of the clientele; it results in a dual structure of tourist profiles. Older hotels and many budget accommodations (rooms and hostels) located in the town still cater to the needs of elderly

Greek visitors who use the mineral springs, whereas foreign tourists – guided usually by tour operators and pre-selected holiday packages – tend to prefer more modern hotel complexes and resorts, away from the centre and the springs, directly on the beach. There, they can enjoy not merely the water and the sun but all the modern paraphernalia of beach tourism, from sun beds, canteens, fast food, Coca-Cola and jet skis to a crass version of folk culture. Promoted over a number of years, this form of beach tourism has resulted in the neglect of other activities like mountain walks on the nearby Gerania ridge, horse riding and so on. In town, a limited range of entertainment sites – only two cinemas, several traditional pastry/coffee shops, and restaurants – cannot compensate for the lack of a theatre, a concert hall, or a multi-purpose cultural centre. The longstanding demand of the more profit-minded local groups to reopen the casino instead was finally satisfied a few years ago as one way of resuscitating tradition and attracting more tourists.

Conclusion

The account presented above on the development of two forms of leisure connected to water and its culture – exemplified by two Greek resorts, Aedipsos and Loutraki – is representative of many other cases in Greece. The essay traced the rise and decline of spa tourism in the nineteenth and twentieth centuries, related to health improvement, and the transition to mass tourism as exemplified by beach culture. Among the several hundred spa locations developed at different points in time in Greece, around forty are still in use today and have been incorporated in recent projects run by local authorities. They were all affected by the more general changes in mentalities, consumer trends and material conditions brought about after the two World Wars. Although the two forms of leisure appear to be mutually exclusive, recent policy changes, despite their shortcomings, have been designed with the purpose of integrating them in the future.

Notes

1. The Greek term used for these baths '*βαλανεῖον*' has survived in the etymology of the French '*balneotherapie*'. Cold baths were indeed already considered a form of bodily discipline.
2. For survival of superstitions and customs from ancient to modern times in Greece related, for instance, to weddings, funerals, new crops, see Ministry of Culture.
3. Nineteenth-century painters have especially portrayed bathers – usually female nudes – and fountains and mythical landscapes, for instance, Courbet, Delacroix, Renoir, Picasso.

Murray's and Baedeker's handbooks for travellers (1840s and 1880s) were based on earlier travel writing by the Grand Tourists and made extensive use of ancient myths.

4. For the various fables associated with Greek springs, cf. Althaus 262–34.

5. Temples of Aesculapius (god of medicine) were built close to springs, and in modern times many churches were built near spas.

6. For bathing during the Byzantine period, cf. A. Berger, passim.

7. Lozato-Giotart has identified the transition with clarity.

8. In 1840, X. Landerer underlined the abundance of Greek mineral waters, urging the government to develop them. In 1862, Althaus referred to the 'many remarkable waters in Greece' visited by 'natives'. Althaus, *passim*.

9. Cf. Polyzoidis, passim. The remark referred to Aedipsos, the largest spa in Greece.

10. Dalezios v. Some of the visitors preferred, however, bathing in the sea.

11. These were Law 2188/1920 on mineral springs; Law 2992/22 concerning concessions of mineral springs and the building of hotels, therapy centres and gambling clubs; as well as a series of decrees between 1921 and 1927 concerning the use of water, the appointment of physicians in baths, particular conditions of the concessions, etc.

12. By 1910 Athens possessed an organized beach in Faleron, where several hotels were established. Wealthy Athenians and affluent Greeks from abroad moved out there for the summer months, and elegant summer residences went up. For bathing times cf. Polyzoidis 157.

15

Rimini and Costa Smeralda: How Social Values Shape Recreational Sites

Patrizia Battilani

Introduction

There is much literature on patterns of industrialization in some Italian regions and even more on the lack of industrial development in others. In particular, several areas of research focus on the major institutional wealth of various regions and on the presence of social involvement, cooperation and reciprocal trust shared by an entire community. Two influential articles are Putnam's essay on institutions and Becattini's on industrial districts (*Mercato*). Putnam emphasizes in particular how civic traditions and the presence of many related non-profit associations improve the efficiency of a region's institutions, above all political ones. However, Becattini's research on industrial districts shows that civic traditions assume the nature of informal relationships, which are formed outside the marketplace and pass through the network of the territory's associations and institutions. According to Becattini, these informal relationships stimulate the collaboration and diffusion of information between small and medium-sized companies and thereby form the basis of their competitive capability.

This essay compares the development of tourism in the Costa Smeralda (Emerald Coast) of Sardinia, an area where, according to Putnam, familism prevails, with that of Rimini, in Emilia Romagna, an area characterized by a strong civic culture. The objective in the case of Rimini is to show that the wealth of institutions and associations in a region contributes both to the creation of entrepreneurial dynamics and to the general population's participation in the process of economic development, including tourism. This, however, affects the characteristics of services offered. In fact, although the different segments of Rimini's population participate in various ways in the region's development, all spend their free time similarly. Therefore, no exclusive tourism exists. Any symbols of the elite's vacations do not represent a social barrier but are accepted and appreciated only because they reflect the area's prosperity and improve its image.

On the other hand, it is easier to create exclusive localities, as in the case of the Costa Smeralda, where the various parts of society are unable to develop tourism on their own and where exogenous investments determine the results. In this case, outside investors do not have to concern themselves with the local customs or community regulations of the other segments of the population. This exclusion makes it easier to create an environment for elite tourism. However, this very separation makes the diffusion of business knowledge and capability – necessary for the growth of tourism in general – inside the region more difficult. It is still possible, however, for local investors to initiate a process of imitation and economic growth in Sardinia's other areas, even though there exists a certain spatial separation. Indeed, although the Costa Smeralda has until now tenaciously defended its exclusivity, other areas of Sardinia have progressively become open to mass tourism.

Rimini and the Impossibility of an Elite Tourism

Two aspects in the development of tourism in Rimini stand out. One is that industrialization is based in small business districts instead of in large corporations. The other is that Rimini's business leaders failed to achieve their pre-First-World-War dream of the city's becoming an exclusive locality, 'the Ostend of Italy', as its publicity proclaimed at the turn of the twentieth century (Masini). Let us begin with the first aspect. The spread of small and medium-sized business networks requires what has been called an 'industrial atmosphere', a condition resulting from the very tight relationship between businesses and a local community. A homogeneous system of values – which is an expression of an ethic of work and activity, of the family and of economic exchange – and a system of institutions and rules exist in the local community. In addition to businesses these systems include family, church, school, local authorities, associations, etc. (Becattini, 'Distretto'). This is the very context in which Rimini's tourism industry developed, and since its beginning it has seen the convergence of various groups: the families of landowners and of the middle class who create and manage the businesses, the city administration, the local banks and the numerous associations.

In 1800 Rimini was an agricultural area with longstanding urban traditions and it depended on the provisions of agriculture for its existence, as did many other Italian cities (Silari). In 1871 71 per cent of its active population was involved in agriculture. This is the context in which Rimini's sea-bathing establishment adventure began in 1843, although its inhabitants had been swimming in the sea since the beginning of the nineteenth century. General chronicles from this period document that all social classes, from craftsmen to soldiers, from police officials to aristocrats, swam in the sea.[1] Their motives were various: to find refreshment from the summer heat, to play, to bathe, to follow the medical advice of doctors who were convinced of salt water's therapeutic effects. During these years Rimini's beaches were not yet popular, in part owing to the uninviting stretches of dunes, shrubs, reeds and marshes and to rubbish carried in by the sea. In 1820 the first bathing-huts, built on piles in the water, appeared and permitted bathers to take their dips completely secluded. These huts were not widely popular but attracted the more aristocratic customers such as princes, dukes and wealthy bourgeois from nearby provinces.

Claudio Tintori, a young exponent from the middle class (his father was a doctor and his mother the owner of a silk mill), was the first to realize a proposal for constructing a sea-bathing establishment. Since he did not have the necessary funds, he involved two friends in the project, the Baldini Counts, who were young descendants of a landowner family. Their models were the beaches of Tuscany, above all Viareggio. In July of 1843 the Privileged Sea Bathing Establishment of Rimini was born. It had six dressing rooms, and a horse and carriage connected it to the city. Initiated with the best of intentions, this endeavour was under the guidance of the Baldini family, sustained by the local bank and blessed by the representative of the Pontifical State, Cardinal Vannicelli Casole (Balzani). The bathing establishment, offering quality services, was directed at moneyed customers. There was a discrete number of bathers – in 1854 the establishment had 354 guests, of which only 12 were outsiders – and it did not become profitable (Porisini). As the demand for local elite tourism in this area was limited, the city could not offer sufficiently prestigious cultural or recreational activities that would attract European aristocracy. Not even the inauguration in 1861 of the Rimini-Milan railroad, connecting the city to the Lombard area, brought in the immediate, expected benefits.

The project was on the verge of ruin when the City of Rimini intervened in 1869. After a heated debate in the City Council, the city bought the establishment and initiated an investment plan for the area by financing a number of related projects: the Kursaal (1870–2) in a park, the nearby Swiss Cabin (a stowaway for the carriages which was transformed into a restaurant in the summer), the hydrotherapeutic establishment (1874–6) and a large, tree-lined boulevard. At the same time the city administration introduced gas lighting and started a telegraph connection between the seaside and the city. These soon added to the city's heavy debts, the increase in taxes and the loans from the Savings Bank of Rimini notwithstanding. The city government, acting as a private company, sustained an economic activity that generated heavy losses.

The Savings Bank of Rimini soon became the other protagonist of the beginnings of tourism in Rimini. Founded in 1841 its charitable mission was to assist the poor and middle classes in saving a small part of their income for times of need. The bank placed particular emphasis on new businesses and made itself available to support new industrial or service-oriented initiatives other than the usual agricultural requalification projects. The Rimini area, however, had very little private industry, while agriculture, dominated by the sharecrop system and by small-farm owners, demonstrated in general little inclination towards innovation. Because of the lack of alternatives for financial investment, the Savings Bank of Rimini, in close collaboration with the city administration, committed itself to lending primarily for tourism-related construction projects (Zamagni).

One of Rimini's tourism problems was its lack of structures for accommodations. In 1882 there were no hotels and fewer than thirty villas that rented out rooms. As a partial solution, the city acquired from the state the area along the coast and in 1885 began to divide it into lots and then sold them at a low price to private owners for homes and villas. The Savings Bank of Rimini participated by granting loans. By 1900 there were only five hotels, and almost all tourist lodgings still remained in private residences.

However, tourism was already acquiring an important role in Rimini's economy, so much so that the House of Commerce's 1872 annual report revealed that the Bathing Establishment had produced an 'increase in all the arts and occupations, and in particular the supply of textiles, clothing, knick-knacks and food items' (Ruffi/Casaretto 33). Twelve years later, in 1884, further evidence that sea bathing was among Rimini's largest industries was the increased influx of outsiders (Silari). The buildings that accompanied the transformation of Rimini into a bathing centre, the Grand Hotel (1908) and the Kursaal with its attached platform for the bathers, had been constructed with the intention of attracting aristocratic customers, as had happened in the rest of Europe. However, Rimini soon proved itself a more attractive vacation resort for the middle class than for the aristocrats.

Only the well-off could afford to stay at the Grand Hotel and the Kursaal. Nonetheless, the middle class considered them an attraction as well and liked to spend time watching the guests who stayed in them. Therefore, less exclusive inns and shops flourished near the Kursaal's Restaurant and the Bathing Establishment. The 1873 advertisement for the Swiss Cabin stated, 'People who like to have a simple meal can eat and drink at reasonable prices' (*Guida ai bagni di Rimini* 54). In 1886 *Italia*, one of the local newspapers, pointed out that restaurants attracted a varied clientele. In addition to the Kursaal and the Swiss Cabin, there were three restaurant huts on the beach to the west of the Bathing Establishment. 'They were naive and rural, but comfortable, democratic and full of people' (*Italia* 8 August 1886). The 1893 illustrated guidebook of Rimini described the possibility to have a satisfying lunch with fine wine at a reasonable price in the canteens close to the beach (*Guida illustrata di Rimini* 32). In 1910, another local paper, *il Gazzettino azzurro*, criticized the proliferation of gypsy-style huts that sold wine, drinks and beachwear to the great detriment of the beach's appearance and decorum (*Gazzettino azzurro* 24 July 1910). Thus, even in its beginning 'the Ostend of Italy' attracted the middle class.

In the Bathing Establishment's first decades of operation, however, Rimini had few attractions for middle-class tourists. There were horse races and frequent archery contests, both especially popular among women, as journals of the era attest. Some sports societies also emerged.[2] These initiatives were not aimed at outsiders but at Rimini's aristocratic class. The same was true for theatrical shows, usually staged in winter when there were no tourists. Rimini's leadership soon realized that the city also needed to offer new leisure activities. However, the city administration, already heavily involved in creating the infrastructure, did not act on this, nor did private businesses, which were interested only in construction. Therefore, the social network of Rimini, that is the associations, took the lead in creating new leisure opportunities. Yet there was no major concentration of recreational activity in the summer months until the 1880s. Founded in 1883, the Rimini Society was financially sustained by shopkeepers, hotel and restaurant owners. Over the next twelve years it vitalized summers for the visitors by organizing enjoyable festivities of various types.

On the whole, a multitude of associations and initiatives blossomed. They were dedicated to organizing the most varied recreational activities: pigeon shooting (often heavily criticized by animal lovers), dancing festivals, concerts, fireworks, theatrical shows, horse shows, boat races, track races for bicycles, aerostatic balloon rides, etc. In 1896 a skating rink opened. In 1900 a Russian resident of Florence founded Rimini's first lawn-tennis club, and the sport quickly enthused vacationers (Gardini et al., vol 2). In 1889 the Arena Theatre opened, for two years located in a small part of the Kursaal, and until 1924 it treated Rimini's summer visitors to assorted performances. Between 1873 and 1903, the Swiss Cabin Restaurant became one of the more popular meeting places in Rimini because it had a café with a musical band and organized events such as wine fairs, thereby entertaining all classes of visitors and residents. 'At one table the Count and the Duke were seen drinking from the same flask as the ironsmith and the cobbler; at another a Countess drank merrily together with some farmers who, with black and calloused hands, had come to exhibit their wines' (*Italia* 10–11 August 1886). The birth of several new journals, some specifically written for tourists, attested to the dynamic nature of Rimini's society. These were often single issues with captivating titles: *Waves of the Beach*, *Pearl of the Adriatic*, *Spider Fish*, *The Sail*, *The Beach*, etc., which publicized the many amusements available to vacationers.[3]

Therefore, if the pattern of investments, on the one hand, demonstrated the city administration's desire to create a place for elite tourism, Rimini's social life and leisure activities, on the other, continually mixed the various social classes, thereby creating the foundation for middle-class tourism. Even in the years characterized by aristocratic tourism, it was possible for middle-class visitors to stay in religious convents at modest prices. Until the First World War, the many opportunities for fun and pleasure notwithstanding, aristocrats who summered in Rimini preferred

213

to spend evenings at the various private villas constructed specifically for them along the green boulevards by the sea. Only the Kursaal seemed to offer activities sufficiently exclusive for these guests, such as concerts and balls.

The need to construct a luxury hotel still existed, but the city would have had to go even further into debt to finance it. In 1906 a Milanese society, the Smara, agreed to manage and renovate the Bathing Establishment and to build a large luxury hotel. In exchange, the Smara became the only authorized company to manage lodgings near the Bathing Establishment over the next twenty years. In 1908 the society decided to build the Grand Hotel, having 250 rooms. Until the 1930s, however, the Bathing Establishment and the Grand Hotel were sources more of debt than of profit, so much so that in 1927 and 1931, respectively, the city administration was again forced to assume their management in order to avoid total failure. Luxury tourism in Rimini, therefore, was not lucrative, and this was a reality neither public nor private investment could alter. Why then did the city allow the Bathing Establishment and the Grand Hotel to survive for so long? The motive was very simple: their very presence guaranteed Rimini a promotional image that attracted middle and lower classes. In other words, these establishments' exclusivity created the positive external conditions that permitted middle-class tourism to flourish. In fact, the entire bathing industry at Rimini is characterized by the dichotomy between the indebted luxurious structures and the increase in tourists who arrived because of them but could not use them (Silari).

The first phase of Rimini's tourist boom was the period between the two wars. The number of bathers increased from 18,750 in 1922 to 74,953 in 1933. Hotels and, above all, boarding houses quickly grew, thanks to the success of all-inclusive pricing. Again, the luxurious amenities, which attracted, for instance, Mussolini and numerous exponents of Italy's fascist government to vacation there, had a promotional function for the whole locality. At the same time the increase in the number of smaller, cheaper and less prestigious boarding houses confirmed Rimini as a tourist destination for the middle class. The number of villas, homes and apartments also grew. Their owners were generally shopkeepers or professionals who used rental fees to supplement their main income. The tourists who came to Rimini were 90 to 95 per cent Italian. This was also the era when summer camps spread; in 1937 they welcomed almost 40,000 children from working-class parents, which reinforced once again Rimini's popular reputation. All kinds of associations and companies promoting leisure sprang up: the tennis club, the automobile club, the air club, the sports club Libertas. Musical events, sporting events and other recreational activities flourished. Above all, dancing was everywhere. 'It is a miracle that the chairs don't dance' the local fascist journal, *The People of Romagna*, reported in 1928. By then, the dream of making Rimini 'the Ostend of Italy' was completely gone, and the locality had decisively taken the path of middle-class tourism.

In the first years after the Second World War the city intervened once again. The so-called New Rimini Plan was to create a new lodging infrastructure along the coast. The plan concentrated on two types of accommodations, villas with gardens near the coast (some already existed) and large hotels to be constructed behind the villas. This model, representing a radical change from that of the 1930s, failed.

In the 1950s, lacking regulations to protect the coast's natural environment, Rimini became a city of boarding houses and small hotels constructed so closely together that no space was left open. In 1949 there were 236 lodging establishments (201 of them boarding houses), and in 1961 there were 1,373; overnight guests in 1950 numbered more than a million, and in 1961 five million. Tourism and construction, both based on the initiative of private business, triumphed. Rimini's major economic venture throughout the 1950s was to build hotels and the venture remained tied to the tourism monoculture. The Savings Bank of Rimini continued to contribute to the growth in number of hotels. Altogether, 90 per cent of the bank's investments in the first years of the 1950s were hotel loans. It also financed the renovation of two prestigious public hotels, the Grand Hotel and the Park Hotel, and the transformation of another hotel into a hotel school. This model reached its first crisis in the 1970s, when the number of tourists began to decline (see Table 15.1). Once again, Rimini's economic and social network responded rapidly with a very articulated strategy.

Table **15.1** Overnight guests (in thousands) in all the reception structures in Rimini and in Sardinia

	Sardinia	Rimini
1955	350	2683
1965	1587	5822
1975	3424	6828
1985	5238	7397
1995	7415	7775

Source: Provincia di Rimini; Annuario statistico italiano, 1955–2000

On the one hand, Rimini's leaders tried to reinforce bathing tourism by expanding its entertainment infrastructure, its variety making Rimini unique in the entire Mediterranean bay. The crisis of a hotel surplus and a more restrictive urban plan, approved in 1965 and applied during the 1970s, moved investments from construction to entertainment. Table 15.2 shows the strong increase in the number of discos, restaurants, bars and theme parks.[4]

215

Table 15.2   The province of Rimini-Forlì: the building of a leisure district

	1977	1978	1983	1988	1992
Discos and arcades	54	138	113	167	165
Restaurants and 'pizzeria'	413	639	813	773	893
Bars and pubs	857	1369	1223	1184	1239
Theme parks ('000 square metres)	209	209	209	524	1062

Source: Nomisma

On the other hand, there was an attempt to improve the beauty of Rimini's surround-ings. Many villages on the hill above it were renovated. Their castles, old churches and museums were promoted as tourist attractions, and different kinds of fairs and festivals were organized during the summer season. In addition, the tourist season was lengthened by promoting conferences and other special events. A second crisis, culminating in 1989 and generated by the presence of mucilage in the seawater, made clear that Rimini could lose its tourists forever. Overnight guests numbered fewer than six million, in comparison to the eight-and-a-half million in 1988. The realization of Rimini's competitive disadvantage that city admin-istrators, associations and consultants had stressed since the 1970s stimulated a new wave of investments back into construction, and this led to extensive hotel renovation. It included new amenities, such as swimming pools and other attract-ions, and improvements in quality of service. This contributed to an increase in tourism in the 1990s.

Costa Smeralda: Inventing Exclusive Seaside Resorts

It is not surprising that the economic and social context for developing tourism in Sardinia is different from that in Emilia Romagna. Investments in Sardinia's bathing establishment in the second half of the 1800s targeted local customers. The very first establishment, inaugurated in the summer of 1862 with twelve bathing huts, was at Alghero, one of the few towns on Sardinia's coast. Renovated many times and surviving financial difficulties, Alghero's bathing establishment was described in 1890 by a local journalist as 'elegant, gracious, pretty, lively . . . able to compete with the establishments of the Adriatic and Mediterranean' (Oliva 186). It was also a lively social centre because of the dance festivals organized every Sunday. There were essentially two disadvantages to this early form of tourism: the brief duration of the bathing season, from the beginning of July to the middle of August, and the fact that the majority of tourists were commuters who did not spend the night. A railroad connected Alghero, the most important seaside resort, to Sassari, the most important interior town, and in the months of July and August supplementary trains were scheduled, especially on Sundays, so as to satisfy the commuters' vacation needs.

There were no accommodations, however. According to travellers' diaries, the situation in the mid 1800s was dreadful to say the least. 'This time I found room and board in a place . . . which is useless to discuss . . .' (Marmora 399). 'Certainly much travel has made me indulgent in matters of lodging . . . but I cannot speak without horror of the Golden Lion in Alghero . . . horrible food, bothersome flies, intolerable mosquitoes, repulsive insects, terrible sheets and absolute lack of tranquillity . . .' (Delessert 77).

The situation in southern Sardinia was no different. In 1863 the Bathing Establishment of Perdixedda Point was founded on the Gulf of Cagliari. Two others were established on the gulf between 1878 and 1895, while in 1892 the first bathing establishment of Carloforte began operation (Price). The uniqueness of Sardinia in 1900 was not so much connected to backwardness, since this was more or less true everywhere in Italy, as to the fact that this continued on into the following decades. At the dawn of the First World War the situation concerning accommodations in Alghero was still appalling. The only new buildings offering lodging were one boarding house with ten beds and another with eleven; otherwise, lodging was private. There were fewer than 250 beds and fewer than ten to twelve thousand annual guests (Simon 1959). The situation did not improve even in the inter-war period. The Italian Touring Club guide stated in 1932 that, 'the coast of Sardinia, from the bathing point of view, is largely ignored and not used. Only recently do we see signs of effort directed towards giving life to well-equipped bathing stations' (Touring club italiano 171). The author was referring to Poetto, on the coast of Quarto, Cagliari, where two bathing establishments had been completed between 1913 and 1914. A steam ferry connected Poetto to Cagliari, and Poetto soon became an attraction for the local aristocracy. The touring guide cited two other tourist destinations, Porto Torres and Marina di Bosa. 'All of these bathing stations are, however, frequented by residents, and there are no hotels. Only Bosa City has two small hotels. Elsewhere you must search for apartments or furnished rooms' (Touring club italiano 172). There was thus no basis for tourism in Sardinia before the Second World War, and the few existing establishments had not been able to attract outsiders.

The development of tourism began in earnest in the 1950s and was concentrated in uninhabited areas rather than in the few towns on the coast. Among the first to understand the potential for tourism in Sardinia were the Club Mediterranean, which five years after its founding in France inaugurated its first vacation village in Sardinia in 1955, and Horizon Holidays, the English travel agency, which has included Sardinia in its charter cruises to Corsica since 1954. It was not a coincidence that many foreign tourists were French and English up to the 1970s.

At that time Italian coasts were becoming more and more attractive to European tourists looking for 'sun, sand and sea', and Sardinia also benefited from this new trend. It offered uncontaminated nature, wonderful coves and the feeling of being among the first to discover the island. In 1949 even Sardinia's regional administration began to promote tourism. It tried to promote hotel construction (95 per cent of the hotels built in the 1950s were regionally financed) as well as to advertise Sardinia's natural and cultural beauty and to improve professionalism by opening various hotel schools. These promotional efforts, however, were quite limited (Price).

For all practical purposes tourism still did not exist in Sardinia, as Table 15.1 makes evident. Sardinia's economic backwardness, however, affected everything, not just tourism. Sardinia, one of the less densely populated parts of Italy, is characterized by an inhospitable terrain, mostly rocky with some swampy areas, and for a long time it was infested with malaria. These territorial features heavily influenced agriculture, which centred around sheep breeding and, in a few more favourable areas, the cultivation of vineyards, orchards, grain fields and oak groves for cork. Although the area was rich in mineral resources, mining did not stimulate the development of other industrial activities. The only industry developed on the island was the chemical industry, begun in the 1950s by state-owned enterprises.

This was the context in 1960 when a group of private companies, named Consorzio Costa Smeralda, made large investments to invent the Costa Smeralda. The project involved a large, uninhabited territory – about 45 km along the coast – with extraordinary natural resources but without facilities, that is roads, electricity and water. Karim Aga Khan IV, an Ishmaelite Moslem and Harvard graduate, led the Costa Smeralda operation by investing his own financial and technical capital. The project began in a casual way. After Karim Aga Khan had bought a vast expanse of territory in northern Sardinia, he realized it could never become his second residence because it took him almost a day to reach it. Given the alternatives, to sell or to build, he opted for the second (Panerai). The *consorzio* did not incorporate existing seaside resorts but created them. No cities, no houses, nothing existed on this coast. The Consorzio Costa Smeralda had the resorts, including Porto Cervo, built. It also coordinated all city offices, organized common facilities, directed construction and protected the use of the 'brand' name Costa Smeralda (Scaramuzzi). The *consorzio*, through a public act, the Building Regulations, guaranteed the protection of the landscape, environment and monuments. All construction had to conform to and enhance the natural beauty of the area, and nothing could detract from the panorama or the abundant geological formations. This project had a strong environmental impact on Sardinia's virgin coastal area.

The first hotels opened in 1962–3, and the promotional campaign was begun simultaneously. The Costa Smeralda was promoted as the new destination of elite tourism. 'Costa Smeralda: the closest thing to another world', 'Acquire a piece of the biggest emerald in the world', 'An almost pristine oasis with every comfort' were advertisements that presented Costa Smeralda to the world (Bandinu). Wilderness, exclusivity, proximity to Europe made the Costa Smeralda the meeting place for international high society. Poor accessibility and lack of tourism traditions transformed the island into an exotic and exclusive site where the wealthy could share the myth of 'sun, sand and sea' far from the mass tourism resorts.

In just a few years many jet-setters began to make reservations on the Sardinian coast, and advertisements for it appeared in newspapers throughout the world. The Costa Smeralda was characterized, especially in the beginning, as an enclave, a territorial oasis. Even the labour was mostly imported because of a lack of adequately skilled workers on the island. Nevertheless, contrary to the initial fears of many locals, the project represented an important breakthrough in Sardinia's tourism history. In fact, an economist's study from the 1980s (Camagni, 'L'impatto') on the economic impact of the Consorzio Costa Smeralda's investments between 1963 and 1980 gave surprising results. The income multiplier for tourism was higher than that of the chemical industry[5], although it was still low. This was probably due to the area's scant industrialization, which made it necessary to import most of the products and services consumed by tourists.

The Costa Smeralda project, however, has had three notable successes. It functioned as an ice-breaker in a region with few tourism traditions and stimulated development in other areas of the island. It also furnished a positive model for local businesses by providing an example of effective management and by introducing professionalism. Third, 'it showed evidence of the necessity to adopt, at least in the early phases of tourism development, integrated projects, which require remarkable financial resources but make it possible to start with a strong [tourism] demand and to provide the necessary infrastructure' (Camagni, 'L'impatto', 399). Only the huge financial and promotional commitment and perhaps the publicity promoting the region to international high society allowed the *consorzio* to create a real bathing myth from nothing. It is worth noting that other small tourism projects in the 1960s and 1970s were completed in various parts of Sardinia, but only the Costa Smeralda produced an image for the entire island. One of the strong points in the project's success was clearly the extraordinary beauty of the coastline, but it was extraordinarily beautiful before the *consorzio*, though few had vacationed there then.

In conclusion, the Costa Smeralda project, operating in a region lacking any type of tourism investment, generated business from the outside (e.g., publicity at international levels, new professionalism, a network of infrastructures), and led to the spread of tourism – no longer of the elite but of the masses – over the rest of the island, as is revealed by data (*Statistiche sul turismo*, 1999). The development of mass tourism has created new challenges, foremost the protection of Sardinia's natural beauty, its most precious asset.

Patrizia Battilani

Concluding Comments on the Different Courses of Tourism Growth

The comparison between the Emilia Romagna and Sardinia tourism models permits the following general observations. First, not all coastal cities follow the same pattern of tourism development and growth. The Italian experience in particular presents at least two possible paths. One path of development progresses more or less slowly and is based on endogenous business capacity and financial resources. It also requires the presence of a community with shared rules and values, all of which are affirmed in the creation of numerous associations. As Becattini pointed out in 1987:

> The most important trait of the local community is its relatively homogeneous system of values and views, which is an expression of a work and activity ethic (this means that all must search incessantly for the type of activity that best fits their aspirations or abilities), of family, of reciprocity and of change . . . Parallel to this system, a system of institutions and rules must develop in such a way as to spread the values throughout the district. (Becattini, *Mercato* 39)

In this case the accumulation of many small and medium-sized investments primes the development of tourism services and attracts customers from a variety of social classes. Another path is based on external finances and professionals. In this second case it is necessary both to start with a very large investment and to promote an effective image of a given locale.

Clearly, the social and economic impact of these two developmental models is profoundly different. In the case of Rimini, all parts of society have participated in the development of tourism, which has always been considered a source of wealth. Studying newspapers from the late 1800s reveals that the only concern about vacation trends was the fear that they could cause a certain relaxation of morals. 'At the bathing-huts on the beaches, which are only for women, men and soldiers come and go. It is shameful; something should be done . . . All should know that public decorum is a part of people's dignity . . . at this rate only loose women and the men worthy of them will go to the sea' (*Italia* 6–7 and 14–15 July 1883).

In Sardinia, it was much more difficult for the locals to accept the cumbersome presence of a tourist industry presented as a foreign body. Also difficult, in the initial phases, was the fact that very little of the added value produced in Costa Smeralda remained on the island, since the invested capital and part of the labour came from abroad. 'Away with Aga Khan and all the imperial bastards' (Ruju 205), was a slogan that tourists saw for years written on the plaza of a famous locality near Sassari. It represented the sentiments of a good part of the population.

The economic impact of tourism on Rimini and the Costa Smeralda was also very different. The great social and economic vitality at Rimini proved incompatible with elite tourism but permitted the creation of a true leisure district, with numerous businesses offering ample and diversified entertainment. In addition, tourism developed ties to other economic activities. All of this results in a very high economic impact. It has taken a long time for Sardinia to develop its own business capability, be it in tourism or in manufacturing. The lack of opportunities to spend money and the absence of industry have produced quite a low tourism income multiplier, and only in recent years has the region enjoyed a major economic upswing.

Costa Smeralda differs entirely from Rimini in yet another aspect: physical geography. In Rimini the seaside was an extension of the urban landscape, and those living in the city had easy access to it. As a local historian pointed out some years ago, 'the identity of that large, ever-growing linear city behind the beach was based on the idea of accessibility' (Farina 152). Nothing could have stopped the middle and working classes, or local entrepreneurs, from progressively conquering the beach. Therefore, tourism soon became an economic opportunity to seize. Conversely, Costa Smeralda was an uninhabited and inaccessible area that built its identity on the idea of exclusiveness. Those living in this part of Sardinia ignored the seaside as a place of leisure and as an economic opportunity. The sea functioned only as the Sardinian border. No wonder the development of tourism had to depend on the arrival of foreign investments and professionals.

In conclusion, different perceptions of water and seaside affect the social and economic impact of tourism as well as the model of tourism growth.

Notes

1. In the 1920s and 1930s the journals report death by drowning of a Ravenna shoesmith (July 1823), a Rimini printer (July 1826), a handcarver (July 1830), three elderly men (July 1836), a noble (July 1836), a soldier (August 1831), a police official (July 1830) (*Storia di Rimini* VI:11).

2. In 1844 a society of horserace lovers and a society that organized shooting contests were founded.

3. 62 papers appeared between 1860 and 1900 (20 for tourism), 101 between 1900 and 1918 (21 for tourism.)

4. *Fiabilandia* (fairytale-land) was the first amusement park in 1969. The following year *Italia in miniatura* was inaugurated. It was created by a small entrepreneur, Ivo Rambaldi, who invested the whole family's estate in it. In 1993, after his death, his sons took the lead. In 1996 *Italia in miniatura* registered 600,000 visitors; its revenues reached 13 billion lire. In 1992 *Mirabilianda* (wonderland) opened and registered 830,000 visitors in 1993. Although it is located near Ravenna, it belongs to the Rimini leisure district.

5. The results of such research gave rise to heated debate; see Cecaro 'Investimenti commento' and 'Investimenti replica'.

16

Vacationing on France's Côte d'Azur, 1950–2000

André Rauch

Introduction

Vacations have been leading the French masses towards the sea. The number of holidaymakers staying at the coast has increased considerably in the last half century, and they have sought out the Mediterranean shores more than any others. Inspired by the landscapes of Florida, the Côte d'Azur has attracted an increasing number of visitors each year.[1] What kinds of leisure practices have been attracting the French to the Côte? In order to respond to this question, it is fitting first to look at French vacation destinations as a whole and next to analyse key developments linked to the journey to the coast and the sun. At the end of the vacation route lie the beach, bathing, partying and sociability. Each of these themes is of importance to anyone seeking to describe and interpret the vacationing practices of French society.

As I have described in *Vacances en France*, the end of the twentieth century was marked by established vacation styles, and yet the emergence of new practices is being borne by new generations of vacationers (Rauch 227–50). These practices are often affected by American consumer culture, its influence ever so present among France's youth. In addition, French vacation tastes are changing: family budgets, market offers and the evolution of living conditions are bringing about profound transformations in concepts and practices. In short, this essay aims to investigate the many facets of one type of leisure, one that is typically French in the sense that, for the French, spending summer vacation on the Côte is always desirable, no matter how many times they have been there before.[2] It also seeks to inscribe this type of leisure in time: in the collective time of the second half of the twentieth century as well as in the duration of each individual's vacation. Finally, it treats the relationship that the French, in accordance with each individual's age or sociocultural origin, maintain with pleasure on the Côte.

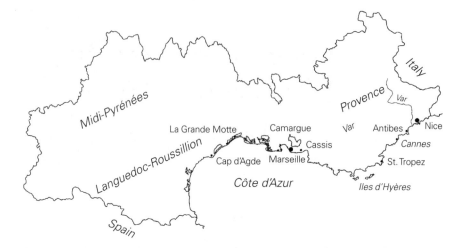

Figure 16.1   Map of Côte d'Azur, created by Graphic Arts Service, University of Oregon, Eugene

Freeway to the Mediterranean, Paradise of the French

Surveys and statistics appearing in the press since the beginning of the 1990s provide a general framework for the vacationing habits of the French. First of all, of the two-thirds of the population that goes somewhere, 85 per cent vacation between 1 July and 30 August (30 per cent of these departures take place in the month of August), a percentage almost unique in Europe. Second, in 1993 almost 80 per cent of French vacationers remained in France, attracted by the wealth of tourist opportunities in their own country, by the variety of their country's heritage and by possibilities to indulge in their refined language and delicate palate. In 2000 this percentage was about the same. Third, more than 50 per cent of holidays are spent at the shore: sea, sun and beach remain the most common destinations for the French, and refusing to spend some days there each year approaches sacrilegious contempt (Rauch 279–87). This has not always been the case; until the early 1970s the countryside was the destination of choice (Bodier/Crenner 403).

While the holidays of the French masses are changing destinations and mentalities, they are often repeating inherited savoir-faire. Visiting places that have borne the dreams of past generations or those of one's parents is a must, that is 'to do' the Côte d'Azur: the English Promenade at Nice, the port of Saint Tropez in Var, the coves of Cassis near Marseille, etc. Crowds, traffic jams, postcards, photo-souvenirs have entered into vacation rituals. And waves of holidaymakers suggest metaphors of invasion. As J. D. Urbain emphasizes, describing holidaymakers with words like 'hordes' (understood to mean barbarians), 'flocks' (in other words, sheep), 'packs' (indisputably gregarious) suggests the 'decline' at the base of modern leisure society (Urbain, *L'idiot* 39, 108). Holidays also reveal a contra-diction: 'my holiday' falls under legitimate right; holidays of 'others' resemble colonization. Travelling some hundred kilometres by car transforms a 'freed' employee into an invading tourist: departing makes him beam; arriving turns him into a devastating force.

In the meantime, the vacation route to the sun has been enhanced. Beginning in 1950, after a period of economic stagnation, special funding for highway investment allowed the French to develop a network of freeways. Since then, the summertime flow of tourists has required the use of main highways over that of rail. From 1960 to 1975, during the years of great expansion, the vacation route became either a freeway or a three-lane highway, i.e. a major road that responded to the imperatives of traffic flow and speed. Maintaining traffic flow became the indispensable complement to speed and safety, although, unlike train schedules, it guaranteed less the time of departure than the punctuality of the time of arrival. According to the aero-spatial image of J. Viard, the freeway exit and the entrance onto secondary roads lead, by successive stages, to a 're-entry into the social atmosphere' (Viard 228–9). And on the journey's horizon, outlines of the sea and its landscape are visible.

Crowds on the Côte d'Azur's Beaches

In 1964 one vacationer in three, on average, stayed at the sea (the Mediterranean, the Atlantic or the Channel) in a variety of lodgings. Accommodations with relatives and friends constituted one quarter of the stays, while those in furnished rentals (24 per cent) and in a tent or a camper (23 per cent) were about the same; the rest of the summer visitors were divided equally among hotels, secondary residences and summer camps. The French consider the shores along the Mediter-ranean the most desirable vacation spots. In 1993 the Var province on the Côte d'Azur advertised 40 million nights over the course of the summer, ranking it above the 28 million in the Charente Maritime and the more than 20 million each in the Hérault, the Vendée and the Morbihan on the French Atlantic Ocean ('Perception'). The Côte d'Azur has become a vacation paradise for lovers of sun, beach and excitement, and for all those who take pleasure in overcrowding. The eccentricities of Saint-Tropez, for example, attract hordes of bathers in string bikinis onto the beaches of Pampelonne just as much as they attract the 'faune interlope' (intruding crowds) to the Papagayo, 'the kitschy nightclub of sensational nights', located on the wharf at Épi. There on the Côte generations of high-school and university students and office workers have strolled along the harbour between Vachon and Sénéquier and let their imaginations run free. While Édith Piaf and Jacques Pills, starting in 1952, spent their vacations in Cannes, where Georges Guétary owned a villa, admirers of the new movie stars, literary celebrities and

225

pop stars waited for the appearance of Brigitte Bardot, Roger Vadim and Françoise Sagan at Saint Trop'. When Dalida strolled along the harbour or François Périer gave autographs while lingering for the evening, the crowds went wild. They bowed down to the myth surrounding these idols of leisure, even if they all spurned the idea of yielding to social conventions in other aspects of their life.

Holidaymakers on the Côte d'Azur were becoming more active in the 1960s with different groups selecting different leisure practices. For example, water sports and hiking were more widespread among campers than among villa occupants. The Languedoc-Roussillon shore came into vogue. In the early 1960s developers of this part of the Mediterranean coast aimed at extending it by 135 kilometres. By the authority of the Ministry of Tourism seven new bathing sites were constructed, designed according to the new needs of vacationers: at La Grand-Motte, the giant buildings of the 'Acapulco', 'The Sea Anemone', 'The Fiji', 'The Rose of the Sands' and the 'Gardens of Ulysses' extended beyond a yachting and sailing harbour (Rauch 147–52).

As Urbain has shown, French families prefer a beach that is attractive for children: sand, play and nudity are signs of a return to nature; social conventions and constraints are put in parentheses, that is set aside. Furthermore, the presence of a large crowd does not necessarily undermine a vacation's success. Campers rarely complain about overcrowding. In fact, Urbain reveals that the combination of sun, sea, sand and crowds is most often agreeable to holidaymakers from the bottom of the social scale; overcrowding is, on the other hand, less appreciated by the well-to-do classes, for whom the taste for solitude is considered a sign of distinction, particularly if they dread mixing with 'people who are not from the same milieu' (Urbain, *plage* 259–60). Indeed, what is essential to the great crowds on the beach is the chattering, the games of exchanging glances with people one meets for the first time and opportunities for seduction. Parading the body, no longer seeking benefits from the sunshine but gratifications in it, goes along with the pastime of being able to contemplate the slow evolution of the colour of one's skin and to evaluate its nuances and effects on the people nearby (Urbain, *plage* 228–9). Reading also plays a contradictory role: on the crowded beach, holidaymakers read summer novels, which create paradoxically the fantasy of leaving the crowds and the very place where, the rest of the year, the reader has dreamed of being. But being on holiday is not enough; a holidaymaker has to do something. How have the French steered themselves to fill their leisure time at the seaside with activities?

Bathing and Water Sports at the Côte d'Azur

Between the two World Wars (1918–39) summer camps on the coast inaugurated new physical activities. One was bathing, which was something completely new for a number of child campers. Its leisure value drew as much from its aura of glory, associated with the temerity of throwing oneself in the water, as it did from notions of body hygiene. The Board of Directors of Summer Camps published a small brochure in 1926 with the following rules: 'Ask parents' permission to go swimming. Take care not to eat immediately beforehand. One should neither push nor fight in the water; both are dangerous. All should be ready to obey at the slightest signal from the supervisors. One single disobedience on this point will result in the complete loss of the delinquent's sea-bathing privileges' ('Directoire'). The principle of fasting three hours or more before bathing gave it a hygienic quality; prohibiting pushing and shoving brought bathing into the sphere of ceremony and removed it from ordinary play; the necessity of getting dressed promptly after leaving the water prolonged the suspense of returning to ordinary play; and prohibiting those leaving the water from resting reflected the camp's imperative, which was that a child should never rest except when asleep. The bathing period was short, most often less than a dozen minutes, after which the children dried themselves carefully, especially their ears and feet. Once dressed again, they could walk or run. It was the moment when the afternoon snack was at its best, and bathing justified large 'four-o'clock' sandwiches. During a congress in 1935, Father Rochaix from Lyon gave his opinion on the question of swimming. He recommended paying attention to subtle signs: 'Shivering, due to an organism's reaction to contact with water, is inevitable; it is advisable to reduce it as much as possible by plunging into the sea or river. Further shivering indicates danger. As soon as it occurs, it is necessary to leave the water immediately, for it signifies that the body's reactional forces are exhausted' (Rey-Herme 125, 129). In short, one was not supposed to think only about swimming; one had to pay attention to the body.

After 1950 new aquatic sports aimed at youth accompanied the development of mass tourism in France. In contrast to the careful regimen of swimming and rest, these initiatives in water sports or in outdoor leisure activities demanded serious training and costly equipment. Yachting marinas on the Atlantic Ocean, on the Isle of Giens, or at Niolon near Marseille on the Mediterranean, such as the centre 'Virginie Heriot', near Saint-Jean-de-Luz on the Atlantic Ocean, organized introductory and advanced-level yachting courses. At the Nautical Centre of Glénans, created by former members of the Resistance, boating and sailing classes began in 1947 under the instigation of Philippe Viannay. Trainees were housed in American tents borrowed from the Air Force. Dishes and blankets were supplied by the General Transatlantic Company. Equipped with large motorboats, sailing boats, like Argonauts, Canetons, Caravels and Vauriens, its staff welcomed the trainees for 15 days (Rauch 186–7).

Nautical and outdoor marinas as well as centres in the mountains were managed by the Ministry for Youth and Sports and well-known technical organizations: Union Nationale des Centres de Montagne UNCM, the French Nautical Union

(UNF) – which merged in 1965 to form the National Union of Centres for Outdoor Sports (UCPA), UFOLEP, a section of the League of Education, etc. A dynamic of introductory and advanced-level athletics drove the management of mountain retreats and centres, marinas, and centres for leisure (Rauch 187). Details matter little; the widespread change in views concerning holidays, from an emphasis on rest to one on activity, is of the greatest importance. The focus on youth and its emblematic function in holiday sports have reversed traditional representations and practices in seaside leisure activities. Previously, staying at Hyères or Nice, a holidaymaker used to take time to admire the thousand-year-old landscapes or infinite horizons. Now, to pass time, the holidaymaker sails, dives and plays tennis. To go on a vacation on the Côte d'Azur is to feel young again. Certain enterprises more than others have played an active role in the advent of practices that have come to make up 'the life of vacations'.

The Holiday on the Côte d'Azur

Camping has made the Mediterranean coast accessible to more French holiday-makers because of the growing number and variety of campsites. Diverse organizations and private groups, for example, the Ligue de l'Enseignement, Groupement du Camping Universitaire (GCU), etc., have managed them (see Sirost). Furthermore, modern equipment has made camping more comfortable. Since the late 1950s tents have changed in style and appearance: campers can now stand up in them, and a canopy separates eating area from sleeping quarters. Certain models have separate sections for parents and children, both sections equipped with little windows. Former scouts or members of youth clubs enjoy the contact with nature and no longer fear it causes rheumatism, as generations before them had feared. The average age of campers has risen, and customs from the 'pioneer' era of camping have changed (see Goguel). Camping at the same campsite each year has offered groups of children and teenagers the opportunity to reunite; it has also given campers of the most modest means the feeling of being part of a familiar social milieu. At the more fashionable campsites, residents soon claimed their territory by arranging flowerbeds around their tents; the most original campers planted garden gnomes. In the 1970s television antennas started sticking out at campsites. On special occasions, people assembled at a nearby bar or at the tents of those people who had a television set. While sipping a drink with the neighbours, for example, people watched the first step on the moon, 21 July 1969. When Neil Armstrong stuck one foot in the lunar dust, there was great silence around the television set. Turning towards the spectators, from the distance of the moon, he pronounced the historic words, which were immediately translated into French, 'That's one small step for a man, one giant leap for mankind', and the campsite burst into applause. Campers have also reunited each summer for the stages of the Tour de France, the reunion resembling a patriotic ceremony. Yet, owing to a very French prejudice, the French elite regard all campers as either labourers on 'paid leave' or impoverished students, since they are the most represented groups on French campsites. In contrast, the English, for whom camping is more traditional, and the Germans or the Dutch, who are sometimes former members of youth movements, camp for many other reasons than the low costs. Their campers and tents stand next to their expensive, powerful cars. Camping for them does not exclude prestige or ease, but it turns its back on everyday comforts (Simonnot 198).

For those who can afford it, certain private enterprises sell the 'Vacation-by-the-sea product'. During the 'The Thirty Glorious Years' (1945–75) the innovation of pre-packaged tourism resulted from several mutations. Some tour operators, like Horizon Holidays in England, Touropa in the Federal Republic of Germany, Sterling Airways in Denmark, Hotelplan in Switzerland, Simon Spies in Sweden and Sunair in Belgium promoted pre-packaged tourism. At the same time, the hotel industry opened chains based on the American model: Intercontinental appeared in 1945, Holiday Inn in 1954, etc. The principle French chains were established afterwards: Sofitel in 1962, PLM in 1966, Novotel in 1967, Frantel in 1968, Meridien in 1970, Jacques Borel in 1971. Some tourist enterprises merged or created consortia: Airtour in France starting in 1958, TUI in the Federal Republic of Germany starting the same year; mergers were completed in 1967 and 1972. While the large German tour operators, Neckermann and Reisen, were created in 1964, the British operators, Thomson Holidays (1965), GUT and ITS (International Charter Tour) have been selling package tours to the Côte d'Azur since 1969, e. g., in 1969 Vacances 2000, Touropa France, Cosmovel ou Jet-Tours; in 1970, Planète; in 1972, Euro 7; and in 1973, Voyages-Conseil (cf. Cazes/Lanquar/ Raynouard). Vacation clubs were the most recent to emerge: Butlin in the United Kingdom, Club Mediterranean in France and, a little later, the European Tourism Club, before merging with Club Mediterranean.

Their product having been created for commercial purposes, such clubs have exploited the principle of the holiday village while subjecting it to the laws of the leisure market. It assures their clients of a successful seaside holiday, clients who want the guarantee that there will be no frustrating glitches or setbacks during their stay or who refuse being deprived of any service. Without a doubt, clubs have transformed the tourist market. They incorporate services in an all-inclusive season ticket: hotel industry, catering, business, organized beach activities, shows and other entertainment. Clubs are a commercial monopoly at heart. In short, in an anarchic service market, they introduce the principle of the finished product, the kind of product sought by a number of middle-class managers in French society.

The Touring-Vacations section of TCF, Vacations 2000, the Olympic Club, the Vacation Club, the Relais du Soleil, Vacations Today, Club Mediterranean (which absorbed See and Know in 1966, then the European Tourism Club [CET] in 1970) figured among the service pioneers (Laurent 55). Advertising the 'Magic Villages', with which Club Mediterranean merged in 1956, seemed the appropriate move.[3] Services offered in holiday packages diversified the product and aroused in the holidaymaker the desire to obtain 'everything' for one lump sum. Yet, clients wanted more than not having to keep track of expenses; they also wanted to feel they had made the right choice. As Henri Raymond observes, at 'Club Mediterranean . . . no one explains why he takes a vacation, not even a vacation to Italy, but always how, after making meticulous comparisons, he chose "Club Med", or even more precisely, Palinuro' (Raymond 1037). But for the French, the Club Mediterranean remains the role model and, without doubt, has done the most to revive the imaginary in holidaymaking. The choice of this name is significant in and of itself, for it has made the experience of holidaymaking on the Côte d'Azur into a product (Ehrenberg, 'Club' 126).

The Côte d'Azur as Product: Life at the Club

Club Mediterranean villages are paradises nestled at the edge of the sea, under the sunny climate of the Mediterranean, but most are outside France (in Southern Italy, Sardinia, Sicily, Corfu, etc.). The club provides equipment, planning and operation without necessarily owning the village site. Generally, a local partner furnishes the necessary capital for construction. This plan reduces investment burdens and permits the use of local labour at lower wages. In fact, the use of native workers has become a condition for the club to set up business. The success of this formula has led to its expansion. In 1965, Club Mediterranean owned 26 villages, including 16 summer villages, only two of which were in France. In 1967, it had 31 villages. Members were recruited from large population areas. The Parisian region alone furnished close to three-quarters of the French summer holidaymakers at Club Mediterranean in 1966, more than half of whom were white-collar workers and 35 per cent were in the learned professions. For their holiday, both of these were offered what amounts to a luxury in bourgeois society, a luxury of which they felt deprived the rest of the year.[4]

The Club's vacationers did something new: breaking from the traditional options of cultural tourism or holidays devoted only to rest or entertainment, they experienced a different adventure. For instance, the diet of abundance that the copious breakfasts and self-serve buffets symbolized, where each person chose whatever, or as much as, she desired, had nothing to do with anything cultural. The pleasure of the palate surpassed that of the eye; abundance symbolized at the same time the better life and permissiveness. It was not unusual to see sexual freedom exhibited during evenings spent on the dance floor, a freedom that emphasized liberation from mundane routine and that cultivated a simple hedonism. Coming to the Club meant finding a home for one's longings and opening its doors to one's most hidden desires. The familiarity between the Gracious Member (GM) and the Gracious Organizer (GO) played out an original type of human relations. Ideologies of freedom, of equality and of the return to spontaneity mingled. In fact, at the end of the 1950s, while the French were still thinking of national reconstruction, the Club's novelty arose from a form of human relations that broke away as equally from the constraints of everyday life as from the muffled anonymity of the hotel. The Club's image of Tahiti symbolized the sweetness of living on vacation. At a place where men and women never wore more than bathing trunks or a sarong, the Club's ambience wiped the slate clean of hierarchies. Symbols of proximity to nature and to humankind prevailed.

Although the Club's image is that of summer holidaymaking on the French Côte, the Club as a business enterprise has never been limited to these beaches nor to summer tourism. Today, its villages can be found in the mountains as well as on the coasts of Italy, Greece, Turkey, Tunisia, etc and reach as far as the shores of the Atlantic and Indian Oceans. At all these sites the Club has introduced its ideology of consumption and relaxation. In this sense, in the eyes of the French, the Club Med became a beacon of a new sociability, *à la française*, as it were. Thus, French representations have idealized the Mediterranean as the imaginary Eden of summer leisure.

Straw hats and bungalows in the villages were bound neither to the rustic nature of camping nor to the affected luxury of the hotel. They created the stage setting of a production whose essential element resulted from simple equivalencies: relaxation of body and manners, freeing up of time and activities, liberation from urgent matters and schedules, all according to the cliché: 'I never know what time it is, nor what day it is'. In brief, real living mixed the opulence of consumption with the simplicity of the untamed. Upon depositing one's money and personal effects at the reception, Gracious Members stopped calculating their expenses in order to enter an imaginary world of 'natural' generosity. According to Alain Ehrenberg, 'at the Club, a strange mixture of chateau life and untamed life, members leave the era of savings and scarcity to enter one of consumption and abundance' (Ehrenberg, 'Club' 126). The Club can be summed up in the following rhetoric: it made the French discover an existence that daily life had stolen from them. In opposing conformity they experienced connections to the natural that industrial society, work hierarchy and urbanization had weakened and destroyed. The promise of sun symbolized a vital reaction against the eleven months of grey weather not spent on holiday and inverted the work-leisure relationship. People began to work eleven months of the year to go on holiday, while before they went to the sea once their work was done. More than ever, holidays on the Côte illustrated new leisure values: the affluence of consumption after the years of scarcity and restriction marking the post-war period. Only after the recession of 1974–75 did the French begin to budget and assess the financial value of the 'leisure product'.

The question is: how much adventure could the Club offer, considering the concentration of people in the holiday village? Although the Club placed at public disposal leisure activities that would otherwise be expensive, it offered above all a lifestyle, a relaxation. Scuba diving, underwater fishing or exploration, water-skiing and sailing incontestably livened up the members' holiday activities. They set up the relational context of seduction. These adventures opened to all a way to meet others; the 'true' encounter, that which culminated at the Club, made people imagine they had found their soul mate (in 1966 the average age at the clubs was less than that of French holidaymakers in general; single men were numerous, women in the majority) (Ehrenberg, 'Rapport'). The Club invited one to discover individual differences. It sold an aptitude to make personal ties to individuals, to the milieu of the living and to all of nature. Its advertising did not cultivate nostalgia for a pre-industrial society, nor a romantic return to the source of life. The break from the framework of professional life was supposed to make one forget the image one had of oneself and to consider tacky the need to legitimate one's social position. In brief, it was an existence so different that it isolated its members and evolved outside of time. Yet, this holiday product was situated in the imaginary space of the Club Med's own version of the French Mediterranean, no matter the village's actual location. The question arises as to the compatibility of the image of holidaymaking on the Côte with the political reality in the countries where the Club has villages. This inspired the remark in the left-leaning weekly magazine *Nouvel Observateur*, 'At the Club, one never worries. The cannons may sound in Greece, in Turkey, in Israel, and the Gracious Members do not hear them; the "sound system" and the music cover up everything' (Sery 46). In short, a bad conscience does not a good vacation make . . . Nevertheless, the young generations have unquestionably renewed these old 'vacation dreams'. More Americanized than their elders, young French people have introduced new leisure practices and adopted other rhythms.

Youth Culture on the New Côte d'Azur

At the beginning of the twenty-first century devotees of tanning on the beach know that it is no longer a place of seduction: 'sea, sex and sun are over with' (Levisalles V). In fact, since co-education began in the early 1960s, influenced by US educat-ional doctrines, adolescent boys no longer wait to go to the beach to meet girls (Winock). The liberalization of morals has also greatly modified the rituals of initiating a date. At present, the modus operandi on an ordinary afternoon is lounging on the beach, observing one's tan, applying suntan lotion, picking off grains of sand, exposing both sides harmoniously to the sun, removing one's sunglasses, going swimming, picking up one's towel while smoothing one's hair, holding in the stomach to look taller and thinner. Everything revolves around appearance, but to each his own body: narcissism rules here, and the presence of the other is only secondary.

In France, Hoyle Schweitzer became a hero for introducing the sailboard. At the end of the 1970s devotees of sea and sun on the Côte d'Azur changed their look: sailboard on shoulder, boys and girls in water socks and wetsuits introduced themselves on the beach. Beyond the equipment, one played with appearances: flowered Bermuda shorts and T-shirts printed front and back in colours with the English words 'Fun', 'California' or 'Don't worry' served as rallying points; surfers personalized the board by taping to it the slogan: 'we find the perfect wave'.[5] A generation of surfers spent the summer with their hands clutching at the 'wishbone', making a 'windshield wiper' along the beach where the omnipresent walking-vendor was always chanting: 'Beignets! Chouchous and lemon ice make the girls pretty and the boys nice!' Riveted to their boards, those 'hooked' on surfing imported, on the other hand, a new culture and used a more coded language: words like 'channels', 'pintails', 'footstraps' made them complicit in this culture. (In a few years they abandoned these dull boards to new owners and mounted the 'ultra-short' and 'super-light' boards to shoot two metres above the water.) Instead of returning to the beach under the nose of the bathers, they made figures in the waves, 'donkey kicks', which are a kind of kick above the water. These groups of friends had their own spot, an edge of beach where 2CVs (Citroën deux chevaux) with torn convertible tops and corroded R4s (Renault 4) were parked. A blazing blast of air rose up at the first 'swell', and they started doing 'jibes' and 'bottom turns'; as soon as the wind fell and the sea calmed into small waves, they gathered their equipment. On this isolated slice of shore, the girls tanned themselves and showed off their slim bodies. They moulded themselves into high-cut bathing suits that outlined their androgynous hips. In short, vacations with a board at the feet landed on the French coasts and seduced the youth (Petitjean 44).

In the late 1990s another act in the same drama played out on the Côte d'Azur's 'grand beaches': for their summer jobs, some youths distributed flyers inviting all those dozing under beach umbrellas to come and check out the DJ at a neighbouring discotheque. Days spent in the sun made nightlife essential. Young holidaymakers had a rhythm: beach in the afternoon, bars in the evening, nightclub starting at 1:00 a.m., going to sleep around 7:00–8:00 a.m. For the wealthiest, the evening mode of dress was streetwear sport or extravagant nightclub clothes. Their fashion also consisted of washed-out, fisherman-style pants and 'dockside'-style shoes. The American Teva-style sandal was said to be an innovation. Young girls preferred a Jane Birkin wicker handbag with a crocheted dress. As for sunglasses, there were two influences: little round ones, Katmandu type, John Lennon style; the other curiosity, Yoko Ono goggles, Porsche style. A must: after ear- or nose-piercing; the navel was adorned with a precious stone ('L'Eté' 6–20). In 1996 the 'power-drink' was recommended as the evening drink; one drank it like a soda, but it contained caffeine, guaraná, ginseng, vitamins, etc. It was the ultra-energy drink for those who wanted to party hard. One used to imagine that holidays of youth exposed a personality separate from social roles; now they dramatized an aesthetic of self in well-coded customs.

Girls wore platform shoes and devilishly tight-fitting pants; boys, bandanas around the head, arrived on motorbikes, leather vests clinging to their skin. There were whispers that the visitors smoked hash as others drank the aperitif *pastis* (aniseed). Ice-cream-cone eaters were not welcomed there! When leaving the last nightclub, the group of nocturnals went for breakfast at an after-hours bar on the beach. Radio music overwhelmed them. Each day of the summer, posters advertised tours of featured stars. The introduction of the lambada dance in July 1989 marked the culminating point of this Americanization of youth leisure. The French television network TF1 and *Orangina* (the French answer to Coca-Cola) signed an agreement to produce a clip that the channel pledged to air 250 times: men and women Creole dancers moved their hips side-by-side to the furious rhythm of South-American music. The American broadcasting corporation CBS distributed a record, a cassette and a compact disc of the music. Thirty-five thousand copies were sold on 12 July, the same day as the product was advertised, and the French radio station NRJ made it a summer smash hit. The whole season long, 'popular discos' on the Côte d'Azur distributed these throbbing tunes. Their originality was that they recreated contact between dance partners, whereas before the regulars used to dance without a fixed partner. Thus, the mastery of radio and television communication, a shrewd assembly of powerful producers, an advertising campaign based on sensual images, in short, a mode negotiated according to the principle of big business began to orchestrate summer fads. However, French holidaymakers now have other concerns than just having fun and chasing trends on the Côte d'Azur.

The Downside of Popularity: Fragile Vacations, Aesthetic Sensitivity

An ecological sensitivity has been growing among French holidaymakers since the mid-1970s. Waterfronts have become in turn the target of a criticism exploding against anything that blocks the ocean view, spoils the landscape or grates on the eyes. At Saint-Jean-de-Mont on the Atlantic Ocean, at Cap-d'Agde on the Mediterranean, concrete skeletons bordering the beach today appear decrepit. During the real estate explosion, at the beginning of the Fifth Republic (1958), promoters had sold property to households of modest incomes. According to the director of the French Agency for the Study and Development of Tourism (AFIT), these investments helped to finance the tourist industry. In the meantime, the quality of accommodations has fallen below acceptable norms. Half the buildings need to be renovated, but the owners, many of whom are past their 60s, have grown sluggish. The picture is similar elsewhere: also built during the 1960s, the grand seaside resorts of Languedoc-Roussillon on the Mediterranean are deteriorating. Without further delay, Cap-d'Agde created a plan in 1996 to renovate the buildings (Garin 8). But, besides the structures themselves, the aesthetics of the area have degraded, and the environment has become denatured.

The media have stigmatized all pollution in these areas and the surrounding nature. As a result, preventative politics have been taking the lead in managing the tourist flow. In May 1997 the European Commission published its report on 'the quality of the waters at bathing spots': the European Union normalized the sanitary compliance of the beaches. New physico-chemical criteria readily included oils, suds and phenol as pollutants. In the same year, 93.5 per cent of French beaches were 'in compliance with the microbiological thresholds' of the European standards; in June 2000, the French office of the Foundation for Environmental Education in Europe (FEEE) published a list of districts boasting the 'pavillon bleu' (blue flag), the European environmental label. According to questionnaires, holidaymakers use this qualifier as a criterion: 42 per cent of the French obtain information about it when choosing their holiday location and 65 per cent when choosing their swimming area (Zappi 11). A sign of the times: the sinking of the Erika, which ruined France's Atlantic beaches for the 2000 season and threatened subsequent ones, aroused public opinion. Passions and sensitivities have been reversed: nature – this 'supernatural' of contemporary civilization, whose fury people feared not so long ago – seems fragile today. Protecting nature has become more urgent than protecting oneself from it. French holidaymakers are more concerned with the environment and their physical well-being than they are with a particular holiday destination.

New crusaders are allying themselves against anything that might harm the Mediterranean landscapes grounding national identity: in order to protect exceptional areas, they want to make them into sanctuaries. Twenty kilometres of coves and cliffs form a natural monument from Callelongue, the extreme point of Marseillaise urbanization, to Cassis. Herbaria of *Posidonia* carpet the sea; on land, paths cross fields where salt tolerant plants grow (Leroux 13). Certain associations are demanding that the place be made into a national park, while in Marseille, the city administration wishes to apply the practices of a public-interest group to this stretch of natural sanctuary. Indeed, each region has inherited a patrimony. The propaganda proselytizes its 'Bible': characterized as evil genies of deterioration, the mass of visitors appears like a modern plague (Cadoret). However, this characterization is self-contradictory; for in order to protect, it is necessary to prohibit, that is to suppress, and this does not jibe with the notion of holiday.

The holiday paradise on the Côte d'Azur and other seashores has fallen today from myth to demystification; pollution is threatening tourist areas and seashores. The parasitic invasion of the beach and the pollution induce repulsion for swimming, aversion towards ravaging tourism, horror at the urbanization of the sea and the mountains, and repugnance at the savage exploitation of the country-side. Phobia and disgust are the summer news in journalistic and imaginary literature. Between the luxury of bathing in the nineteenth century and the concern for the ecological quality of life today, nature has become the mirror of a country's life or death. Yet, systems of defence have been developed to fight the cancer of construction sites: already in 1975 the Federal Consumers Union (UFC) published a provocative article in the journal *Que Choisir?* on the 'choices to make for this summer's vacation' (June 1975). The UFC ranked public beaches from 1 (satis-factory) to 5 (mortal danger), based on findings of bacterial pollution. It pointed to Marseille and Collioure as well as to Saint-Jean-de-Luz, La Rochelle, Granville, Cherbourg, Arromanches and Trouville. Spectres of the polluted beach, covered with concrete, converged, in the article, with hatred for summer invaders and financial speculation. In order to set up some anti-concrete and anti-pollution defences, the areas have since been classified and the natural reserves inventoried. The Seashore Law of 3 June 1986 prohibits the construction of coastal roads and forbids building on a strip starting 100 metres from the shore. It also subjects urbanization to the consent of the prefectural office.[6] But this plan of action may well have inspired curiosity more than it kept people from vacationing in certain areas.

A certain type of frequentation is also threatening the Mediterranean coast's aesthetic appeal. In areas shared by holidaymakers, young people from the projects in French cities stick out like sore thumbs, and their invasion continues to be incriminating. When they first arrive, they provoke discrimination from merchants, campground proprietors or nightclub owners, all fearing these urban youths might dislodge the 'good' clientele. At campsites, groups of these youths, not having membership in any official organization, are refused entry. Necessity then obliges: the rebels do not make reservations. Most of them arrive squeezed into a car; one of them registers at the reception; the others rejoin him at the base of the campsites; and all celebrate their clandestine deed. Campsites have then set up surveillance: 'Out of fifty-three salaried employees, a dozen are security guards; this is not our idea of vacationing', complains a campground manager (Subtil 6). Mass vacations presuppose a consensus, a condition of sharing space and lifestyles. Setting up insurmountable borders thus goes against a liberal economy and segregates holidaymakers.

Conclusion: Mass Vacationing on the Côte d'Azur.

The Côte d'Azur used to be an area reserved for the privileged. In the last third of the nineteenth century, for example, aristocratic families from England, Russia or Austria met there to enjoy the mild winters. Foreign nobility and the French upper middle class still claim the most beautiful spots. The advent of mass holiday-making since the 1950s is not to be confused, then, with the hope of a single paradise for all. Those who do not really feel comfortable at certain elite holiday spots prefer to blend into the crowds. Being part of the community at an over-crowded campsite gives others a sense of revenge against their ordinary lives while reinforcing feelings of solidarity. However, the invasion onto surrounding beaches provokes disdain among the privileged, who vacationed there before office workers and employees, these beneficiaries of 'paid leave', broke against the shores. 'Ah! To return to the Estaque from the time of the French writer Colette or the painter Camoin!' is a common sentiment of the wealthy traditionalists.[7]

On the one hand, the general atmosphere of French holidaymaking has produced a norm. In other words, regardless of social status, everyone is doing more of the same. For example, the variation among rates of departure for the socio-professional categories fell from 73 points in 1974 to 47 points in 1994 (Bodier/Crenner 405). The annual business shut-down in the month of August, according to labour legislation, reinforces this tendency. On the other hand, the number of holidaymakers can also create confusion, and the Côte d'Azur proves it. Any one holiday spot has to support multiple or seasonal uses; radical differences exist between campers and villa owners, between devotees of underwater diving or windsurfing and those who tan on the beach; yet they have all come to spend their vacation on the Côte d'Azur. The mixing of these different social categories, with their contrasting experiences, has become central to collective memories of holidaying on the Côte.

Paradoxically, contemporary French vacations have also created places that leave nothing to chance: the protected reserve, the vacation club and the freeway corridor witness only tourists, who establish relationships of consumption. In a period of growth, holidaymakers spend money at the Côte d'Azur without keeping track of it, but when a crisis tightens the purse strings, their holidays have less panache. New emblems now valorize the image of youth and the preference for an active holiday style: no longer loafing around but learning to do something new, no longer the leisurely stroll but the excursion are in vogue. In a word, an ideology of personal progress is giving holidaymakers the pretence of achieving self-realization. 'Vacations on the Côte' find their substance in this reconsideration of uses, and this modifies the image of the person. The desire to have a blast, to shock and to arouse the admiration of others is the reason for these escapes from the social orbit. The goal is to make people dream.

(Translated by Susan C. Anderson and Bruce H. Tabb)

Notes

1. Before the First World War, the Côte d'Azur was only a winter vacation spot created by the English, who considered its summer climate too hot. After it, Europeans discovered the summer as a vacation season. Marc Boyer reports that in 1925 some Americans from the 'Lost Generation' founded the resort of Juan les Pins, which reproduced an American model from funds invested in Florida and California's vacation industries. This introduced new vacation trends in France (Boyer 129–30).

2. See, for example, Normand, who reports that the Côte d'Azur is still the top vacation spot in France among the French. The refrain of French singer Charles Trenet's (1913–2001) popular song, 'Nationale 7' (1955) – 'National 7 that goes from Paris to Sète' – which all French can still hum, illustrates the Côte's enduring popularity in the French imagination.

3. In 1950, the magazine *Elle* advertised the 'Magic Villages' in Tirol and Sicily as places frequented by movies stars and other celebrities (Rauch 169). This was at a time when France was emerging from the period of postwar reconstruction, before becoming a consumer society. Leisure advertising was just beginning.

4. For more information on the Club Med, one should consult the important Archives du Club Méditerranée at its headquarters; for understanding and assessing the role of the Club in how the French imagine leisure, see Ehrenberg 'Rapport'; see also Franco as well as Peyre and Raynouard.

5. The English words in quotation marks remain in English in the lingo of young French surfers.

6. This is an administrative authority for the province.

7. For a better idea of how the coast looked before the advent of mass tourism, see, for example, the collection of French paintings of the Côte d'Azur and Provence in the Musée de l'Annonciade in Saint-Tropez.

Bibliography

Aaland, M. *Sweat*, Santa Barbara, CA 1978.

Acerbi, J. *Travels through Sweden, Finland and Lapland, to the North Cape, in the Years 1798 and 1799*, vol I. London 1802.

Agentia Nationala pentru Atragerea Investitiilor. *Invita la colaborare Moldova*, Chishinau 2000.

Alderson, F. *The Island Resorts and Spas of Britain*, London 1973.

Aldinger, H. 'Der erste Stuttgarter Fabrikgarten', *Die Gartenkunst* 51 (1938), pp. 217–18.

Aleichem, S. *Marienbad: A Novel*, A. Shevrin (tr.) London (1911) 1982.

Algemeen Handelsblad (AH), Amsterdam.

Allen, D.E. *The Naturalist in Britain: a Social History*, 2nd edition, Princeton, NJ 1994.

Althaus, J. *The Spas of Europe*, London 1862.

Ambjörnsson, R. *Det skötsamme arbetaren: Idéer och ideal i ett norrländskt sågverkssamhälle, 1880–1930*, Stockholm 1989.

Amsterdam en de Amsterdammers door een Amsterdammer, (Deventer 1875) Amsterdam 1974.

Amsterdamsche Courant (AmsC), Amsterdam.

Anabitarte, B. *Gestión municipal de San Sebastián, 1894–1900*, San Sebastián 1974.

Anabitarte, B. *Gestión municipal de San Sebastián, 1901–1925*, San Sebastián 1975.

Anderson, M. 'Body Culture and the Ascetic Ideal', in M. Anderson, *Kafka's Clothes: Ornament and Aestheticism in the Habsburg Fin-de-Siècle*, Oxford 1992.

Anderson, S. C. and Tabb, B. H. *Water, Culture and Politics in Germany and the American West*, New York 2001.

Annuario statistico italiano, Roma 1955–2000.

Archivo General de Gipuzkoa (AGG), Tolosa.

Archivo Municipal de San Sebastián (AMSS).

Arnhemsche Courant (AC), Arnhem.

Arscott, C. 'Modern Life Subjects in British Painting 1840–60', PhD diss. University of Leeds, 1987.

Arscott. C. '*Ramsgate Sands*, Modern Life, and the Shoring-up of Narrative', in B. Allen (ed.), *Towards a Modern Art World*, London 1995, pp. 157–68.

The Art Journal (1865), Review of Royal Academy exhibition.

Βιομηχανική Επιθεώρηση (Industrial Review), various issues.

Bachvarov, M. 'End of the Model? Tourism in Post-Communist Bulgaria', *Tourism Management*, 18.1 (1997), pp. 43–50.

Bachvarov, M. *Geography of Tourism in Socialist Countries*, Sofia 1975 (Bulgarian).

Baedeker, K. *Greece, Handbook for Travellers*, London 1889.

Baedeker, K. *Southern Germany and Austria, including the Eastern Alps: Handbook for Travellers*, Leipzig 1873.

Balance of Payments of Bulgaria, Bulgarian National Bank 1999.

Balbian Verster, F. *De Amsterdamsche IJsclub, 1864–1914. Gedenkschrift bij het 50-jarig bestaan*, Amsterdam 1915.

Balzani, R. 'La nascita della villeggiatura di massa nella riviera romagnola', *Il Risorgimento* 2 (1993), pp. 155–66.

Bandinu, B. *Costa Smeralda come nasce una favola turistica*, Milano 1980.

Barnhart, R. T. *Gamblers of Yesteryear*, Las Vegas 1983.

Barringer, T. *The Pre-Raphaelites: Reading the Image,* London 1998.

Bausinger, H., Beyrer, K. and Korff, G. (eds), *Reisekultur*, Munich 1991.

Becattini, G. 'Il distretto industriale marshalliano come concetto socio-economico', *Studie informazioni, Quaderni* 34 (1991), pp. 51–66.

Becattini, G. *Mercato e forze locali: Il distretto industriale*, Bologna 1987.

Becquet, P. "Les mauvais bouillons de nos vacances," *Le Nouvel Observateur* 616, 30 Aug 1976, p. 38.

Bendiner, K. *The Art of Ford Madox Brown*, University Park, PA 1998.

Berger, A. *Das Bad in der byzantinischen Zeit*. Munich 1982.

Berger, P. *Die Nervenschwache (Neurasthenie): Ihr Wesen, ihre Ursachen und Behandlung,* Berlin 1910.

Berman, P.G. 'Body and body politic in Edvard Munch's *Bathing Men*', in K. Adler and M. Pointon (eds), *The Body Imaged: The Human Form and Visual Culture since the Renaissance*, New York 1993, pp. 71–83.

Bijlsma, H. *Ien, twa, trije: fuort! Het kortebaanschaatsen in Friesland*, Heereveen 1985.

Bijlsma, H. *Yn streken. Tachtig jaar Bond van ijsclubs in twee eeuwen Friese schaatssport*, Franeker 1999.

Bilz, F. E. *Das Neue Naturheilverfahren: Lehr- und Nachschlagebuch der naturgemäßen Heilweise und Gesundheitspflege*, Leipzig (1896?).

Blackbourn, D. and Eley, G. *The Peculiarities of Germany History*, Oxford 1984.

Bloch, E. 'Schöne Fremde', in *Das Prinzip Hoffnung*, 5 vols. Frankfurt 1985, Vol. 3, pp. 430–5.

Blos, W. *Denkwürdigkeiten eines Sozialdemokraten*, vol. 2, Munich 1919.

Bodier, M. and Crenner, E. 'Partir en vacances', in INSEE (ed.), *Données Sociales 1996: La société française*, Paris 1996, pp. 403–9.

Bogaers, A. *De kermis op de Maas of Rotterdamse ijsvreugd. Ten voordeele van de armen*, Rotterdam 1838.

Böhme, G. and Böhme, H. *Feuer, Wasser, Erde, Luft: Eine Kulturgeschichte der Elemente*, Munich 1996.

Böhme, H. *Kulturgeschichte des Wassers*, Frankfurt a.M. 1990.

Böhme, H. *Natur und Subjekt*, Frankfurt a. M. 1988.

Boissonnas, F. *Le Tourisme en Grèce*, Genève 1930.

Böröcz, J. 'Travel Capitalism: The Structure of Europe and the Advent of the Tourist', *Comparative Studies in Society and History* 34 (1992), pp. 708–41.

Bortas, A. M. *Storskiftet I Dalarna 1803–1894*, Leksand 1992.

Bothe, R. (ed.), *Kurstädte in Deutschland: Zur Geschichte einer Baugattung*, Berlin 1984.

Bourke, John, *The Sea as a Symbol in English Poetry*, Alden and Blackwell (Eton) Ltd. 1954.

Boyer, M. *Le tourisme de l'an 2000*, Lyon 1999.

Brewer, J. and Porter, R. (eds), *Consumption and the World of Goods*, London 1993.

Brewster, Sir D. *Memoirs of the Life, Writings, and Discoveries of Sir Isaac Newton*, 2 vols. London 1855.

Bruchis, M. *The Republic of Moldavia: From the Collapse of the Soviet Empire to the Restoration of the Russian Empire*, L. Treptow (tr.), New York 1996.

Buzinkay, G. *An Illustrated History of Budapest*, Budapest 1998.

Cadoret, A. (ed.), *Protection de la nature: Histoire et idéologie. De la nature à l'environnement*, Paris 1985.

Calvo Sánchez, M. J. *Crecimiento y estructura urbano de San Sebastián*, San Sebastián 1983.

Camagni, R. P. 'L'impatto sull'economia sarda della spesa e dell'investimento turistici in Costa Smeralda', *Quaderni sardi di economia* 4 (1982), pp. 371–403.

Camagni, R. P. 'Investimenti turistici e investimenti industriali in Sardegna: Un controcommento', *Quaderni sardi di economia* 4 (1983), p. 348.

Campbell, C. *The Romantic Ethic and the Spirit of Modern Consumerism*, Oxford 1987.

Cannadine, D. *The Decline and Fall of the British Aristocracy*, London 1990.

Caspar, H. 'Bäderkonzeption für Sport und Freizeit', *Archiv des Badewesens* (1979), pp. 9–10.

Cassou, J. 'Du voyage au tourisme', *Communications* 10 (1967), pp. 25–6.

Castellan, A.L. *Lettres sur la Grèce*, Paris 1811.

Cazes, G. *Les nouvelles colonies de vacances? Le tourisme international à la conquête du Tiers-Monde*, Paris 1989.

Cazes, G., Lanquar R. and Raynouard Y. *L'aménagement touristique*, Paris 1986.

Cecaro, M. 'Investimenti turistici e investimenti industriali in Sardegna: un commento', *Quaderni sardi di economia*, 1–2 (1983), pp. 83–92.

Cecaro, M. 'Investimenti turistici e investimenti industriali in Sardegna: replica a Camagni', *Quaderni sardi di economia* 1 (1984), pp. 346–7.

Chandler, R. *Travels in Asia Minor and Greece*, Oxford 1825.

Claridge, R. *Hydropathy or the Cold Water Cure, as Practised by Vincent Priessnitz at Graefenberg, Silesia, Austria*, London 1842.

La Constancia, San Sebastián.

Contreras Poza, L. *Estudios sanitarios en la costa guipuzcoana*, San Sebastián 1977.

Corbin, A. *The Lure of the Sea: The Discovery of the Seaside in the Western World*, Cambridge 1994.

Cosgrove, D. and Daniels, S. *The Iconography of Landscape*, Cambridge 1988.

Croutier, A. L. *Taking the Waters: Spirit, Art, Sensuality*, New York 1992.

La Cruz, San Sebastián.

Csapó, K. 'Szórakozás a budai fürdôkben', *Tánctudományi Tanulmányok* (1996–7), pp. 70–9.

'A császárfürdô Budán', *Vasárnapi Ujság* 10 (1863), pp. 184–5.

Curman, C. 'Några allmänna betraktelser öfver bad- och brunnskurer', *Nordisk Lommebog for Laeger* 20 (1901), pp. 3–8.

Curman, C. *Om Bad*, Stockholm 1871.

Δήμος Μυτιλήνης, *Το Άγιο Νερό. Οι ιαματικές πηγές της Λέσβου* ('The Holy Water, The Mineral Springs of Lesbos'). Athens,1996.

Dagblad van Zuid Holland en 's-Gravenhage (DZHS), The Hague.

Dalezios, O. Ιαματικά Λουτρά της Ελλάδος (Mineral Waters of Greece), Athens 1891.

Damas (F. Baron van Hogendorp), *Haagsche omtrekken*, II, 's Gravenhage 1886.

Davidoff, L. *The Best Circles: Society, Etiquette and the Season*, London 1973.

De Jong, H. *De barre winter van 1890–1891*, Franeker 1990.

Delessert, E. *Six semaines dans l'Iles de Sardaigne*, Paris 1885.

della Marmora, A. *Itinerario dell'isola di Sardegna, Cagliari*, Cagliari (1868) 1971.

El Diario de San Sebastián (*DSS*), selected issues.

Dickens, C. 'Our Watering Place', *Household Words*, 2 August 1851, in M. Slater (ed.), *The Dent Uniform edition of Dickens' Journalism: Vol III: 'Gone Astray' and Other Papers from Household Words, 1851–9*, London 1998, pp. 9–18.

Dickens, C. 'The Tuggses at Ramsgate', first published 31 March 1836, in M.Slater (ed.), *The Dent Uniform edition of Dickens' Journalism: Vol I: Sketches by Boz, and Other Early Papers, 1833–9*, London 1994, pp. 330–41.

'Directoire des Colonies de Vacances', *Revue des Patronages* (1926), cited by Rey-Herme, p. 125.

Dolmetsch, C. *'Our Famous Guest': Mark Twain in Vienna*, Athens and London 1992.

Douglas, M. *Purity and Danger*, London 1966.

Doukakis, G.A. *Ο Τουρισμός της Νήσου Λέσβου* (Tourism of the Island of Lesbos), Athens 1959.

Dritsas, M. 'The Advent of the Tourist Industry in Greece during the Twentieth Century' in F. Amatori et al. (eds), *Deindustrialization and Reindustrialization in 20th-Century Europe*, Milano 1999.

Dritsas, M. 'Foreign Capital and Greek Development in Historical Perspective', *Uppsala Papers in Economic History*, 1993, pp. 1–33.

Dritsas, M. 'Formas de Esparcimiento en Grecia durante el periodo de Entreguerras', *Erytheia* 16 (1995), pp. 143–54.

Bibliography

Bibliography

Bibliography

Dutton, G. *Sun, Sea, Surf and Sand: The Myth of the Beach*, London 1985.

Dwyer, P. *A Handbook to Lisdoonvarna and Its Vicinity*, Dublin 1998.

Ελληνικός Οργανισμός Τουρισμού (EOT; National Tourist Organization)

Eade, J. and Sallnow, M. *Contesting the Sacred: The Anthropology of Christian Pilgrimage*, London 1990.

Éber, L. 'A Gellért-Fürdô', *Magyar Iparmûvészet* 21 (1918), pp. 140–3, 145–51, 165.

Edelsward, L. M. *Sauna as Symbol: Society and Culture in Finland*, New York 1991.

Edvinsson, S. *Den osunda staden: Sociala skillnader i dödlighet i 1800-talets Sundsvall*, Stockholm 1992.

Ehrenberg, A. 'Le Club Méditerranée, 1935–1960', in Ouvry-Vial, B. and Louis, E. (ed.), *Revue Autrement*, Paris (1990), pp. 117–29.

Ehrenberg, A. 'Rapport d'Enquête', Archives du Club Méditerranée, Paris 1987.

Encke, F. 'Parkanlage am Klettenberg in Köln', *Die Gartenkunst* 8.5 (1906), pp. 91–5.

Enit, *7° Rapporto sul turismo*, Roma 1998.

Στατιστική Ιαματικών Πηγών, (Statistics on Spas 1970–1997).

La Epoca, Madrid.

'L'Eté 1996: Guide', *Nouvel Observateur*, Paris 4–10 Jul 1996, pp. 6–20.

Farbaky, P. 'Architecture during the Tripartition of Hungary I: 1540–1630', in D. Wiebenson and J. Sisa (eds), *The Architecture of Historic Hungary*, Cambridge, MA 1998.

Farina, F. *Le Sirene dell'Adriatico*, Milano 1995.

Ferro, A. de, 'Translator's Preface' in S. Kneipp, *My Water Cure through Thirty Years*, A. de Ferro (tr.), Edinburgh (1886) 1893.

Filippakopoulos, N. *Το Λουτράκι (Loutraki)*, Athens n.d.

Finden, W. and E. *Views of Ports and Harbours, Watering Places, Fishing Villages, and Other Picturesque Objects on the English Coast*, London (1838) 1974.

Fischer, R. 'Der Schillerpark zu Berlin', *Die Gartenflora* 58 (1909), pp. 207–13.

Floyer, J. *The Ancient Psykhroloysia Revived: or, an Essay to Prove Cold Water Bathing Both Safe and Useful*, London 1701/2.

Fokas, E. *Γενικαί Αρχαί Υδροθεραπείας και Ιατρικής Κλιματολογίας* (General Principles of Hydrotherapy and Medical Climatology), Athens 1957.

Francis, J. G. *Beach-Rambles in Search of Sea-side Pebbles and Crystals*, London 1859.

Franco, V. *La Grande aventure du Club Méditerranée*, Paris, 1970.

Frankfurter Rundschau magazine 22 Apr. 1989.

Frith, W. P. *My Autobiography and Reminiscences*, 2 vols, London 1887.

Fuhs, B. *Mondäne Orte einer vornehmen Gesellschaft*, Hildesheim 1992.

'Fürdôk ma és régen', *Vasárnapi Ujság* 35 (1888), pp. 589–90.

Furnée, J.H. 'Bourgeois Strategies of Distinction. Leisure Culture and the Transformation of Urban Space: The Hague, 1850–1890', in S. Gunn and R.J. Morris (eds), *Identities in Space: Contested Terrains in the Western City since 1850*, Aldershot 2001, pp. 204–27.

Gardini, A., Gattei, G. and Porisini, G. *Storia di Rimini dal 1800 ai nostri giorni*, 5 vols, Rimini 1977.

Garin, C. 'Les stations balnéaires tentent de réhabiliter leur front de mer', *Le Monde*, Paris, 25 Aug 1998, p. 8.

Gazzettino Azzurro 24 July 1910.

Gennep, A. van, *The Rites of Passage*, London (1908) 1960.

Georgiev, D., Dereliev, C., Yankov, P. and Profirov, L. 'Shablenski ezeren kompleks' (Shabla Lake Complex), in Kostadinova, I. (ed.): *Ornitologichno vazhni mesta v Bulgaria* (Ornithologically Important Places in Bulgaria), Prirodozashtitna poreditsa 1, Sofia 1997, pp. 145–7.

Georgiev, G. *Biogeograpfski osobenosti na vlazhnite zoni v Bulgaria* (Biogeographical Characteristics of wetlands in Bulgaria), Blagoevgrad 1999.

Gerbod, P. 'Le loisir aristocratique dans les villes d'eaux françaises et allemandes au XIXe siècle (1840–1870)', in Werner (ed.), *Hof, Kultur und Politik*.

Gijswijt-Hofstra, M. 'Conversions to Homeopathy in the Nineteenth-Century: The Rationality of Medical Deviance', in M.Gijswijt-Hofstra, H.Marland and H.de Waardt (eds), *Illness and Healing Alternatives*, London 1997, pp. 161–82.

Gijswijt-Hofstra, M., Marland, H. and de Waardt, H. (eds), *Illness and Healing Alternatives*, London 1997.

Gil de Arriba, C. *Casas para baños de ola y balnearios marítimos en el litoral montañes*, Santander 1992.

Gilman, S. *The Jew's Body*, London/New York 1991.

Girouard, M. 'The Birth of a Seaside Resort', in Girouard, *Town and Country*, London 1992.

Goguel, C. 'Les Vacances des Français', *Revue Communications* 10 (1967), pp. 3–19.

Goldmerstein, J. and Stodieck, K. *Thermenpalast: Kur-, Erholungs-, Sport, Schwimm- und Badeanlage*, Berlin 1928.

Gosse, P. H. *The Ocean*, London 1849.

Gosse, P. H. and E. *Sea-side Pleasures*, London 1853.

Gouw, J. ter, *De volksvermaken*, Haarlem 1871.

Graburn, N. 'Tourism: The Sacred Journey' in V. Smith (ed.), *Hosts and Guests: The Anthropology of Tourism*, Oxford 1989, pp. 17–32.

Graetzer, J. *Lebensbilder hervorragender schlesischer Ärzte*, Breslau 1889.

Graham, R. *Graefenberg: or, a True Report of the Water Cure, with an Account of its Antiquity*, London 1844.

Grand Hotel: The Golden Age of Palace Hotels. An Architectural and Social History, New York and Paris 1984.

Granville, A. B. *The Spas of Germany*, 2 vols, London 1837.

Graves, C. *Trip-tyque*, London 1936.

Gröning, G. and Wolschke-Bulmahn, J. 'Zur Entwicklung und Unterdrückung freiraumplanerischer Ansätze der Weimarer Republik', *Das Gartenamt* 34.6 (1985), pp. 443–58.

Gröning, G. and Wolschke-Bulmahn, J. *Grüne Biographien: Biographisches Handbuch zur Landschaftsarchitektur des 20. Jahrhunderts in Deutschland*, Berlin and Hannover 1997.

Große Welt reist ins Bad 1800–1914: Eine Ausstellung des Adalbert Stifter Vereins München in Zusammenarbeit mit dem Österreichischen Museum für angewandte Kunst, Wien, catalogue, Munich 1980.

Grove, D. *Hungary's Unrivalled Leisure Resource*, Budapest 1977.

Guida ai bagni di Rimini, Rimini 1873.

Guida illustrata di Rimini, Rimini 1893.

Gunder, G. 'Die Aufgaben der Deutschen Gesellschaft für Gartenkunst', *Die Gartenkunst* 48 (1935), p. 101.

Gundle, S. 'Mapping the Origins of Glamour: Giovanni Boldini, Paris and the Belle Epoque', *Journal of European Studies* 29 (1999), pp. 269–95.

Hahn, G. von and Schönfels, H-K von, *Wunderbares Wasser: Von der heilsamen Kraft der Brunnen und Bäder*, Aarau 1980.

Hahn J. S. *Unterricht von der Heilkraft des frischen Wassers* (1738), rev. and coll. by Prof. Oertel, Nuremberg 1834.

Hamilton, C. I. *Anglo-French Naval Rivalry 1840–1870*, Oxford 1993.

Harvey, W. H. *The Sea-side Book: Being an Introduction to the Natural History of the British Coasts*, London 1849.

Hasebroek, J.P. 'De Schaatsenrijder', in: *De Nederlanden. Karakterschetsen, kleederdragten, houding en voorkomen van verschillende standen*, Haarlem 1841, pp. 85–8.

Heilig, W. 'Das Gedächtnismal im Park und Garten', *Die Gartenkunst* 30.1 (1917), pp. 4–6.

Hennebo, D. 'Der deutsche Stadtpark im 19. Jahrhundert', *Das Gartenamt* 20.8 (1971), pp. 382–91.

Herbel, A. 'Das Freizeitbad – Resümee einer Besichtigungsreise', *Archiv des Badewesens* (1978), pp. 158–63.

Herbert, R. L. *Monet on the Normandy Coast: Tourism and Painting, 1867–1886*, New Haven 1994.

Hobsbawm, E. J. and Ranger, T. (eds), *The Invention of Tradition*, Cambridge 1983.

Hoffmann, H. *Der Badeort Salzloch, seine Jod-, Brom-, Eisen- und salzhaltigen Schwefelquellen und die tanninsauren animalischen Luftbäder nebst einer Apologie des Hasardspiels. Dargestellt von Dr. Polykarpus Gastfenger, Fürstlich Schnackenbergischem Medicinalrathe und Brunnenarzte, Mitglied der Aquatischen Gesellschaft, des Deutschen Douche-Vereins, des Casinos und des Kegelklubs zu Schnackenberg, sowie vieler anderer gelehrten Gesellschaft correspondierem und Ehrenmitgliede, usw.* Frankfurt am Main 1860.

Hogarth, P. *Arthur Boyd Houghton: Introduction and Checklist of the Artist's Work*, London 1975.

Holmberg, A.E. 'Bohuslän', in *Läsebok för folkskolan* (1868), pp. 194–7.

Houghton, Rev. W. *Sea-side Walks of a Naturalist with His Children*, London 1870.

Howell, S. *The Seaside,* London 1974.

Hufeland, C.W. *The Art of Prolonging Human Life,* E. Wilson (ed. and tr.), London (1797) 2nd edn, 1859.

Hüfner, G. *Die Sozialkur und ihre statistische Erfassung: Ein Beitrag zur Erhebung und Auswertung von Bäderstatistiken aus den Jahren 1875 bis 1965,* Kassel 1969.

Igglessis, G. *Οδηγός της Ελλάδος (Guide to Greece) 1949–1950,* Athens 1950.

Igglessis, G. *Οδηγός της Ελλάδος (Guide to Greece) 1955–1956,* Athens 1956.

Ilmonen, A. 'Sauna in Finnish Pictorical Art', in Teir, H. Collan, Y. and Valtakari, P. (eds), *Sauna Studies. Papers read at the VI International Sauna Congress in Helsinki on August 15–17.1974,* Vammala 1976, pp. 24–33.

Iordanova, M. 'Hidrolozhki usloviya i resursi' (Hydrological Conditions and Resources), in *Bulgarsko Chernomorsko kraibrezhie* (Bulgarian Black Sea Coast), Sofia 1979, pp. 54–74.

Istat, *Statistiche sul turismo,* 1955–2000.

Italia 8 August 1886.

Iván, E. 'Régi Fürdôk Pest-Budán', *Vasárnapi Ujság* 61 (1914), p. 72.

Ivanov, B. The Birds of the Shabla and Tuzlata Lakes. In: Golemansky, V. and W. Naidenov (eds) *Biodiversity of Shabla Lake System.* Sofia 1998.

Izaguirre, R. de, *Estudios acerca de la bahia de San Sebastián,* Pasajes de San Pedro 1933, pp. 71–109.

Jacobs, M. *Budapest: A Cultural Guide,* Oxford 1998.

Jensen, H. 'Zeitgemäße Aufgaben der Zeitschrift Gartenkunst', *Die Gartenkunst* 46.9 (1933), pp. 138–43.

Jensen, J. 'Die Lichtung', *Die Gartenkunst* 50.9 (1937), pp. 171–80.

Johnson, J. *Pilgrimages to the Spas in Pursuit of Health and Recreation,* London 1841.

Joll, J. *1914: The Unspoken Assumptions,* London 1968.

Jung, H. R. 'Die städtischen Gartenanlagen von Altona', *Die Gartenkunst* 5.12 (1903), pp. 205–7.

Kaplan, M. A. *The Making of the Jewish Middle Class: Women, Family and Identity in Imperial Germany,* Oxford 1991.

Kazachka, D. 'Teritorialnoto razpredelenie na balneolozhkite rekreatsionni resursi v Bulgaria' (Territorial Distribution of the Balneological Recreational Resources in Bulgaria), *Annals of Sofia University* 2.80 (1986), pp. 167–79.

Kenneally, C. 'Simmer Palaces', *Travel Holiday* 180 (1997), pp. 46–9.

King, C. *The Moldovans: Romania, Russia, and the Politics of Culture,* Stanford, CA 2000.

Kingsley, C. *Glaucus; or, The Wonders of the Shore,* Cambridge 1855.

Kingsley, C. *Westward Ho!,* London (1855) 1967.

Klenze, H. *Taschenbuch für Badereisende und Kurgaste,* Leipzig 1875.

Kneipp, S. *My Water Cure, through Thirty Years,* A. de Ferro (trans.), Edinburgh (1886) 1892.

Kneipp, S. *Thus Shalt Thou Live: Hints and Advice for the Healthy and Sick on a Simple and Rational Mode of Life and a Natural Method of Cure*, London (1889) 1894.

Kohl, H. (ed.), *Briefe Ottos von Bismarcks an Schwester und Schwager*, Leipzig 1915.

Kolbrand, F. 'Schönheit am Arbeitsplatz: Ein Weg in die Zukunft der Gartengestaltung', *Die Gartenkunst* 48 (1935), pp. 173–9.

Koldo Mitxelena J.U. 5280, Acción Católica de la Mujer en Guipúzcoa, July 1934, pp. 5–7; August 1934, p. 5; May 1936, pp. 9–10.

König, G. M. *Eine Kulturgeschichte des Spaziergangs,* Vienna 1996.

Konold, W. and Rolli, E. 'Was tun mit maroden Freibädern? Rückbau zum Naturweiher', *Garten und Landschaft* 103.8 (1993), pp. 41–3.

Kos, W. 'Zwischen Amusement und Therapie: Der Kurort als soziales Ensemble' in H. Lachmeyer, S. Mattl-Wurm and C. Gargerle (eds), *Das Bad, eine Geschichte der Badekultur im 19. und 20. Jahrhundert*, Salzburg 1991.

Kósa, L. *Fürdôélet a Monarchiában*, Budapest 1999.

Koshar, R. '"What Ought to Be Seen": Tourists' Guidebooks and National Identities in Modern Germany and Europe', *Journal of Contemporary History* 33.1 (1998), pp. 323–40.

Kostadinov, D. and Karakolev D. *Glavni balneologichni kurorti* (Principal Balneological Resorts), Sofia 1983.

Kostadinova, I. 'Mezhdunarodni merki za prirodozashtita' (International Environmental Protection Measures), *Ornitologichno vazhni mesta v Bulgaria. BDZP. Prirodozashtitna poreditsa*, 1, 1997.

Kostov, E. 'Istinata za bulgarskiya turizam: vchera, dnes i utre' (The Truth About the Bulgarian Tourism: Yesterday, Today and Tomorrow), unpublished, Sofia 1995.

Kostova, A. 'Razdavai i vladei e printsip, vlastvasht v "Slanchev bryag"' (Give Out and Rule Is the Principle that Governs in "Slanchev Bryag"') *Duma Daily* (Sofia) 27 January 1994, p. 13.

Koukoulas, A.G. *Λουτράκι και Θερμαλισμός* (Loutraki and Thermalism), Loutraki 1991.

Koukoulas, A.G. *Στ' Αχνάρια του Τόπου μου* (Tracing My Home Country), Loutraki 1990.

Koulov, B. 'Political Change and Environmental Policy' Bell J. (ed.) *Bulgaria in Transition*, Oxford 1998, pp. 143–64.

Krantz, C. 'Kurgäster, fiskare och turister', *Svenska Turistföreningens Årsskrift* (1948), pp. 263–84.

Krasnobaev, B. I., Robel, G. and Zeman, H. (eds), *Reisen und Reisebeschreibungen im 18. und 19. Jahrhundert als Kulturbeziehungsforschung*, Berlin 1980.

Kraus, J. *Carlsbad and its Natural Healing Agents*, London 1877.

Krieger, F. 'Neue Freizeitkonzeptionen für öffentliche Bäder: Angebot und Nachfrage – Entwürfe und Ausführungen', *Archiv des Badewesens* (1979), pp. 458–61.

Kruisinga, C. and P. de Groot, *IJsvermaak in Leeuwarden. Geschiedenis van Koninklijke Vereeniging 'De IJsclub'*, Leeuwarden 1999.

Kuhnert, R. *Urbanität auf dem Lande: Badereisen nach Pyrmont im 18. Jahrhundert*, Göttingen 1984.

Kurlansky, M. *The Basque History of the World*, London 1999.

Küster, C. L. 'Mit der Bahn an die See', in *Saison am Strand: Badeleben an Nord- und Ostsee. 200 Jahre Altonaer Museum in Hamburg/Norddeutsches Landesmuseum*, Herford 1986.

Kynast, 'Wasserspielgarten im Parkgürtel Neu-Tempelhof', *Garten und Landschaft* 65.8 (1955), p. 6.

Laaksonen, T. Yhteissaunominen Suomessa (Joint Saunabath of both sexes in Finland), MA-Thesis 1994. Dept. of Ethnology, University of Turku, Finland.

Lagerlöf, E. 'Ackes konst I kriternas ljus', in *J.A.G. Acke,* Stockholm 1960, pp. 189–211.

Landmann, 'Schönheit der Arbeit', *Die Gartenkunst* 51 (1938), pp. 115–17.

Lange, W. 'Garten und Weltanschauung', *Die Gartenwelt* 4.31 (1900), pp. 361–4.

Lange, W. 'Das Wasser in der Landschaft', *Die Gartenwelt* 5 (1901), pp. 438–40, 459–61, 557–9.

Langer, P. *Gottfried Hahn, Pastor an der Schweidnitzer Friedenskirche und seine Familie*, Liegnitz 1903.

Larrinaga, C. *Actividad económica y cambio estructural en San Sebastián durante la Restauración, 1875–1914*, San Sebastián 1999.

Laszowska, E. de, Letter (1896), Blackwoods Archive, National Library of Scotland MS. No. 4647: 271.

Laurent, A. *Libérer les vacances?* Paris 1973.

Lázár, I. *An Illustrated History of Hungary*, Budapest 1998.

Leeuwan, T.van, *The Springboard in the Pond*, Cambridge, MA/London 1998.

Leimu, P. 'Acerbi, l'Europa di Mezzo e la sauna', De Anna, L. G. Lindgren, L. and Peso, H. (eds), *Giuseppe Acerbi tra clarissimo e restaurazzione*, Atti del Convegno 31.5.–2.6.1996, Seili, Finlandia, Publicazioni di lingua e cultura italiana n. 8, Universitá di Turku, Turku 1997, pp. 169–81.

Leimu, P. 'Die finnische Sauna-Tradition', in Fritsche, W. (ed.), *Internationales Sauna-Archiv: Zeitschrift für Forschung und Praxis des Sauna-Bades und verwandter Fachgebiete* 4 (1994) Bielefeld 1995, pp. 117–22.

Leimu, P. 'The Finnish Sauna Tradition', *Informaatio* 4 (1994) (University of Turku, Ethnology), pp. 13–16.

Leimu, P. 'The Sauna as an Instrument of Socialization', *Ethnologia Scandinavica* (1983), pp. 79–83.

Leimu, P. 'On the Sauna-Bathing Habits of Finnish Soldiers from the Beginning of the 19th Century to the Present Day', *Sauna '86: Developments*. International Sauna Congress. Holland, 4–5–6 February 1986. Kon. Ned. Jaarbeurs, Utrecht 1986, 5 pp.

Lenček, L. and Bosker, G. *The Beach: The History of Paradise on Earth*, New York 1998.

Leonardi, A. 'L'importanza economica dei "Kurorte" nello sviluppo del turismo austriaco', in Prodi, P. and Wandruszaka, A. (eds), *Il luogo di cura nel tramonto della monarchia d'Asburgo*, Bologna 1995, pp. 173–218.

Lepenies, W. *Melancholy and Society*, Cambridge, MA 1992.

Lepowitz, H. Waddy, 'Pilgrims, Patients and Painters', *Historical Reflections/ Réflexions Historiques* 18: 1 (1992), pp. 121–45.

Leroux, L. 'Les Marseillais unanimes pour défendre leurs calanques', *Le Monde*, Paris, 24 Jul 1997, p. 13.

Lesser, L. *Volksparke heute und morgen*, Berlin-Zehlendorf 1927.

Levertin, A. *Svenska Brunnar och Bad,* Stockholm 1892.

Levisalles, N. *Libération* 22 Jul 1999, p. V.

Lieven, D. *The Aristocracy in Europe 1815–1914*, London 1992.

Lindsay, I. *Dressing and Undressing for the Seaside*, Hornchurch, Essex 1983.

Lindwall, F.W. 'Bohuslän', in *Läsebok för folkskolan*, Stockholm 1912, pp. 443–53.

Lockhart, D. and Drakakis-Smith, D. W. (eds) *Island Tourism: Trends and Prospects*, London 1997.

Löfgren, O. *On Holiday: A History of Vacationing*, Berkeley, CA/London 1999.

Löschburg, W. *Von Reiselust und Reiseleid: Eine Kulturgeschichte*, Leipzig 1977.

Lôvei, P. 'Architecture before Hungary: First Century A.D. to ca. 895', in D. Wiebenson and J. Sisa (eds), *The Architecture of Historic Hungary*, Cambridge, MA 1998.

Lozato-Giotart, J.-P. *Mediterranée et tourisme*, Paris 1990.

Lukács, J. *Budapest 1900: A Historical Portrait of a City and Its Culture*, New York 1988.

Luz, Christof, 'Wasser zwischen Gestaltung und Ökologie', *Garten und Landschaft* 99.7 (1989), pp. 17–21.

Maasz, H. *Der Garten – Dein Arzt: Fort mit den Gartensorgen*, Frankfurt/Oder 1927.

MacCannell, D. *The Tourist: A New Theory of the Leisure Class*, London 1976.

Mansén, E. 'Forum, An Image of Paradise; Swedish Spas in the Eighteenth-Century', *Eighteenth-Century Studies* 31 (1998), pp. 511–16.

Mappes, M. letter to Jens Jensen, 22 July 1936, Archive of the Morton Arboretum (see the complete text of the letter in Gröning/Wolschke-Bulmahn, *Grüne Biographien* p. 242).

Marcuse, J. *Bäder und Badewesen in Vergangenheit und Gegenwart*, Stuttgart 1903.

Marinov, V. 'Commercial Tourism', in *Geography of Bulgaria*, Sofia 1997.

Masini, M. *La stagione dei bagni: Rimini nelle cronache della Bella epoque*, Rimini 1986.

Mathieson A. and Wall, G. *Tourism: Economic, Physical and Social Impacts*, New York 1982.

Mattson, O. 'Badgäster och infödingar', in *Svenska Turistföreningens Årsskrift* (1964), pp. 183–201.

Bibliography

Mayer, A. J. *The Persistence of the Old Regime*, London 1981.

McKendrick, N. Brewer, J. and Plumb, J. H. *The Birth of a Consumer Society: The Commercialization of Eighteenth-Century England*, London 1982.

Meijerman, A.M. *Hollandse winters*, Hilversum 1967.

Mennell, S. *All Manners of Food: Eating and Taste in England and France from the Middle Ages to the Present*, Oxford 1985.

Meraklis, M. 'Νερό Φρέσκο που ξεπήδαγε από τους αιώνες: Η χθόνια φυση του νερού' (Fresh Water Springing from the Centuries: The Subterranean Nature of Water), in Ministry of Culture/Museum of Greek Folk Art, *Το Νερό πηγή Ζωής, κίνησης, καθαρμού. Πρακτικά Επιστημονικής Συνάντησης*, Athens 1999.

Merkatis, J, '*Τα ιαματικά νερά της Ελλάδος*' ('The Mineral Waters of Greece'), *Viomechanike Epitheorisi* 325.11 (1961), pp. 35–48.

Mermet, G. *Francoscopie*, Paris 1994, pp. 422–30.

Merrylees, J. *Carlsbad and its Environs*, London 1886.

Mikoletsky, J. 'Zur Sozialgeschichte des österreichischen Kurorts im 19. Jahrhundert: Kurlisten and Kurtaxordnungen als sozialhistorische Quelle,' in *Mitteilungen des Instituts für österreichische Geschichtsforschung* 99: 3 (1991), pp. 393–433.

Milchev, B. 'Prouchvane na zimuvashtite vodolyubivi ptitsi v Stranja planina i prilezhashtoto chernomorsko kraibrezhie' (Study of the Waterfowl Wintering in Stara planina and the Adjacent Black Sea Coast), *Annals of Sofia University* 85.1, Zoology (1994), pp. 277–91.

Millar, Oliver, *The Victorian Pictures in the Collection of Her Majesty the Queen*, Cambridge 1992.

Ministry of Culture/Museum of Greek Folk Art, *Το Νερό πηγή ζωής, κίνησης, καθαρμού. Πρακτικά Επιστημονικής Συνάντησης*, ('Water as Source of Life, Movement, Catharsis', Proceedings of a scientific conference), Athens, 1999.

The Ministry of Foreign Affairs, *The Republic of Moldova*, Chishinau 1999.

Mirbeau, O. *Die Badereise eines Neurasthenikers*, Budapest 1902.

Mishev, K., Popov, V. and Tishkov, H. 'Prirodnite rekreatsionni resursi na Bulgarskoto chernomorie i ratsionalnoto im izpolzvane' (The Natural Recreational Resources of the Bulgarian Black Sea Coast and their Rational Utilization), *Problems of Geography* 1.1 (1983), pp. 15–27.

Moldova through the Ages, Chishinau 1999.

Mora, A. *Dax Ville D'Eau: Exposition, Galerie D'Art Municipale*, Dax 1984.

Móra, I. *Budapest: Then & Now*, Budapest 1997.

Mosse, G. *The Image of Man: The Creation of Modern Masculinity*, New York 1996.

Mosse, G. *Nationalism and Sexuality: Middle-Class Morality in Modern Europe*, Madison 1985.

Murray, J. *A Handbook for Travellers in the Ionian Islands, Greece, Turkey, Asia Minor and Constantinople*, London 1840.

Mytilene, The Town of *Το Άγιο Νερό. Οι ιαματικές πηγές της Λέσβου* (*The Holy Water: The Mineral Springs of Lesbos*), Athens 1996.

National Bank of Greece Historical Archives, Series XXXIV, folders 0–034, B–61, B–64.

Neuenschwander, E. *Schöne Schwimmteiche*, Stuttgart 1993.

'New Tourism Law in Moldova and Its Tourism Firms', *Bulletin BASA-Press*, Moldova, 7 June 2000 (Russian).

Niel, A. *Die großen k. u. k. Kurbäder und Gesundbrunnen*, Graz 1984.

Nieuwe Rotterdamsche courant (NRC), Rotterdam.

Nolan, M. 'Pilgrimage Traditions and the Nature Mystique in Western European Culture', *Journal of Cultural Geography* 7: 1 (1986), pp. 4–20.

Nomisma, Rimini, 'quale sviluppo per il prossimo decennio', mimeo, 1995.

Nordau, M. *Degeneration*, London (1892) 1895.

Normand, J-M. 'Les vacances, une conquête sociale encore inachevée,' *Le Monde*, Paris, 7 Jan 2002, p. 17.

Nowotny, O. 'Heilung durch Wasser: Zum Gedanken an Pfarrer Sebastian Kneipp', *Österreichische Apotheker Zeitung* 51 (1997), pp. 550–3.

Nungesser, M. *Das Denkmal auf dem Kreuzberg von Karl Friedrich Schinkel*, Berlin 1987.

Oberthaler, G. *Das Ultental und seine Bader: eine Historie in Wort und Bild*, Museumsverein Ulten 1997.

Oliva, G. 'Luoghi di pena-luoghi di svago: La villeggiatura ad Alghero', *Il Risorgimento* 2 (1993), pp. 177–94.

Opaschowski, H. W. 'Freizeit in öffentlichen Schwimmbädern: Ursachen des Besucherrückgangs', in BAT-Freizeitforschungsinstitut (ed.), *Lösungsansätze zur Profilierung als Freizeitbad, Projektstudie zur Freizeitforschung*, Hamburg 1983, pp. 1–18.

Orsenna, E. and Terrasse, J-M, *Villes D'Eaux*, Paris 1981.

Az Osztrák-Magyar Monarchiá Irásban és Képben, Budapest 1887–1901.

Palmer, F. H. E. *Austro-Hungarian Life in Town and Country*, London 1903.

Panerai, P. 'Karim d'Italia', *Il Mondo* 25 dicembre 1997.

Paulson, R. *Rowlandson: A New Interpretation*, London 1972.

Payer, L. *Medicine and Culture: Notions of Health and Sickness in Britain, the US, France and West Germany*, London 1989.

Pearce F. 'Hungary's Spas in Hot Water', *New Scientist* 144/1955 (1994), pp. 22–5.

Pemble, J. *The Mediterranean Passion: Victorians and Edwardians in the South*, Oxford 1988.

'La perception du littoral par les touristes français', *Les Cahiers de l'Observatoire du tourisme*, Paris, Jul 1993.

Peter, P. and Roemer, L. *Wasserbecken im Garten*, Munich: Schriftenreihe der Deutschen Gesellschaft für Gartenkunst und Landschaftspflege, no. 4, 1958.

Petitjean, G. 'Planche: Le creux de la vague', *Nouvel Observateur* 975, Paris, 15 Jul 1983, p. 44.

Peyre, C. and Raynouard, Y. *Histoire et légendes du Club Méditerranée*, Paris 1971.

Pietikäinen, T. Sauna yhteisössä – saunominen sosiaalisen kanssakäymisen muotona (The sauna in community – saunabath as a means of social inter-course), Proseminarium thesis 1991. Dept. of Ethnology, University of Turku, Finland.

Pimlott, J. A. R. *The Englishman's Holiday: A Social History*, Trowbridge (1947) 1976.

Pindar. *The Odes of Pindar, Vol. 1, Olympian Odes, Pythian Odes*, E. H. Warmington (ed.), Loeb Classical Library, London 1968, I.1, 4

Pohlenz, H. F. 'Ein Wasserscheiben-Brunnen', *Die Gartenschönheit* 8 (1927), p. 159.

Pointon, M. 'The Representation of Time in Painting: A Study of William Dyce's *Pegwell Bay: A Recollection of October 5th, 1858'*, *Art History* 1.1 (March 1978), pp. 99–103.

Pointon, M. *William Dyce 1806–64: A Critical Biography*, Oxford 1979.

Polyzoidis, Th. *Εγχειρίδιον περί Λουτρών* (*Manual of Baths*), Athens 1878.

Porisini, G. 'Nascita di una economia balneare (1815–1914)', in A. Gardini, G. Gattei and G. Porisini, *Storia di Rimini dal 1800 ai nostri giorni*, vol.II, Rimini 1977, pp. 55–102.

Porzó (Ágai, A.), *Utazás Pestrôl-Budapestre 1843–1907*, Budapest 1908.

Price, R. *Una geografia del turismo: paesaggio e insediamenti umani sulle coste della Sardegna*, Cagliari 1983.

Prignitz, H. *Vom Badekarren zum Strandkorb: Zur Geschichte des Badewesens an der Ostsee*, Leipzig 1977.

Prodanov, K., Dencheva, K. and Ivanov, L. 'Vidovoto raznoobrazie na ribite v bulgarskite chernomorski vodi' ('Diversity of the Fish Species in the Bulgarian Black Sea Waters'), in *Natsionalna strategiya za opazvane na biologichnoto raznoobrazie* (National Strategy for Biodiversity Protection) 1, Sofia 1993, pp. 7–34.

Prodi, P. and Wandruszaka, A. (eds), *Il luogo di cura nel tramonto della monarchia d'Asburgo*, Bologna 1995.

Profirov, L., Michev, T., Dimitrov, M., Nikolov, K., Yankov, P. and E. Stoinov, 'Atanasovsko ezero' ('Atanasovo Lake'), in *Ornitologichno vazhni mesta v Bulgaria* (Ornithologically Important Places in Bulgaria), Prirodozashtitna poreditsa 1, Sofia 1997.

Provincia di Rimini, Assessorato al turismo, 'Dinamica delle presenze turistiche complessive annuali (1946–2000)', mimeo, 2000.

Provinciale Groninger Courant (PGC), Groningen.

El Pueblo Vasco (PV), San Sebastián, selected issues.

Putnam, R. *Making Democracy Work*, Princeton, NJ 1993.

'A 'Ráczfürdô' Budán', *Vasárnapi Ujság* 11 (1864), pp. 241–2.

Rae, W. F. *Austrian Health Resorts and the Bitter Waters of Hungary*, London 2nd edn.1889.

Rauch, A. 'Les usages du temps libre', in Rioux, J.-P. and Sirinelli, J.-F. (eds), *La Culture de masse en France de la Belle-Époque à aujourd'hui*, Paris 2002, pp. 352–409.

Rauch, A. *Vacances en France de 1830 à nos jours*, Paris 2001.

Raymond, H. 'Hommes et dieux à Palinuro', *Esprit* (Jun 1959), pp. 1037–47.

Read, B. *Victorian Sculpture*, London 1982.

Reader, I. and Walter, T. *Pilgrimage and Popular Culture*, Basingstoke 1993.

'Recreation and Leisure Zones around Chishinau Do Not Fulfill Sanitary Requirements', *Bulletin BASA-Press*, Moldova, 12 June 2000 (Russian).

Reis, V. van der, *Die Geschichte der Hydrotherapie von Hahn bis Priessnitz*, Berlin 1914.

Republic of Moldova – 1998. National Human Development Report, *UNDP* 1999.

Rey-Herme, A. *Les colonies de vacances en France de 1906 à 1936*, Paris 1961.

Ribner, 'Our English Coasts, 1852: William Holman Hunt and Invasion Fear at Midcentury', *Art Journal* 55.2 (Summer 1996), pp. 45–54.

Ricks, C. (ed.), *The Poems of Tennyson*, London 1969.

Ridder, J.H. de, 'Schaatsenrijden', in: *Het ijsvermaak op de Maas te Rotterdam in februarij 1855*, Rotterdam 1855, pp. 17–23.

Rodríguez Ranz, J. A. *Guipúzcoa y San Sebastián en las elecciones de la II República*, San Sebastián 1994.

Romdahl, A. review in *Svenska Dagbladet* 26 May 1907, p. 6.

Royal Academy exhibition catalogue, 1854, no.1370.

Rubovszky, A. 'A Szent Gellért Szálló Históriája', *Világszövetség*, II/14 (1993), p. 15.

Ruffi, E. and Casaretto L. *Seconda relazione industriale-commerciale-statistica per l'anno 1872 presentata al ministero d'Agricoltura, Industria e commercio dalla Camera di Commercio ed Arti di Rimini*, Rimini 1874.

Ruju, S. *Società, economia e politica dal 2° dopoguerra ad oggi, Sardegna*, Torino 1998.

Rumbold, H. *Recollections of a Diplomatist*, vol. 2, London 1902.

Ruskin, J. *The Harbours of England*, London 1856, in E.T.Cook and A. Wedderburn (eds), *The Works of John Ruskin*, vol 13, London , pp. 1–76.

Sacher-Masoch, F. *Venus in Furs*, Harmondsworth (1870) 2000.

Sada, J.M. and Hernandez, T. *Historia de los csinos de San Sebastián*, San Sebastián 1987.

Sandell, K. 'Naturkontakt och allemansrätt: Om friluftslivets naturmöte och friluftlandskapets tillgänglighet i Sverige 1880–2000', in *Svensk Geografisk Årsbok* 73 (1997), pp. 31–65.

Sarholz, H-J, *Geschichte der Stadt Bad Ems*, Bad Ems 1994.

Scaramuzzi, I. *Inventare i luoghi turistici, analisi di alcune esperienze significative*, Padova 1993.

Schivelbusch, W. *The Railway Journey*, Oxford 1980.

Schmid, A. S. 'Stadtgrün zwischen Ökologie und Gartenkunst', *Garten und Landschaft* 96.1 (1986), pp. 17–19.

Schmid, H. and Stieler, K. *The Bavarian Highlands and the Salzkammergut with an Account of the Hunters, Poachers and Peasantry of Those Districts*, London 1874.

Schmid, H. O. 'Die Struktur der Bäder und ihrer Kurgäste in früherer und heutiger Zeit', *Heilbad und Kurort. Zeitschrift für das gesamte Bäderwesen* 14.6 (1962).

Schmidt, E. 'Der Naturgarten – Ein neuer Weg?', *Garten und Landschaft* 91.11 (1981), pp. 877–84.

Schmitt, M. *Palast-Hotels. Architektur und Anspruch eines Bautyps, 1870–1910*, Berlin, 1982.

Schomburg, E. *Sebastian Kneipp*, Bad Wörishofen 1976.

Schönherr, M. 'Bademusik', in *Große Welt reist ins Bad 1800–1914*, pp. 24–32.

Sery, P. 'Chères et sacrées vacances', *Nouvel Observateur*, 552, Paris, 15 Jun 1975, p. 46.

Shields, R. *Places on the Margin: Alternative Geographies of Modernity*, London 1991.

Shorter, E. *From Paralysis to Fatigue: A History of Psychosomatic Illness in the Modern Era*, New York 1992.

Silari, F. I bagni ed altro. 'L'evoluzione dell'industria e dei servizi nel riminese dalla metà dell'Ottocento alla fine del Novecento', in A. Varni and V. Zamagni (eds), *Economia e società a Rimini tra '800 e '900*, Rimini 1992, pp. 97–189.

Simon, A. 'Relazione illustrativa del P.R.g. di Alghero', mimeo, 1959.

Simonnot, P. *Ne m'appelez plus France*, Paris 1991.

Singer, W. 'Sport- und Badeplätze in den städtischen Anlagen', *Die Gartenkunst* 11.3 (1909): pp. 42–5.

Sirost, O. (ed.), 'Habiter la nature? Le camping', *Revue Ethnologie Française* 31 (Oct–Dec 2001).

Sisa, J. 'Hungarian Architecture from 1849 to 1900', in D. Wiebenson and J. Sisa (eds), *The Architecture of Historic Hungary*, Cambridge, MA 1998.

Sisa, J. 'Neoclassicism and the Age of Reform: 1800–1848', in D. Wiebenson and J. Sisa (eds), *The Architecture of Historic Hungary*, Cambridge, MA 1998.

Smith, V. 'The Quest in Guest', *Annals of Tourism Research* 19 (1992), pp. 1–17.

Söder, H-P. 'Disease and Health as Contexts of Modernity: Max Nordau as a Critic of Fin-de-Siècle Modernism', *German Studies Review* 14: 3 (1991), pp. 473–87.

Sombart, W. *Luxus und Kapitalismus*, Munich 1913.

Sontag, S. *Illness as a Metaphor*, London 1983.

Sörlin, S. and K. Sandell, 'Naturen som ungdomsforstrare' in Sörlin and Sandell (eds), *Friluftshistoria: Från 'härdande friluftslif' till ekoturism och miljöpedagogik*, Stockholm 2000, pp. 27–46.

Spacks, P. M. *Boredom: The Literary History of a State of Mind*, Chicago 1995.

Sperber, J. 'Bürger, Bürgertum, Bürgerlichkeit, Bürgerliche Gesellschaft: Studies of the German Upper Middle Class and Its Sociocultural World', *Journal of Modern History* 69: 2 (1997), pp. 271–97.

Spitzer, K. 'Naturgärten im Stadtmilieu: Natural Gardens in an Urban Milieu', *Garten und Landschaft* 98.7 (1988), pp. 457–62.

Statistical Yearbook of the Commercial-Industrial Chamber of the Republic of Moldova, 2000 (Russian).

Statistiche sul turismo, Roma 1955–2000.

Steendijk-Kuipers, J. *Vrouwen-beweging. Medische en culturele aspecten van vrouwen in de sport, gezien in het kader van de sporthistorie, 1880–1928*, Rotterdam 1999.

Steiner, A. *'Das nervose Zeitalter'*: *Der Begriff der Nervösität bei Laien und Ärzten in Deutschland und Österreich um 1900*, Zürcher medizingeschichtliche Abhandlungen, Neue Reihe, Nr. 21, Zurich 1964.

Steinhauser. M. 'Das europäische Modebad des 19. Jahrhundert – Eine Residenz des Glücks', in L. Grote (ed.), *Die deutsche Stadt im 19. Jahrhundert*, Munich 1974.

Sternberger, D. *Panorama of the Nineteenth Century*, Oxford 1977.

Stevenson, S. *Hill and Adamson's The Fishermen and Women of the Firth of Forth*, Edinburgh 1991.

Steward, J. 'The Spa Towns of the Austro-Hungarian Empire and the Growth of Tourist Culture: 1860–1914', in P. Borsay, G. Hirschfelder and R-E. Mohrmann (eds), *New Directions in Urban History: Aspects of European Art: Health, Tourism and Leisure since the Enlightenment*, Münster 2000, pp. 87–127.

Stieler, K. 'Tourists in the Country' in Schmid and Stieler, pp. 155–66.

Stieler, K. 'Traun and Ischl' in Schmid and Stieler, pp. 82–6.

Stowe, W. W. *Going Abroad: European Travel in Nineteenth-Century American Culture*, Princeton, NJ 1994.

Subtil, M.P. 'Les jeunes des banlieues accusés de troubler les vacances au bord de l'océan', *Le Monde*, Paris, 22 Aug 1998, p. 6.

Süddeutsche Zeitung, 8 June 1990.

Sustainable Development – A Challenge for Moldova, UND 2000.

Sustainable Tourism Development Project, UNDP-Moldova 2000.

Sutton, P.C. *Masters of 17th Century Dutch Landscape Painting*, Amsterdam 1987.

Svenvonius, G. 'Inledning' in *STFÅrsbok* (1886), pp. 1–84.

Talve, I. *Bastu och torkhus i Nordeuropa* (The Sauna and the Drying House in Northern Europe), Nordiska Museets Handlingar 53, Stockholm 1960.

Talve, I. *Finnish Folk Culture*, Tampere 1997.

Tawada, Y. *Wo Europa anfängt*, Tübingen 1995.

Theweleit, K. *Male Fantasies*, Vol 1: *Women, Floods, Bodies, History* (1977), trans. S. Conway, Minneapolis 1987.

Tissot, S. A. *Advice to People in General, with Respect to Their Health* (Avis au people (sic) . . .) Edinburgh (1761) 1772.

Titterington, C. 'John Dillwyn Llewelyn: Instantaneity and Transience', in M. Weaver (ed.), *British Photography in the Nineteenth Century*, Cambridge 1989, pp. 65–78.

Török, A. *Budapest: A Critical Guide*, London 1998.

Tóth, I. 'Hungarian Culture in the Early Modern Age', in L. Kósa (ed.), *A Cultural History of Hungary From the Beginnings to the Eighteenth Century*, Budapest 1998.

Touring club italiano, *Guida pratica ai luoghi di soggiorno e di cura: Le stazioni di mare*, Milano 1933.

Tourism, Annual Bulletin, Sofia 1999, 2000, 2001.

'Tourism Law of the Republic of Moldova', *Monitorul Oficial al Republicii Moldova*, 12 May 2000 (Russian).

'Tourist Business Needs Special Skills', *Chishinau News* 2 June 2000 (Russian).

Towner, J. *An Historical Geography of Recreation and Tourism in the Western World, 1540–1940*, Chichester 1996.

Troev, T. 'Survey of Bulgaria', *The Financial Times Daily* 5 May 1993, p. 15.

Turner, B. *The Body and Society: Explorations in Social Theory*, London 1996.

Turner, V. and E. *Image and Pilgrimage in Christian Culture: Anthropological Perspectives*, Oxford 1978.

Ukraine and Moldavia, Moscow 1978 (Russian).

La Unión Vascongada (*UV*), San Sebastián.

Urbain, J.-D. *L'idiot du voyage: Histoires de touristes.* Paris 1993.

Urbain, J.-D. *Sur la Plage: Moeurs et coutumes balnéaires (XIXe–XXe siècles)*, Paris 1994.

Urquia, J.M. *Historia de los balnearios guipuzcoanos*, Bilbao 1985.

El Urumea, San Sebastián.

Utrechtsche Provinciale en Stedelijke Courant (UPSD), Utrecht.

Het Vaderland (VL), The Hague.

Vallas, J-L, *Cauterets: Mille ans d'histoire et d'idylle*, Cauterets 1982.

Van der Woude, D.M. *Vrouwen in de hardrijdersbaan*, Assen 1947.

Van Schuppen, N. 'Van vrouwenvermaak tot damesrekreatie. Een overzicht van de Nederlandse ontwikkeling van sportbeoefening door vrouwen in de negentiende eeuw', *Jaarboek voor vrouwengeschiedenis* 1 (1980), pp. 12–45.

Veblen, T. *The Theory of the Leisure Class*, New York 1899.

Venbrux, E. 'Op het ijs kent men 's lands wijs. Over de betekenis van het schaatsen', in H. de Jonge (ed.), *Ons soort mensen. Levensstijlen in Nederland*, Nijmegen 1998, pp. 273–311.

Viard, J. *La révélation vacancière*, Paris 1981.

Volkmann, Hans (ed.), *Die künstlerische Verwendung des Wassers im Städtebau*, Berlin 1911.

La Voz de Guipúzcoa (*VG*), San Sebastián.

Waissenberger, R. 'The Biedermeier mentality' in R. Waissenberger ed. *Vienna in the Biedermeier Era: 1815–1848*, London 1986, pp. 51–92.

Wallin, J. *Handbok för badgäster*, Göteborg 1858.

Walton, J.K. 'Consuming the Beach: Seaside Resorts and Cultures of Tourism in England and Spain', in E. Furlough and S. Baranowski (eds), *Tourism and Consumption in Modern Europe*, Ann Arbor, Michigan 2001.

Walton, J. K. *The English Seaside Resort: A Social History, 1750–1914*, Leicester 1983.

Walton, J. K. 'Popular Entertainment and Public Order: The Blackpool Carnivals of 1923–4', *Northern History* 34 (1998), pp. 170–88.

Walton, J. K. 'The Seaside Resorts of Western Europe, 1750–1939', in S. Fisher (ed.), *Recreation and the Sea*, Exeter 1997, pp. 36–56.

Walton, J. K. 'Tradition and Tourism: Representing Basque Identities in San Sebastián and Its Province, 1848–1936', in N. Kirk (ed.), *Northern Identities*, Aldershot 2000, pp. 87–108.

Walton, J. K. and Smith, J. 'The First Century of Beach Tourism in Spain: San Sebastián and the playas del norte, from the 1830s to the 1930s', in M. Barke et al (eds), *Tourism in Spain: Critical Perspectives*, Wallingford 1996, pp. 35–61.

Walton, J. K., Blinkhorn, M., Pooley, C., Tidswell, D. and Winstanley, M. J. 'Crime, Migration and Social Change in North-West England and the Basque Country, c. 1870–1930', British Journal of Criminology 39 (1999), pp. 103–4.

Walvin, J. *Beside the Seaside: A Social History of the Popular Seaside Holiday*, London 1978.

Warner, M. *The Victorians: British Painting 1837–1901*, Washington 1997.

Water in Moldovan Nature and Economics, Chishinau 1981 (Russian).

Waugh, F. A. *Book of Landscape Gardening*, New York 1928.

Wechsberg, J. *The Lost World of the Great Spas*, London 1979.

Weininger, O. *Sex and Character*, (trans. anon.), London (1903) 1906.

Werner, K. F. (ed.), *Hof, Kultur und Politik im 19. Jahrhundert*, Bonn 1985.

Wichers, J. van Buttinga, *Schaatsenrijden. Geschiedkundig overzicht met beschrijvingen van sneeuwschoenen, benen- en ijzeren schaatsen en koude winters. Handleiding voor het hardrijden, figuurrijden en het oefenen op het ijs. Met aardige oude prenten geïllustreerd*, 's-Gravenhage 1888.

Wiener, M. *English Culture and the Decline of the Industrial Spirit*, Cambridge 1981.

Wiepking-Jürgensmann, H. F. 'Jahresschau deutscher Gartenkultur Hannover', *Die Gartenschönheit* 14.9 (1933), pp. 162–7.

Wiklund, T. Det tillgjorda landskapet: En undersökning av förutsättningarna för urban kultur i Norden, Göteborg 1995.

Williams, A. and Shaw, G. 'Tourism: Candyfloss Industry or Job Generator?' *TPR* 59 (1988), p. 1.

Winock, M. *Chroniques des Années 60,* Paris 1987.

Wolf, A. 'Ein Teichbiotop im Garten: A Garden Pond Habitat', *Garten und Landschaft* 89.6 (1979), pp. 443–6.

Wolf, U. 'Die Düsseldorfer Wasserspielplätze', *Garten und Landschaft* 66.11 (1956), pp. 325–30.

Wolschke-Bulmahn, J. 'Avantgarde und Gartenarchitektur in Deutschland', *Zolltexte* 7.26 (1997), pp. 11–17.

Wolschke-Bulmahn, J. '"The Peculiar Garden" – The Advent and the Destruction of Modernism in German Garden Design', R. Karson (ed.), *The Modern Garden in Europe and the United States: Proceedings of the Garden Conservancy Symposium, New York, 1993, Masters of American Garden Design*, vol. III, Cold Spring New York 1994, pp. 17–30.

Wolschke-Bulmahn, J. 'The Search for "Ecological Goodness" among Garden Historians', in M. Conan (ed.), *Perspectives on Garden Histories: Dumbarton Oaks Colloquium on the History of Landscape Architecture*, vol. 21, Washington D.C 1999, pp. 161–80.

Wolschke-Bulmahn, J. and Gröning, G. 'The Ideology of the Nature Garden: Nationalistic Trends in Garden Design in Germany during the Early Twentieth Century', *Journal of Garden History* 12.1 (1992), pp. 73–80.

Wordsworth, C. *Greece: Pictorial, Descriptive and Historical*, London 1839.

Yankov, P. 'Pomoriisko-Burgaski kompleks' in Michev, T. (ed.), *Natsionalen plan za prioritetni deistviya po opzvane na nai-znachiimite vlazhni zoni v Bulgaria* (National Priorities' Action Plan for Protection of the Most Important Wetlands in Bulgaria), Sofia 1993, pp. 33–44.

Yankov, P., Dimitrov, M., and Kostadinova, I. 'Ornitologichno vazhnite mesta v Bulgaria' ('Ornithologically Important Places in Bulgaria'), Prirodozashtitna poreditsa 1, Sofia 1997, pp. 118–19.

Zamagni, V. 'La cassa di risparmio di Rimini fra passato e futuro', in A. Varni and V. Zamagni (eds), *Economia e società a Rimini tra '800 e '900*, Rimini 1992, pp. 19–93.

Zappi, S. 'La qualité des eaux de baignade s'améliore sur le littoral', *Le Monde*, Paris, 3 Jul 1997, p. 11.

Notes on Contributors

Susan C. Anderson, Professor of German at the University of Oregon, specializes in twentieth-century German literary and cultural studies, with emphasis on questions of collective identities and multiculturalism; she is co-editor of *Water, Culture, and Politics in Germany and the American West* (2001).

Patrizia Battilani is visiting professor for the Economic History of Tourism at the University of Bologna, Italy. Her publications include *Vacanze di pochi, vacanze di tutti* (2001) and *La creazione di un moderno sistema di imprese* (1999).

David Blackbourn is Coolidge Professor of History at Harvard. The author of five books on modern German history, including *Marpingen* and *The Long Nineteenth Century: A History of Germany, 1780–1918*, he is currently completing the project 'The Conquest of Nature: Water and the Making of the Modern German Landscape'.

Margarita Dritsas is Professor in European Economic and Social History, School of Humanities, Hellenic Open University, Patras, Greece. She has published extensively on issues of Greek economic and business history. Her more recent research includes the history and development of the tourist industry in Greece.

Michelle Facos is Associate Professor of Art History at Indiana University, Bloomington (USA). She has published widely on late nineteenth-century Swedish art, and is currently writing the Symbolism volume for Phaidon's Art & Ideas series.

Jan Hein Furnée is affiliated with the Department of History, University of Groningen, The Netherlands. He is completing his doctorate on leisure culture in the Dutch residential capital The Hague, 1850–1890.

Gert Gröning is Professor for Urban Horticulture and Landscape Architecture and Executive Director, Institute for History and Theory of Design, University of the Arts, Berlin. His main fields of interest include the history of garden and landscape architecture, social science aspects of open space planning, and design of open spaces.

Boian Koulov is an adjunct professor at George Washington University. He received a Ph.D. in economic and social geography at the Bulgarian Academy of Sciences. His areas of interest are environmental and political geography, tourism, and Southeastern Europe.

Pekka Leimu, Professor and Chair of Ethnology and Vice Dean of the Faculty of Humanities at the University of Turku, specializes in military history/sociology, Finnish sauna, industrial communities, urban culture, European cultural borders and culture areas, and modernization of rural culture.

Vassil Marinov is Associate Professor in the Department of Tourism, Sofia University; Procurist for the National Center for Regional Development, Sofia; Vice-Chairman of the UN Commission for Human Settlements; and Consultant for the Bulgarian Ministries of Economy and of Regional Development. He is an expert in geography of tourism, tourism planning and policy, market research in tourism, regional development and policy, sustainable development, project management.

Christiana Payne is Senior Lecturer in History of Art at Oxford Brookes University. She is currently working on representations of the coast and the sea in nineteenth-century British art.

André Rauch is Professor at the University Marc Bloch in Strasbourg, France. He teaches history and sociology of culture. His most recent books are *Vacances en France de 1830 à nos jours* (2001) and *Le premier sexe: Mutations et crise de l'identité masculine* (2001).

Jill Steward, University of Northumbria, is a member of the European Urban Culture Group and researches the cultural history of tourism and travel writing, focusing on Austro-Hungary before the First World War. Recent publications focus on tourism in modern Europe and on the literature of tourism.

Terri Switzer, Assistant Professor of Art History at St. Ambrose in Davenport, Iowa (USA), specializes in Central European art (particularly Hungarian) from the mid-nineteenth century to ca. 1920 and recently completed her PhD dissertation, 'Nationalism in Hungarian art, 1860–1920', at Indiana University.

Bruce H. Tabb, Associate Professor at the University of Oregon Library, oversees cataloguing operations for rare books and special collection materials and serves as bibliographer for Germanics. He is co-editor of *Water, Culture, and Politics in Germany and the American West* (2001).

Maria Vodenska is Associate Professor in the Department of Tourism at Sofia University and Dean of the Faculty of Geology and Geography. Her research specialties are theory and practice of tourism, tourism impacts, socio-economic factors for tourism development and regional geography of tourism.

John K. Walton is Professor of Social History at the University of Central Lancashire, Preston, UK. He has published extensively on seaside tourism, sport and regional identities in England and Spain. His most recent books are *Blackpool* (1998), *The British Seaside: Holidays and Resorts in the Twentieth Century* (2000) and (edited with F.J. Caspistegui) *Guerras danzadas: futbol e identidades locales y regionales en Europa* (2001).

Joachim Wolschke-Bulmahn, Professor in the History of Landscape Architecture and Open Space Planning, Department of Landscape Architecture and Environmental Development, University of Hannover, focuses his research on the recent history of landscape architecture, particularly during the time of National Socialism. His most recent book is *Byzantine Garden Culture*, co-edited with A. Littlewood and H. Maguire (2002).

Index

Note: An italicized page number refers to an illustration on that page.

Index

tourism, 1, 2, 3, 4, 23, 24, 28, 31, 34,
35n5, 37, 39, 42, 44, 46, 47, 48, 111,
114, 149, 150, 156, 157, 158, 161,
162, 165–79, 181, 182, 183, 186,
187, 189, 190, 192, 196, 198, 199,
201, 204, 205, 206, 207, 209–21,
223–38
see also *environmental issues: eco-tourism*
travel, 2, 9, 12–14, 16, 23, 24, 28–29, 30,
35n2, 37, 38, 39, 87, 88, 108, 114, 143,
150, 157, 158, 176, 181, 191, 193, 196,
199, 201, 202, 206, 211, 216–7, 218,
224–5
'travel capitalism', 14
Tsaldaris, Panagis, 203
tuberculosis, 28, 32, 34, 169
Turgenev, 9
Twain, Mark: see *Clemens, Samuel*

vagrants, 15
Venbrux, Eric, 55, 56, 68n1
Venizelos, Eleftherios, 203
Venus de Milo, 76

Wallin, J., 108, 114
Walton, J.K., 103n4
Waugh, Frank A., 119
Weekes, Henry, 89, 97–8
The Young Naturalist, 89, 96, 97, 102

Weininger, Otto, *Geschlecht und Charakter* [Sex and Character], 34
Wellington, 92
wells, 37, 150
Wernher, George, 153
wetlands, 168–9, 170–1, 172, 177, 183
Wiepking, Heinrich, 132
Wilde, Oscar, 14
Wilden, Josef, 162n3
Wilhelm I, 18, 20
Wilhelmson, Carl, 114
William III, 66
Winternitz, Wilhelm, 28
Wolf, Ulrich, 135
Wollstonecraft, Mary, 108
women's emancipation, 63, 126
Wordsworth, 98, 99
Wright, William, and the 'Wright Regime', 11
Wurth, Kiene Brillenburg, 68n

Ybl, Miklós, 158, 159

Zille, Heinrich, 16
Zola, 9
Zorn, Anders, 109–110, 114, 115, 116
Out of Doors in Dalarö, 109, 110, *110*, 115, 116
Zorreguieta, Máxima, 69n5
Zsigmondy, Vilmos, 158, 159–60